BLACK INTELLECTUAL THOUGHT IN MODERN AMERICA

BLACK INTELLECTUAL THOUGHT IN MODERN AMERICA

— A Historical Perspective —

Edited by Brian D. Behnken,
Gregory D. Smithers, and Simon Wendt

UNIVERSITY PRESS OF MISSISSIPPI / JACKSON

Margaret Walker Alexander Series in African American Studies

www.upress.state.ms.us

Designed by Peter D. Halverson

The University Press of Mississippi is a member of the Association of American University Presses.

Copyright © 2017 by University Press of Mississippi
All rights reserved

First printing 2017

∞

Library of Congress Cataloging-in-Publication Data

Names: Behnken, Brian D., editor. | Smithers, Gregory D., 1974– editor. | Wendt, Simon., editor.
Title: Black intellectual thought in modern America : a historical perspective / edited by Brian D. Behnken, Gregory D. Smithers, and Simon Wendt.
Description: Jackson : University Press of Mississippi, 2017. | Series: Margaret Walker Alexander series in African American studies | Includes bibliographical references and index. |
Identifiers: LCCN 2017012606 (print) | LCCN 2017016658 (ebook) | ISBN 9781496813664 (epub single) | ISBN 9781496813671 (epub institutional) | ISBN 9781496813688 (pdf single) | ISBN 9781496813695 (pdf institutional) | ISBN 9781496813657 (cloth : alk. paper)
Subjects: LCSH: African Americans—Intellectual life. | African American intellectuals—History. | African American philosophy—History. | African Americans—Civil rights—History. | African Americans—Social conditions.
Classification: LCC E185.89 .I56 (ebook) | LCC E185.89 .I56 B55 2017 (print) | DDC 323.1196/073—dc23
LC record available at https://lccn.loc.gov/2017012606

British Library Cataloging-in-Publication Data available

CONTENTS

Introduction - 3 -
BRIAN D. BEHNKEN, GREGORY D. SMITHERS, SIMON WENDT

CHAPTER ONE
"All the Science and Learning"
Black Intellectual History in the United States - 11 -
GREGORY D. SMITHERS

CHAPTER TWO
Black Marxism - 35 -
MINKAH MAKALANI

CHAPTER THREE
The Quest for Racial Change
African American Intellectuals and the Black Liberal Tradition - 80 -
BRIAN D. BEHNKEN

CHAPTER FOUR
Black Conservative Thought in the Post-Civil Rights Era - 107 -
DANIELLE L. WIGGINS

CHAPTER FIVE
Steps In and Places Outside
The Reception of Black Feminist Intellectuals and Black Feminist Theory in Modern America - 138 -
BENITA ROTH

CHAPTER SIX
Intellectual Predicaments
Black Nationalism in the Civil Rights and Post-Civil Rights Eras - 170 -
SIMON WENDT

CHAPTER SEVEN
Afrocentric Intellectuals and the Burden of History   - 206 -
TUNDE ADELEKE

Contributors   - 237 -

Index   - 241 -

BLACK INTELLECTUAL THOUGHT IN MODERN AMERICA

INTRODUCTION

BRIAN D. BEHNKEN, GREGORY D. SMITHERS, SIMON WENDT

In 2013, the African American philosopher Lewis R. Gordon wrote, "Black intellectuals face a neurotic situation." Like African American writers before him who paused to consider the place of black intellectuals in American society, Gordon understood that black intellectuals face a dilemma: on the one hand, they are routinely questioned about whether "there are black thinkers on a par [with](or beyond) those of the Western canon ranging from Plato and Aristotle to Hegel and Marx and on to recent times such as Sartre and Foucault." On the other hand, those African Americans who do devote themselves to a life of the mind open themselves to criticism for being "too bookish and for failing to be 'in the streets,' where 'the struggle' is being waged."[1] In our current era of urban unrest, the media exposure of police violence in predominantly black communities, and the rise of the Black Lives Matter movement, this latter concern seems particularly prescient.[2]

Due to the current state of social and political life in the United States, the need for black intellectuals and African American ideas remains as pressing as ever. But what types of ideas are needed? Indeed, what type of education should black Americans seek out? Should education and knowledge be purely utilitarian in their function, or can one seek out all of the science, art, and learning in the world for the sake of learning? As Gordon reminds us, these are not new questions, but they are enduring ones. Gordon spoke to these questions by reflecting on the apparent need for black intellectuals to justify their existence—whether in terms of comparing the quality of black thought to that of Western (read: white) thinking, or in relation to the gritty reality of the inner city. Moreover, since World War II the urban environment has acted as a synonym for "street cred," "keepin' it real," and what in popular culture is considered an "authentic" African American experience, which again underscores how racial perceptions remain operational in American life just as black intellectuals work to foster historical understanding, deconstruct racialized thinking, and devise sociological and political strategies for meeting the myriad needs of black communities.[3]

The challenges associated with being an articulate, well-educated black man or woman in the United States are fairly well known. Black intellectualism adds an additional obstacle to the lived experience of many African Americans. From abolitionists, such as Frederick Douglass, to Barack Obama, whose navigation of the overwhelmingly white world of American politics to rise to become the president of the United States, questions about intellect and racial "authenticity" and "legitimacy" have often followed prominent black intellectuals and political leaders as they pursue knowledge and work to apply their knowledge in communities throughout the United States. Indeed, white Americans are often unable to resist the urge to mix what they understand as compliments with a thinly veiled racialism when asked to characterize prominent African American intellects and leaders.

Take for example the characterizations that have dogged President Obama during his time in the White House. Obama, like black leaders who came before him, has been portrayed as a figure of the United States' "salvation" on the one hand, and an agent for the republic's decline on the other. While interviewing a group of eighteen-to-twenty-four-year olds about the contradictory perceptions white people have of Obama, African American scholars H. Samy Alim and Geneva Smitherman identified one white American's description of the president as emblematic of the terms used to describe him. Responding to Alim and Smitherman's questionnaire, the respondent wrote that Obama was "[d]ignified yet humble, assertive yet calm/collected, stern yet compassionate, and formal while authentic, President Obama's language transcends the typical blandness of modern politicians (at least the old, white, male variety) and I believe he is truly able to inspire hope and confidence through his speeches."[4] Obama, it would seem, can only be certain things if he is positioned against white, male politicians.

Few academics would label Obama as purely an intellectual. While he has a law degree from Harvard University and worked for a time as a faculty member at the University of Chicago's School of Law, he is first and foremost a politician. Yet his various publications and his education certainly qualify him as an intellectual. Nonetheless, the above quotation highlights the often-contradictory ways in which some Americans perceive black Americans of cultivated intellect and who rise to become spokespeople "for the race" and, in the case of President Obama, for the nation.[5]

Such questions and concerns do not seem to plague other segments of black intellectual and political leaders. In particular, black conservatives do not seem to have to validate their own positions in the way that a liberal leader such as President Obama does. For instance, Dr. Ben Carson had excelled throughout late 2015 as a conservative leader and as a possible frontrunner for the Republican primary race. Carson's conservative viewpoints caused no great concern for his Republican constituents. Moreover, he has avoided, in some instances deliberately, topics that either deal with race or that concern African Americans. It could be argued that Carson is a cipher for white Americans; a black man who appeals to white conservative voters by seemingly operating within a white (i.e., not racialized) framework. Such a position means that his primarily white supporters can avoid many of the assumptions and opinions that dog a liberal such as Obama.

Despite optimistic projections that the United States had turned a racial corner and was about to embark on a "post-\racial" era following Barack Obama's historic election to the presidency in 2008, as well as the prominence of black conservatives such as Ben Carson, race and the lived realities of racism remain a determining factor in the ways black intellectuals perceive America and are perceived by Americans.[6] Lewis Gordon is thus not alone in making the above observations about the place of black intellectuals in American social, cultural, and academic life. Since the civil rights movement of the 1950s and 1960s, prominent black intellectuals and social theorists have made similar observations. From Harold Cruse in the late 1960s, to Manning Marable, William J. Moses, Vernon J. Williams, and Cornell West in more recent decades, the significance of black intellectualism to African American leadership, and black intellectuals to the nurturing of black cultural and academic life, has been a source of sometimes intense interest.[7] As the critical race theorist David Theo Goldberg observes, the frenzied attention that black intellectuals occasionally attract can be attributed to the role that intellectuals such as Cornell West take in being both scholar and public figure.[8]

Black intellectualism has often only been visible during these frenzied moments, which is additionally problematic for black scholars. Historian Jonathan Scott Holloway, for example, has noted that African American intellectuals seem to operate within what he calls a "crisis cannon," and writing about black intellectuals has followed a similar crisis trajectory. "Writing about black intellectuals," Holloway observes, "almost always revolves around a crisis of the moment or the crisis of living in a world where many believe the words 'black' and 'intellectual' are mutually exclusive."[9] Holloway's observations are twofold. First, his explanation of the "crisis canon" brings to light the invisibility of black intellectuals, who are only made visible when a crisis or need for their existence arises. Second, he underscores how the term "black intellectual" is popularly understood as incongruent or misaligned. In his analysis, African Americans are both popularly and academically conceived of, if they're conceived of at all, as either black or intellectual, but rarely both at the same time.

Such misconceptions are not new. African American intellectuals and political leaders have been construed in such ways for generations. Perhaps there is no better example of this than the so-called divide between W. E. B. Du Bois and Booker T. Washington. These individuals have been viewed as mirror opposites: Du Bois the radical race leader who sought to progressively advance black people, and Washington the accommodationist (read Uncle Tom) who sought to teach black people industrial and craft skills. But this understanding of Washington and Du Bois is basically an ahistorical construction that pits two titans of black thought against one another. Du Bois certainly opposed Washington's accommodationism, and he developed a different academic program, the Talented Tenth, to help black Americans progress. But he also spoke highly of Washington, congratulated him on his speech at the Atlanta Cotton Exposition (where Washington famously encouraged black people to accommodate themselves to life in the United States), pursued for a short time an academic position at Washington's Tuskegee Institute, and even acknowledged the value of a technical or industrial education. Washington, for his part, not only seems to have respected Du Bois, he attempted to attract him to Tuskegee. He also never opposed Du Bois's Talented Tenth concept.[10] Du Bois's famous essay "Of Mr. Booker T. Washington and Others," in his book *The Souls of Black Folk*, has been held up as the definitive critical statement on Washington and his ideas. Du Bois certainly criticized Washington, but he did so in an exceedingly thoughtful manner, acknowledging Washington's successes while critiquing his failures.[11] In short, the Washington–Du Bois "divide," "controversy," or "rivalry" has largely been overstated. In conceiving of their differences in this manner, scholars have replicated the artificial divisions within black leadership, have missed the nuances of both Du Bois's and Washington's viewpoints, and have, more problematically, obscured other voices, especially that of the far more militant anti-Washington thinker William Monroe Trotter.

The Washington–Du Bois example also underscores how black intellectuals are frequently reduced to only one or two groupings, or as having a single, correct position. In short, black people, black intellectuals specifically, are largely viewed by those outside the community as liberal, and perhaps secondarily as conservative. As noted above, such a conception misses other intellectuals, such as Trotter. His criticisms of Washington, for example, were vicious. He referred to Washington as "the Benedict Arnold of the Negro Race" and asked acerbically, "[A]re the rope and the torch all the race is to get under your leadership?"[12] Trotter also went beyond criticism to actively protest Booker T. Washington. Why then do scholars not discuss the Washington-Trotter disagreement? Trotter's challenges to Washington reveal an additional layer of black intellectual thought, and while Trotter is regularly discussed in black history and African American studies courses, he does not merit the same legacy in the pantheon of black leaders as do Du Bois and Washington. Trotter, in short, does not fit the reductive model of black intellectual leadership.

This reductive thinking is problematic because it focuses almost exclusively on black liberal intellectuals. But what of the radical, the feminist, the Marxist, or the conservative, among other intellectual types? Black intellectualism has also been largely understood as a male domain, but what of black female intellectuals? Surely other forms of intellectualism exist, but their existence has largely been in a vacuum, hidden from the public. Part of our goal with this volume is to make these other forms of black intellectualism visible. This collection represents an intervention in the history of black intellectualism in the United States. Rather than revisiting the well-trodden ground of the contradictory popular and academic perceptions that continue to follow black intellectuals, the contributors attempt to reorient our focus to the sources of the historical and theoretical underpinnings of black intellectualism in modern America.

In the first chapter, "All the Science and Learning": Black Intellectual History in the United States," Gregory D. Smithers provides a broad overview of black intellectual thought from the late eighteenth to the early twentieth centuries. He notes that it was during this time, particularly the nineteenth century, that most of the types of black intellectualism developed, such as liberalism, Marxism, feminism, and conservatism.

In the second chapter, "Black Marxism," Minkah Makalani explores the radical, and often hidden, role of African American Marxists. Makalani seeks to correct an intellectual and political myopia that either ignores black Marxists or sees them simply as pawns in the international Cold War. He also rightly notes that scholarship on black Marxists has tended to be bound by limits on its breadth of inquiry. Marxists are often analyzed solely within the purview of the Communist Party, which obscures other aspects of black

Marxism. In particular, Makalani highlights the role of race, anticolonialism, and the civil rights concerns of black Americans within the Marxist tradition, altering Marxism's seemingly colorblind and class-based focus with an appreciation of African American thought.

In chapter three, "The Quest for Racial Change: African American Intellectuals and the Black Liberal Tradition," Brian D. Behnken explores the history of black liberalism. Itself the most often recognized form of black intellectualism, liberalism, Behnken asserts, is far more complex than is commonly understood. Black liberals imbibed the notions of American democracy and constitutional government, albeit with black people included equally within that constitutional or political framework. Black liberals have had a multiplicity of goals and tactics, from integration to voting rights, from public scholarship to political leadership. But their most important endeavor was rooted in the concept of racial change. Racial change symbolized a transformation of American life that, at its most basic, meant the complete evolution of black equality in the United States.

In the fourth chapter, "Black Conservative Thought in the Post–Civil Rights Era," Danielle L. Wiggins reminds us of the diversity that characterizes the African American intellectual community, focusing on black conservative thinkers' attacks on liberalism and their efforts to offer conservative alternatives. Wiggins shows that their critique of the US government's efforts to intervene on behalf of African Americans and to assist black individuals and communities was a peculiar amalgam of black intellectual traditions and the ideology of the New Right that emerged in the 1970s and 1980s. Conservatives of color tapped into a reservoir of black conservative thought that dates back to the nineteenth century but merged it with the anti–civil rights impetus of white conservatives who welcomed their contributions but marginalized them within organizations of the New Right. Despite the fact that black conservatives were a marginal presence in white institutions and were immensely unpopular within the African American community, their thought left a lasting imprint on political thought in the United States.

The fifth chapter, Benita Roth's "Steps in and Places Outside: The Reception of Black Feminist Intellectuals and Black Feminist Theory in Modern America," analyzes black feminist thought that grew out of civil rights–era activism. Roth notes that while there is a broad scholarly understanding of black feminism, black feminists have often been hidden from public view. However, she avers that black women and black feminists have done much to alter what it means to be black and female in the United States. She highlights especially the origins of intersectionality in black feminist scholarship and the role that intersectionality continues to play in feminist discourses.

Her chapter underlines not only the diversity of African American women's lived experiences—what it means to be simultaneously a racially minoritized individual but also a woman—but also the multiplicity of oppressions that black women experience—from racism to sexism and beyond.

In chapter six, "Intellectual Predicaments: Black Nationalism in the Civil Rights and Post–Civil Rights Eras," Simon Wendt analyzes black nationalist thought from the 1950s to the 1990s. "Black nationalism" has been a term fraught with inaccuracies and misconceptions. The term would seem to indicate a desire for a separate nation-state, but this was only one (and often one with very limited support) aspect of black nationalism. Wendt adopts an understanding of black nationalism that emerged from the Black Power era, calling for racial solidarity and black self-determination, and he highlights its postcolonial or anticolonial nature. Wendt focuses specifically on "paraintellectuals": black thinkers who did not necessarily originate in academia and who viewed the lived experience of black people as the best route to overcome the problems of black America. Thus, paraintellectuals refuted the notion that analysis of African American issues could come from traditional forms of education or learning. Instead, analysis would come from the everyday experiences of black thinkers who lived in what they perceived as a colonial world within the United States.

The final chapter, Tunde Adeleke"'s "Afrocrentic Intellectuals and the Burden of History," is a lively intellectual history of a concept that has divided African American intellectuals as much as it has brought them together. Afrocentrism has a long history in African American thought. It is a way of narrating the past that is at once an example of myth-making and historical narration, while also a source of racial identification for some. Not only does Adeleke detail the long history of Afrocentrism, but he also comments on the divisive and often critical reception that Afrocentrist scholars have experienced, especially in regards to the bifurcation in the field between advocacy and scholarship.

Taken together, the chapters in this volume seek to complicate how black intellectualism is academically and popularly understood. As opposed to simply looking at those "crisis" moments or at the most popular intellectual leaders, we view black intellectualism broadly, and attempt to highlight the diversity of the differing traditions. Black intellectuals were not just individuals with advanced degrees housed in ivory towers; they were grassroots leaders, civil rights activists, politicians, everyday men and women. They represented virtually all aspects of black American life. Their words and thinking had relevance in the times in which they lived and continue to have relevance today.

NOTES

1. Lewis R. Gordon, "Africana Philosophy and Philosophy in Black," *The Black Scholar* 43, no. 4 (Winter 2013): 46.

2. Keeanga Taylor, *From #BlackLivesMatter to Black Liberation* (Chicago: Haymarket Books, 2016).

3. Robin D. G. Kelley, *Yo' Mama's Disfunktional!: Fighting the Culture Wars in Urban America* (Boston: Beacon, 1997), 26; Shawn Taylor, *Big Black Penis: Misadventures in Race and Masculinity* (Chicago: Chicago Review Press, 2008), 70; Jeffrey O. G. Ogbar, *Hip-Hop Revolution: The Culture and Politics of Rap* (Lawrence: University Press of Kansas, 2007); Manning Marable, *Living Black History: How Reimagining the African-American Past Can Remake America's Racial Future* (New York: Basic Civitas Books, 2006).

4. H. Samy Alim and Geneva Smitherman, *Articulate while Black: Barack Obama, Language, and Race in the U.S.* (New York: Oxford University Press, 2012), 4.

5. Such a contradiction in the way black intellectuals are perceived was explored in detail by Harold Cruse in his now iconic *The Crisis of the Negro Intellectual: A Historical Analysis of the Failure of Black Leadership* (Boston: Beacon, 1967), 10.

6. Clarence E. Walker and Gregory D. Smithers, *The Preacher and the Politician: Jeremiah Wright, Barack Obama, and Race in America* (Charlottesville: University of Virginia Press, 2009); Howard McGary, *The Post-Racial Ideal* (Milwaukee: Marquette University Press, 2012); F. Michael Higginbotham, *Ghosts of Jim Crow: Ending Racism in Post-Racial America* (New York: New York University Press, 2013).

7. William J. Moses, *Afrotopia: The Roots of African American Popular History* (New York: Cambridge University Press, 1998); Manning Marable, ed., *Dispatches from the Ebony Tower: Intellectuals Confront the African American Experience* (New York: Columbia University Press, 2000); Vernon J. Williams Jr., *The Social Sciences and Theories of Race* (Urbana: University of Illinois Press, 2006); Cornell West, *Race Matters* (New York: Vintage, 1994).

8. David Theo Goldberg, "Whither West? The Making of a Public Intellectual," in *Education and Cultural Studies: Toward a Performative Practice*, ed. Henry A. Giroux and Patrick Shannon (New York and London: Routledge, 2013), 34–35.

9. Jonathan Scott Holloway, "The Black Intellectual and the 'Crisis Canon' in the Twentieth Century," *Black Intellectuals: Commentary and Critiques*, a special issue of *The Black Scholar* 31, no. 1 (Spring 2001): 2–13.

10. On Du Bois's and Washington's viewpoints of one another, see Raymond Wolters, *Du Bois and His Rivals* (Columbia: University of Missouri Press, 2002) and Raymond W. Smock, *Booker T. Washington: Black Leadership in the Age of Jim Crow* (Chicago: Ivan R. Dee, 2009).

11. W. E. Burghardt Du Bois, *The Souls of Black Folk: Essays and Sketches* (Chicago: A. C. McClurg, 1903), chap. 3.

12. Manning Marable and Leith Mullings, eds., *Let Nobody Turn Us Around: An African American Anthology* (Lanham, MD: Rowman and Littlefield, 2009), 183; Stephen Tuck, *We Ain't What We Ought to Be: The Black Freedom Struggle from Emancipation to Obama* (Cambridge: Harvard University Press, 2010), 120.

- CHAPTER ONE -

"ALL THE SCIENCE AND LEARNING"

Black Intellectual History in the United States

GREGORY D. SMITHERS

In 1895, Edward Austin Johnson published a revised edition of his popular *A School History of the Negro Race in America from 1619 to 1890*. Johnson's book was a primer for black school children. Like other history primers written for African American children, *A School History of the Negro Race in America* emphasized the antiquity of the African people, noted their historical accomplishments—"*The pyramids of Egypt*," Johnson instructed readers, "were either built by Negroes or people closely related to them"—and highlighted the uneasy relationship between the cultural development of black Americans and slavery. Johnson thus wrote, "*All the science and learning* of ancient Greece and Rome was, probably, once in the hands of the foreparents of the American slaves."[1]

The phrase "*All the science and learning*" was a derivation of the more commonly used "science and learning." Both phrases were popular in nineteenth-century intellectual and educational discourses, punctuating the writing of scholars in the hard sciences and the rapidly professionalizing academic disciplines in the humanities and social sciences.[2] To produce and possess "science and learning" was a marker of accomplishment. Through diligent experimentation, empirical analysis, and the accumulation and dissemination of knowledge, human understanding was expanded, and civilization was improved. For Johnson to assert that African people had once possessed "*All the science and learning*" was at once a boast about the intellectual accomplishments of black America's African ancestors and a reminder to readers about the variety of intellectual and cultural influences that constituted the diversity of African American intellectualism.[3]

Significantly, Johnson insisted that African people had once aspired to, and achieved, great feats of learning and understanding. If future generations of black American scientists, scholars, and leaders were to rise up from the ash heap of slavery and the subsequent violence and economic marginalization that followed under the system of Jim Crow segregation in the South and West, African American school children would need to engage with a life of the mind by first recognizing that their African ancestors—no matter how distant—had once overcome great odds in contributing to the civilized world's store of knowledge and understanding. Such history lessons balanced an Africa-centric understanding of the past with recognition of the impact that racial slavery—and the Eurocentric forms of knowledge that made it possible—continued to have on black Americans. Like the authors of other black history primers, Stewart was determined to underscore the idea that black children were not racially inferior to their white contemporaries; instead, African American children did in fact possess the capacity to call on, and develop, ideas about religion, science, the arts and humanities, and politics, to achieve great scientific and intellectual accomplishments.

This chapter presents a historical overview of black intellectual thought between the late eighteenth century and the outbreak of World War II. The following analysis is by no means a comprehensive summation of black intellectualism during this extended period—such analysis would require a book-length treatment. Instead, the chapter charts some of the main currents in black thought with the goal of providing the general historical context for post–World War II black Marxism, liberalism, conservatism, feminism, nationalism, and Afrocentrism.

For much of the nineteenth century, Christianity and liberal intellectual and political thought dominated black intellectual history. Black churches and their ministers were assumed to play a central role in African American social, political, and cultural life; providing spiritual comfort and ethical guidance; and nurturing one of the few spaces in American life where black people could come together and nurture their political consciousness. Indeed, black churches, and the syncretic brand of Christianity that emerged within them, provided African American people with communal spaces in which they could worship, socialize, and develop political and intellectual traditions.[4]

African American interpretations of Christianity had the potential to complement liberal intellectualism and republican thought as much as they could clash with politically radicalized forms of Christianity—something that became particularly clear in the 1960s and 1970s when the emergence of liberation theology presented African Americans with a radical intellectual and political alternative to traditional forms of black church memberships and Christian thinking.[5] However, for much of the nineteenth century, classical liberalism punctuated black abolitionism and played a major role in the formation of a black political and middle class during the late nineteenth and early twentieth centuries.[6] At the same time, the forces of conservatism (and at times, reaction) produced theories about racial separatism and emigration that went against the grain of the black intelligentsia's preference for liberalism throughout much of the nineteenth and early twentieth centuries. Alternatively, Marxist theory challenged the "progressivism" of black liberalism during the late nineteenth and early twentieth centuries, just as black feminist thinking struggled with the double-bind of racism and gender discrimination in American history. Black intellectual history is therefore not monolithic; it is diverse and complex. It reflects the resilience and vibrancy of black culture, and it spotlights the United States' social, economic, political, and cultural shortcomings. The ideas that black intellectuals have written and spoken about since World War II belong to a rich tradition that began in an era when slavery was part of the fabric of American life.

THE FORMATION OF A BLACK INTELLECTUAL CLASS AND THE FIGHT AGAINST SLAVERY

Black American intellectual life traces its origins to the African medicine men and priests who were captured in West Africa, transported to the Caribbean and the Americas, and enslaved on plantations. Medicine men and priests played important roles in transmitting knowledge and keeping cultural practices alive in what Europeans referred to as the New World. As plantation slavery developed in North America during the seventeenth and eighteenth centuries, and the brutal discipline of the slave system intensified, slave owners viewed enslaved "priests" as a threat to the maintenance of a pliant slave labor force. As a result, slave religion became what one historian refers to as the "invisible institution" of the slave plantation complex.[7] Medicine men, or "conjurers," endured among the slave populations of Britain's, and ultimately, the American republic's southern colonies and states. They, along with slave women, continued to be the bearers of medicinal folk remedies and taught slave children maxims for the maintenance of good health and well-being.[8]

The African and African American medicine men and priests who toiled under slavery's brutalities transmitted knowledge from one generation to the next through oral and performative means. Folktales, mythology, and cultural practices were learned orally, aurally, and visually through storytelling, song, and dance.[9] In the seventeenth and early eighteenth centuries, colonial lawmakers worried about the implications of enslaved Africans and African Americans gathering in small congregations to transmit the knowledge contained in these stories, songs, and dances. Much as slave owners worried that "priests" would foment rebellion among other slaves, both lawmakers and slave owners worried that the congregation of blacks could foster a sense of community, providing the cohesiveness needed for rebellion. For example, in urban areas, especially in and around cities such as Charles Town, Richmond, and New York, large congregations of "Negroes" were often seen gathered on the city streets, in taverns, or in the "dramshops." These meetings represented an opportunity for intellectual exchange. The sense of conviviality and community that such gatherings fostered among free and enslaved blacks, and between skilled black tradesmen and working-class white populations, had the potential to undermine the authority of an emerging planter elite.[10]

Planter elites in North America became increasingly concerned during the eighteenth century about the possibility of rebellious slaves cultivating disaffection among their fellow bondsmen.[11] Europeans and Euro-Americans with an interest in the expansion of the slave system wanted to prevent violence and unrest among slave populations to ensure that the socioeconomic and cultural life that slave labor made possible throughout the Atlantic World would not only continue, but expand. The result was an increasingly rigid policing of slave societies. Slave laws, and the policing of those laws, were designed to ensure a subservient slave population.[12] In this increasingly oppressive context, not only did whites frown upon black intellectual activity, but they also attempted to crush it wherever it existed.

Historians and anthropologists have written a great deal about the formation of slave culture in North America during the eighteenth and nineteenth centuries. This scholarship dates back to the days of slavery and the decades immediately following its abolition. Since the civil rights movement in the 1950s and 1960s, however, the scholarly discourse about slave culture and its relationship to the development of black intellectual traditions has produced some intense academic debates. Some scholars argue that cultural retentions from Africa influenced the cultural and intellectual development of black America. Sterling Stuckey, for example, argued that the "final gift of African 'tribalism' in the nineteenth century was its life as a lingering memory in the minds of American slaves."[13] Through the development and transmission of

African oral traditions, music, and dance, New World slaves kept the memory of a life outside of slavery alive. Such memories enabled individuals to forge a sense of community where only back-breaking labor would have otherwise existed.[14]

The notion that African cultural retentions shaped nineteenth-century slave culture remains historically contested.[15] In the early twentieth century, the anthropologist Melville Herskovits tackled this subject by focusing on the acculturation of the "New World Negro." He contended that in the United States, African cultural retentions were particularly weak.[16] Subsequent research by Sidney Mintz and Richard Price urged students of slavery to approach the intellectual and cultural life of diaspora blacks with greater nuance and subtlety, moving our historical understanding beyond the narration of superficial cultural expressions.[17]

Mintz and Price's call has resulted in a rich historiography. Some scholars have echoed Stuckey's analysis and see African retentions in the cultural practices, intellectual formations, and agricultural knowledge of the enslaved.[18] Other scholars, such as Stuart Hall, Paul Gilroy, Philip Morgan, and James Sidbury argue that black cultural and intellectual life in the Caribbean and Americas formed in a syncretic process that resulted from the diasporic migrations of African peoples. Prior to the abolition of the international slave trade, the overwhelming majority of these diasporic migrants were coerced.[19] Millions endured the middle passage and New World slavery, experiences that continue to give meaning to African American intellectual traditions in the United States.[20] Tunde Adeleke refers to the importance of the trans-Atlantic slave trade and New World slavery in the emergence of black cultural and intellectual traditions as the "slavocentric" perspective. Adeleke argues that in nineteenth-century America, slavery "was the essence of the new identity cherished by leading black American thinkers."[21] Indeed, slavery inspired acts of rebellion—both large and small—among the enslaved and framed the activist scholarship of black America's leading antislavery activists, journalists, and community leaders in the decades prior to the outbreak of the Civil War in 1861.[22]

Black intellectualism was thus inflected from its very beginning with an antislavery activism. From the poetry of Phillis Wheatley, David Walker's *Appeal to the Colored Citizens of the World* (1829) to resist "abject slavery and wretchedness," the pioneering journalism of Samuel Cornish and John Russwurm, and the memoirs of enslaved men and women—such as Octavia V. Rogers' *The House of Bondage* (1890)—slavery, or more specifically, slavery's abolition, was fundamental to the emergence of an African American intellectual tradition.[23] As Russwurm so eloquently declared in an 1829 editorial, "Give as much importance as we may to other subjects, to us SLAVERY is the all absorbing one."[24] Russwurm and Cornish's antislavery editorials appeared primarily in the pages of their newspaper, *Freedom's Journal*, a publication that appeared four years prior to the first edition of white abolitionist William Lloyd Garrison's *The Liberator* (1831). Like the black abolitionists who followed their journalistic lead, Russwurm and Cornish were determined to both oppose slavery and publish a black-owned and operated newspaper "devoted to the dissemination of useful knowledge among our brethren, and to their moral and religious improvement."[25]

Black abolitionists led efforts to end slavery and develop strategies to "improve" the race. During the first third of the nineteenth century they did this by emphasizing the language of "moral suasion."[26] Black leaders recognized that for their version of moral suasion and ideas for racial uplift to meet success, significant changes in the United States' social and cultural environment were needed.[27] African American articulations of moral suasion and racial uplift were shaped by the racial realities of American life and reports of slave resistance;[28] but they were also influenced by nineteenth-century romantic literature, Christian theology, classical liberalism, and empirical scholarship that refuted "scientific" theories about "negro inferiority" and justified slavery. Such works as Henri-Baptiste Grégoire's *An Enquiry Concerning the Intellectual and Moral Faculties, and Literature of Negroes and Mulattoes, Distinguished in Science, Literature and the Arts* (1810) appealed to black abolitionist thinkers for the way in which it helped them formulate arguments refuting the racism and pseudoscientific findings of the American School of Ethnology. For example, black abolitionist James McCune Smith used a statistical methodology to refute the arguments of proslavery ideologues. Smith analyzed census data and concluded that the proslavery argument about free blacks in the North suffering from greater incidences of mental illness compared to those enslaved African Americans in the South was false.[29]

Russwurm, Cornish, and McCune Smith were among the leading public intellectuals in the North prior to the Civil War. Their dual focus—abolishing slavery and racial uplift—was aided by the formation of black institutions dedicated to these causes.[30] Among the most important of these institutions was Richard Allen's African Methodist Episcopal Church; the African Baptist Missionary Society (ABMS); the American Moral Reform Society, founded by Robert Purvis and William Whipper; and the Negro Convention Movement.[31]

The Negro Convention Movement is particularly noteworthy in understanding the formation of nineteenth-century black thought. The Negro Convention Movement brought together black ministers, journalists, businessmen, social activists, and intellectuals. Not all of the men who joined the movement were activist-scholars, but all were determined to end slavery, overthrow de facto forms of segregation in the North, and develop strategies to uplift the race. Drawing on the Bible, and taking what they understood to be a scientific approach to the observation of "Negro" physiognomy and intellectual capacity, long-held prejudices used to justify slavery could be overcome. In particular, black leaders pursued this line of argumentation to reinforce the significance attached to examples of "Negro" accomplishment, economic achievement, and cultural refinement.[32] For example, William Whipper, Alfred Niger, and Augustus Price, prominent members of the movement, positioned their arguments in opposition to "scientific" theories about the "Negro's" racial inferiority. In one particularly powerful refutation of antiblack racism, Whipper, Niger, and Price stated, "The general assertion that superiority of the mind is the natural offspring of a fair complexion, arrays itself against the experience of the past and present age, and both natural and physiological science."[33]

Associated with theories about the "natural" inferiority of black Americans were cultural assumptions: they were considered lazy, stupid, ill-disciplined, lascivious, and so forth. The leaders of the Negro Convention Movement recognized the power that such cultural assumptions had on American racial opinion and encouraged African Americans to engage in activities—such as formal education, commercial enterprise, and moral reform societies—that would make a lie of racist assumptions. By becoming successful in business, for example, black men would dispel the racist stereotypes that racial "scientists" pedaled in American popular and academic culture. Thus, the leaders of the Negro Convention Movement insisted that by embracing the qualities of industry, thrift, sobriety, and Christian morality, black Americans would ultimately prove, through their accomplishments, that they were worthy members of the American body politic.[34]

As sectional political debate over slavery intensified between the 1830s and 1861, prominent black abolitionists such as Frederick Douglass, William Wells Brown, Henry Bibb, Harriet Jacobs, and Harriet Tubman strove to persuade Americans of the importance of ending slavery. They also worked to underscore to black Americans the importance of material and moral uplift.[35] Brown, for instance, typified the way in which black abolitionists criticized slavery as corrosive of "religion, liberty, national strength, and social order."[36]

Bibb, like black female abolitionists Sojourner Truth and Harriet Jacobs, emphasized the debilitating emotional effects that slavery had on enslaved women and black family life.[37] Bibb argued that ending slavery would end the forced breakup of enslaved families and halt the immoral treatment of enslaved women. "Female virtue could not be trampled under foot with impunity, and marriage among the people of color kept in utter obscurity," Bibb insisted, with slavery abolished.[38]

Through the publication of memoirs and antislavery narratives, black men and women in the North evidenced their intellectual and organizational commitment to abolishing slavery. Once runaways had escaped along the "underground railroad," or, preferably, slavery was abolished from the republic, the work of overcoming the debilitating effects of bondage began. The Reverend Richard Allen, the founder of the African Methodist Episcopal Church, argued in 1831 that racial uplift should focus on the cultivation of "our mental and physical qualities" in "agriculture and mechanical arts." Acting on such ideas would enable African American men to support strong family units and "give us the standing and condition we desire."[39] Similar arguments were hammered out by the delegates from the Committee on Commerce within the Negro Convention Movement. In an 1847 statement, the Committee on Commerce urged black people to embrace commercial activity because "Commerce [is] the great lever by which modern Europe has been elevated from a state of barbarism and social degradation, whose parallel is only to be found in the present condition of the African race."[40]

Black economic development, however, went hand-in-hand with access to American institutions designed to protect citizens' civil and political rights. Frederick Douglass recognized this when he observed, "Slavery and free institutions can never live peaceably together." According to Douglass, liberty "must either overthrow slavery, or be itself overthrown by slavery."[41] Douglass, a former Maryland slave who escaped to freedom and became the most important black abolitionist of the antebellum era, embodied the way in which black leaders consistently opposed slavery while simultaneously wrestling with arguments about how best to abolish it. Indeed, Douglass's thinking on the relationship between "moral suasion" and "political action" changed noticeably over the course of the 1840s and 1850s.[42] Douglass recognized that the rhetoric of moral suasion lacked the necessary force to inspire political, and, if necessary, military action, to abolish slavery. Moreover, black abolitionists grew increasingly impatient with the anemic efforts of their white counterparts—particularly the so-called "gradualists"—to uplift the poor and uneducated in free black communities.[43] Unsurprisingly, then, Douglass and fellow black abolitionists replaced the language of moral suasion with a more urgent political rhetoric during the 1850s and early 1860s. In an 1862 speech, for example, Douglass demanded "the unrestricted and complete Emancipation of every slave in the United States whether claimed by loyal or disloyal masters."[44]

Historian Waldo Martin, one of Frederick Douglass's biographers, notes that Douglass reiterated his commitment to civil and political equality in the decades immediately after the Civil War. Continuing his long-held opposition for racial separatism, Douglass called on black Americans to strive for an "empirical equality," a legal and economic condition that demanded the extension of equal opportunity and protection before the law for black as well as white Americans. According to Douglass, black America's policy "should be to unite with the great mass of the American people in all their activities, and resolve to fall or flourish with our common country."[45]

Douglass's statements represented the most articulate rendering of the dominant black intellectual position on slavery, freedom, and racial uplift. His was an assimilationist position, informed by the tenets of bourgeois self-help and nineteenth-century liberalism. It was not, as Booker T. Washington would ultimately espouse, an accomodationist position. Nonetheless, while a majority of black Americans shared Douglass's views between the 1850s and the 1870s, not all black thinkers fell into line.[46] Martin Delany, for example, became famous for his espousal of black nationalism and a "separatist" ideology. Other nineteenth-century black intellectuals espoused variants of black nationalism, most notably Alexander Crummell, who, as historian Wilson J. Moses observes, can be viewed as a source for both black nationalist thought and black conservatism.[47] Delany, however, is worth emphasizing because of the varied intellectual life he led—addressing topics such as African history, slavery, and the racial origins of humankind—and for his intellectual disagreements with Frederick Douglass.[48] Delany's version of black nationalism, while also concerned with racial "uplift," counseled emigration out of the United States.[49] Delany's racial separatism did not center on Africa, however. He rejected emigration to Liberia, labeling it "no place for the colored freedmen of the United States."[50] Instead, he insisted, "The advantages of the colored people of the United States, to be derived from emigration to Central, South America, and the West Indies, are incomparably greater than that to any other parts of the world at present."[51]

But Delany was arguing against the tide of most black intellectuals during the 1850s, 1860s, and 1870s. Delany's racial and geographical separatism thus proved distasteful to most black abolitionist and political leaders. Frederick

Douglass's position more accurately captured the idealism of most black Americans. His vision of the American republic was of a biracial nation, a national self-imagining that did not become commonplace until after the Second World War. "The black and the white—the negro and the European—these constitute the American people," Douglass argued shortly after the Civil War, "and, in all the likelihoods of the case, they will ever remain the principle inhabitants of the United States, in some form or other."[52]

BLACK INTELLECTUALS AFTER SLAVERY

The composition of the American body politic emerged as one of the most important topics of discussion for both black and white intellectuals after the Civil War. The Civil War changed the United States in that militarily, the slave South was defeated, slavery was abolished, and thanks to the Fourteenth and Fifteenth Amendments to the US Constitution, black Americans enjoyed the protections of the law and political equality for the first time. In the late 1860s and the 1870s, as Americans "reconstructed" their nation, former slaves voted, and black men such as John Lynch, P. B. S. Pinchback, Mumford McCoy, Hiram Revels, and Blanche K. Bruce, were elected to political office at the state and/or federal level. For the United States, and the South in particular, the emergence of elected black officials was nothing short of revolutionary. Douglass's biracial prophecy was becoming a reality.[53]

The emergence of a cadre of elected black officials afforded a unique opportunity to transform black thought into policy. The liberal ideals of political and legal equality, coupled with integration into America's capitalist system, held sway among black thinkers.[54] But the legacy of slavery loomed large. Politically, whites deployed physical force and intimidation to keep blacks away from the ballot box or from running for elected office. Economically, tens of thousands of black Americans found themselves locked into a system of sharecropping and debt peonage that looked and felt little different from slavery. Socially, racial violence undermined African American enterprise and disrupted the nurturing of stable black families. And culturally, millions of white Southerners remained "unreconstructed," refusing to accept the outcome of the Civil War, while millions more throughout the United States continued to believe that "the Negro is not equal to the white man." The fear of "Negro rule" that gripped white Americans in the decades after the Civil War gave rise to terrorist groups such as the Ku Klux Klan, segregation laws, the white primary, and the disenfranchisement of millions of black Americans. By the late 1880s, Douglass's biracial prophecy was being picked apart by reactionary forces in American politics and cultural life.[55]

The challenges that Jim Crow segregation ultimately posed for black thinkers were manifold: political powerlessness; labor exploitation; violence, particularly in the form of lynching; and racist caricatures that vacillated between happy-go-lucky, watermelon-eating "negras," to corrupt and power-hungry black men whose true ambition was to rape and/or intermarry with white women. These challenges inspired different forms of black intellectual activity at the turn of the century. Many black leaders touted education as the solution to overcoming racial prejudice. But what sort of education best served black Americans? While large numbers of African Americans availed themselves of educational opportunities during Reconstruction, in the segregated world of Jim Crow America black intellectuals split over the most appropriate form of schooling for African American children.

Two dominant schools of thought emerged. On one side, Booker T. Washington championed the idea of industrial education. At the Tuskegee Institute in Alabama, Washington put his plan for industrial education into action. With the financial support of sympathetic whites, Washington oversaw a curriculum that instructed boys in practical skills and trades, and girls in the "domestic arts." His educational philosophy was both practical and pragmatic. Believing that the ethos of self-help was more important to black Americans than ever in the age of Jim Crow, Washington stated of his educational philosophy:

> I would say to the black boy what I would say to the white boy, Get all the mental development that your time and pocket-book will allow,—the more, the better; but the time has come when a larger proportion—not all, for we need professional men and women—of the educated colored men and women should give themselves to industrial and business life. The professional class will be helped in so far as the rank and file have an industrial foundation, so they can pay for professional service.[56]

Under Washington's guidance, industrial education at Tuskegee was a rather vague program. This was intentional. To those whites wanting to see blacks remain the "mud sill" of American society, Washington's curriculum seemed to fit the bill. For black parents wanting to give their children the practical skills to make a living in a hostile white world, Tuskegee offered a model for self-help and individual capitalist enterprise. But for black America's intellectual elites, industrial education reinforced the unenlightened and lowly socioeconomic standing of African American people.[57]

The ideas of W. E. B. Du Bois echoed the main body of opposition to Washington's curriculum of industrial education. While Washington recognized the need for laboring and professional classes in black America, college-bred men such as Du Bois offered increasingly pointed criticisms of the Tuskegee curriculum and its emphasis on materialism and disengagement with the political sphere.[58] Du Bois, who haughtily referred to his class of educated African Americans as "the Talented Tenth," wanted more from black education than the ability to put bread on the table—although he certainly wanted this. He wanted young black people to have a liberal arts education that would help them to become "decent self-respecting citizens."[59]

Du Bois enjoyed a rich life as an activist-scholar. Ever the champion of civil rights, his early academic career was characterized by historical studies of the international slave trade, slavery, Reconstruction, and the sociology of urban race relations and racialized poverty. And Du Bois historical scholarship helped to lift the veil from American memories of slavery. The racial politics driving Du Bois's scholarship was also evident during his time as editor of the NAACP's *The Crisis*. Du Bois used *The Crisis* to present a popularized version of African and African American history, draw attention to campaigns to pass antimiscegenation laws and abolish segregation statutes, and expose the brutalities of lynching in the South and racialized poverty in the North. In both a journalistic and scholarly capacity, Du Bois was a true scholar-activist dedicated to the cause of social justice.[60]

For much of the early twentieth century, Du Bois's thinking reflected the "science and learning" that black Americans coveted. He studied the "Negro problem," as it was called, with the empirical eye of the social scientist and the narrative verve of the historian. In *The Philadelphia Negro* (1899), for instance, Du Bois showcased his skill as a historical sociologist, dissecting the causes of racial poverty, crime, and interracial mixing.[61] It was racial slavery, though, that Du Bois came back to repeatedly to explain disfunction in black families, explore the racial "caste" system in America, and discuss white America's antipathy for "social equality," a not-so-covert euphemism for interracial marriage.[62] On this latter point, all other elements of the "Negro problem" coalesced. As Du Bois noted of national discussions about "social equality":

> [O]ne party hotly begins the discussion by intimating in plain terms that blacks are degenerates and prostitutes, commerce with whom on

any plane is monstrous. The other party retorts with a record of millions of mulattoes and mixed bloods, the deliberate degradation of black womanhood and the criminal lust of the white race the world over. With such beginnings there is no rational end of discussion, no reasonable enlightenment.[63]

Indeed, racial enlightenment seemed well out of reach for most Americans by the early twentieth century. Segregation was the law of the land in the South and West, and the unspoken custom in the North (although there, too, efforts were made at the state level to pass anti-interracial marriage laws).[64] In the South and Midwest, the lynching of thousands of African Americans was popularly assumed to be the manifestation of justifiable white anger about black men lusting after white women. The activist scholarship of black Americans such as Ida B. Wells and Walter White helped expose the broader motives behind lynching, motives that at the end of the day came back to the white South's determination to maintain control of a grotesquely violent and racist society.[65]

The racial realities of late nineteenth- and early twentieth-century America thus inspired black intellectual critiques of race and sexualized racism. Anna Julia Cooper, for instance, became one of the most prescient of black female intellectual voices during this time. Her writings were learned, but they were also deeply affected by the subjective experience of being a racialized woman in the United States. "Only the BLACK WOMAN can say," Cooper famously wrote, "'when and where I enter, in the quiet, undisputed dignity of my womanhood, without violence and without suing or special patronage, then and there the whole negro race enters with me.'" Like Du Bois, Cooper's scholarship spoke to the "problems" of the "whole negro race."[66] She knew the stakes were high. Sexual abuse, violence, impoverishment, and legal invisibility afflicted black American men, women, and children less as individuals and more as members of a family, a community, and a race.

If race and slavery were intertwined factors in black abolitionist demands for the immediate end of slavery in the nineteenth century, they remained—with sexual violence against black women—the enduring historical and sociological obstacles to the overthrow of Jim Crow segregation and the acquisition of legal equality in the twentieth. The liberal integrationist thread of black thought therefore endured into the next century, but the challenges black intellectuals grappled with were in some respects more profound. In large part, this was because ideas about race, coupled with a scholarly and popular antipathy for race mixing, acquired the appearance of scientific truisms in American culture.⁶⁷ In response, black intellectuals began the process of dismantling scientific racism and challenging the social conventions and laws that perpetuated sexual violence against black people.

W. Montague Cobb, one of the early twentieth century's few black physical anthropologists, took an empirical approach to the question of race. Cobb maintained that rigid racial categories were fictitious because studies of human heredity revealed growth, and development remained unaltered in racial "crosses." Du Bois added a historical and sociological perspective to the discussion of racial "types." In 1921, for instance, he pointed out that black Americans had "not asked for amalgamation"; that had been "forced upon us by brute strength, ignorance, poverty, degradation and fraud." Du Bois added that the human races are so malleable that intermixture will inevitably "decrease the contrast between extreme racial forms."⁶⁸

But there was something more at stake than academic arguments about the malleability of racial groupings. According to black activists, legally preventing racial mixing on a sexual or social level ultimately reinforced the socioeconomic disadvantages of black families. African American religious leaders and moral reformers tended to council conformity to bourgeois standards of morality, hygiene, and nucleated family formation as a means of overcoming the racial history that helped to shape white perceptions of black people. This conservative, antievolutionary, approach to racial uplift came increasingly into conflict with black intellectuals, such as Du Bois, who endeavored to weave evolutionary ideas—and to write openly about the utility of eugenics and birth control—into their critiques of race and racial change.⁶⁹

This was an argument that the African American sociologist E. Franklin Frazier linked back to slavery in his path-breaking *The Negro Family in the United States* (1939).⁷⁰ Of more immediate concern to early twentieth-century blacks was the impact that laws against intermarriage would have on black families and communities. Francis Grimke, one of the leading African American campaigners for civil rights during the late nineteenth and early twentieth centuries, was unequivocal in stating his opposition to a proposed antimiscegenation law in Washington, DC. Grimke argued that interracial sex was a product of the racism and exploitation of the slave plantation. To pass laws prohibiting intermarriage would simply perpetuate nineteenth-century immorality in a new century. Thus, Grimke insisted that legal prohibitions on intermarriage create the "conditions where it is safe for a [white] man, who is protected on one side by his color, to do certain things which he would not dare do if he were not protected in that way."⁷¹

The bitter lessons of history were never far from the surface for black activist-scholars during the late nineteenth and early twentieth centuries. This should not be surprising given the segregated nature of black education between the late 1880s and the onset of the civil rights movement. Within the confines of these segregated schoolrooms, black children were exposed to black-authored history primers that fostered both "race pride" and an awareness of slavery's place in American history. In 1882, for example, George Washington Williams, a prominent African American minister, politician, and veteran of the Civil War, published volume 1 of *History of the Negro Race in America from 1619 to 1880*. Williams's primer was attentive to change over time and space, informing students, "For nearly three centuries Africa has been robbed of her sable sons. For nearly three centuries they have toiled in bondage, unrequited, in this youthful republic of the West. They have grown from a small company to be an exceedingly great people,—five millions in number. No longer chattels, they are human beings; no longer bondmen, they are freemen, with almost every civil disability removed."[72] Williams was a black intellectual determined to highlight the social, cultural, political, and economic contributions that people of African descent had made to the American colonies and the "youthful republic." Through generations of coerced migrations across the Atlantic Ocean, Williams detailed how African slaves evolved from saleable "chattel" to "human beings." With emancipation, freedom brought new opportunities for the individual and collective development of African America.

While at pains to emphasize the contribution that people of African descent had made to American history, Williams articulated an awareness shared by many black Americans of his class and education: emancipation did not mean complete freedom for African American people. Williams believed that only with the total removal of "civil disability" would black people be able to rightly avail themselves of "all the science and learning" of the age. He seized on this popular phrase to assert that the former slaves' "weary feet now press up the mount of science. Their darkened intellect now sweeps, unfettered, through realms of learning and culture." And in acknowledgement of the biracial America that Douglass prophesied, Williams added, "With his Saxon brother, the African slakes his insatiable thirstings for knowledge at the same fountain."[73]

African American intellectuals continued to wrestle with the legacy of slavery, the complexities of race and racism, and their own aspirations for "science and learning" throughout the early twentieth century. In the formation of political institutions, mutual aid societies, churches, and scholarly fraternities, such as the American Negro Academy and its dedication to the promotion of "Literature, Science, and Art" among "men of African descent," black thought continued to evolve.[74] It also became more complex. The great migration of blacks from the South to the North during the interwar period, coupled with the influence of the women's suffrage movement on black women's thinking and the spread of Marxist ideologies, meant that how black Americans thought about race and the significance of slavery in their history became increasingly contested. As the following chapters in this volume suggest, the emergence of a distinct form of black feminist thinking and African American understandings of Marxism challenged the historically dominant liberal strain of black thought in the United States.

The Russian Revolution convinced African Americans such as A. Philip Randolph (one of black America's most prominent labor union leaders), activist Bayard Rustin, and academics Claude McKay and the "Angry Blond Negro" Cyril Briggs that they were part of a larger "struggle" against economic exploitation and oppression. To black communists, slavery had constituted the ultimate form of labor exploitation. And the exploitation that engendered poverty and splintered black families continued in modern industrial garb in the twentieth century. These ideas gained considerable traction in Harlem, a crossroads of southern black emigrants and black migrants from the Caribbean. In 1921, communists celebrated one of their greatest recruiting coups when they recruited Cyril Briggs in Harlem. At the time, Briggs had been a member of Marcus Garvey's United Negro Improvement Association (UNIA), a black nationalist organization committed to racial separatism and black emigration "back" to Africa. However, once Briggs embraced communism he parted with UNIA because of his dislike of Garvey's procapitalist views.[75] Emblematic of black socialist thought as it developed during the first half of the twentieth century, the idea that capitalism perpetuated the legacies of slavery rang true for black Marxists such as Briggs.

Black women also tested, and expanded, the intellectual boundaries of black liberalism during the late nineteenth and early twentieth centuries. Ida B. Wells, Mary Church Terrell, Anna Cooper, and scores of lesser-known black women developed ideas designed to challenge racism and gender discrimination. These intellectual efforts were supported by a growing number of black women's clubs during the early twentieth century. The members of these institutions voiced their opposition to segregation, lynching, and poverty, and they joined the fight for civil and political rights. Two organizations in particular, the National Federation of Afro-American Women and the National League of Colored Women, led these efforts. They eventually merged, forming the National Association of Colored Women (NACW) in 1896. Mary Church Terrell, the first president of NACW and an advocate for liberal integrationism, was a tireless campaigner for civil rights and desegregation. Like the growing numbers of black women who joined political clubs and social organizations during the early twentieth century, Terrell insisted that "the evil of segregation" must fall.

CONCLUSION

In the 1950s, 1960s, and 1970s, the civil rights movement and the black studies movement transformed America. They brought together the major threads in black intellectual thought—liberalism, socialism, feminism, conservatism, and Afrocentrism—that continue to punctuate intellectual discourse in the twenty-first century. In the 1950s, 1960s, and 1970s, though, the challenge for black intellectuals was to articulate arguments that would buttress efforts to undermine racist discourses in the United States and transform the discriminatory practices that had become endemic in American institutions. As the following chapters demonstrate, black intellectuals played, and continue to play, a key role in reorienting the ways in which all Americans talk and have talked about race, racism, and history. It is fitting, therefore, to conclude with the words of Harold Cruse, who observed in his thought-provoking *The Crisis of the Negro Intellectual* (1967): "The peculiarities of the American social structure, and the position of the intellectual class within it, make the functional role of the negro intellectual a special one. The negro intellectual must deal intimately with the white power structure and cultural apparatus, and the inner realities of the black world at one and the same time." Significantly, Cruse added that the "functional role of the negro intellectual demands that he *cannot* be absolutely separated from either the black or the white world."[76]

NOTES

1. Edward A. Johnson, *A School History of the Negro Race in America from 1619 to 1890, with a Short Introduction as to the Origin of the Race; also a Short Sketch of Liberia* (revised edition, Chicago: W. B. Conkey, 1895), 9.

2. A. W. Coats, *The Sociology and Professionalization of Economics: British and American Economic Essays*, vol. 2 (New York and London: Routledge, 1993), 234–35; Peter Novick, *That Noble Dream: The "Objectivity Question" and the American Historical Profession*

(New York: Cambridge University Press, 1988),47–48; Mary O. Furner, *Advocacy and Objectivity: A Crisis in the Professionalization of American Social Science, 1865–1905* (1975; rpr. New Brunswick: Transaction, 2011), xii–xiii; Sonja Olin Lauritzen and Robert Ohlsson, "Transformations of Risk Knowledge: The Medical Encounter and Patients' Narrative Construction of Meaning," in *Education, Professionalization, and Social Representation: On the Transformation of Social Knowledge*, ed. Mohamed Chaib, Berth Danermark, and Staffan Selander (New York and London: Routledge, 2011), 185–86.

3. On this point, see Gregory D. Smithers, *Slave Breeding: Sex, Violence, and Memory in African American History* (Gainesville: University Press of Florida, 2012); Edward Baptist, *The Half Has Never Been Told: Slavery and the Making of American Capitalism* (New York: Basic Books, 2014), chap. 7; Trevor G. Burnard, *Planters, Merchants, and Slaves: Plantation Societies in British America, 1650–1820* (Chicago: University of Chicago Press, 2015), 195.

4. Wallace D. Best, *Passionately Human, No Less Divine: Religion and Culture in Black Chicago 1915–1952* (Princeton: Princeton University Press, 2005), 3; Clarence E. Walker and Gregory D. Smithers, *The Preacher and the Politician: Jeremiah Wright, Barack Obama, and Race in America* (Charlottesville: University of Virginia Press, 2009), 23; Paul Harvey, *Through the Storm, through the Night: A History of African American Christianity* (Lanham, MD: Rowman and Littlefield, 2011), 2; Edward Blum and Paul Harvey, *The Color of Christ: The Sons of God and the Saga of Race in America* (Chapel Hill: University of North Carolina Press, 2012), 87.

5. John Sallient, *Black Puritan, Black Republican: The Life and Thought of Lemuel Haynes, 1753–1833* (New York: Oxford University Press, 2003); Sylvester Johnson, "The African American Christian Tradition," in *The Oxford Handbook of African American Theology*, ed. Katie G. Cannon and Anthony B. Pinn (New York: Oxford University Press, 2014), 73–74; Blum and Harvey, *The Color of Christ*, 238.

6. At the same time, I agree with Manisha Sinha, that acts of slave resistance proved absolutely critical to the cause of emancipation. Manisha Sinha, *The Slave's Cause: A History of Abolition* (New Haven: Yale University Press, 2016), 1.

7. Albert J. Raboteau, *Slave Religion: The "Invisible Institution" in the Antebellum South* (New York: Oxford University Press, 1978), xiii; William M. Banks, *Black Intellectuals: Race and Responsibility in American Life* (New York: W. W. Norton, 1996), 3–4.

8. Todd L. Savitt, *Medicine and Slavery: The Disease and Health Care of Blacks in* (1978; rpr. Bloomington: University of Illinois Press, 2002), 120; Marie Jenkins Schwartz, *Birthing a Slave: Motherhood and Medicine in the Antebellum South* (Cambridge, MA: Harvard University Press, 2006), 111; Herbert C. Covey, *African American Slave Medicine: Herbal and Non-Herbal Treatments* (Lanham, MD: Rowman and Littlefield, 2008), 50.

9. Banks, *Black Intellectuals*, 6–7.

10. Orville W. Taylor, *Negro Slavery in Arkansas* (Durham: Duke University Press, 1958), 6; Patricia Woods, "The French and the Natchez Indians in Louisiana: 1700–1731," *Louisiana History* 19 (Fall 1978): 414; Philip D. Morgan, *Slave Counterpoint: Black Culture in the Eighteenth-Century Chesapeake and Lowcountry* (Chapel Hill: University of North Carolina Press, 1998), 20, 305–6, 352, 413–14; Jane Landers, *Black Society in Spanish Florida* (Urbana: University of Illinois Press, 1999), 31.

11. Gwendolyn Hall, *Africans in Colonial Louisiana: The Development of Afro-Creole Culture in the Eighteenth Century* (Baton Rouge: Louisiana State University Press, 1992), 189; David J. Libby, *Slavery and Frontier Mississippi, 1720–1835* (Jackson: University Press of Mississippi, 2004), 11–12; Ira Berlin, *Generations of Captivity: A History of African-American Slaves* (Cambridge, MA: Belknap Press of Harvard University Press, 2003), 39–42.

12. Thomas D. Morris, *Southern Slavery and the Law, 1619–1860* (Chapel Hill: University of North Carolina Press, 1996).

13. Sterling Stuckey, *Slave Culture: Nationalist Theory and the Foundations of Black America* (New York: Oxford University Press, 1987), 3.

14. Laura Tanna, "African Retentions, Yoruba and Kikongo Songs in Jamaica," *Jamaica Journal* 16 (August 1983): 47–52; John Thornton, *Africa and Africans in the Making of the Atlantic World, 1400–1800* (New York: Cambridge University Press, 1998).

15. Tommy L. Lott, *The Invention of Race: Black Culture and the Politics of Representation* (Malden, MA: Blackwell, 1999), 23.

16. Melville J. Herskovits, "On the Provenience of New World Negroes," *Social Forces* 12 (December 1933): 247–62; Melville J. Herskovits, *The New World Negro: Selected Papers in Afroamerican Studies*, ed. Frances S. Herskovits (Bloomington: Indiana University Press, 1966), 305–14.

17. Sidney W. Mintz and Richard Price, *The Birth of African-American Culture: An Anthropological Perspective* (1976; rpr. Boston: Beacon, 1992), 54–56.

18. Works that focus on African "agency" and cultural retention in black American culture include Lawrence W. Levine, *Black Culture and Black Consciousness: Afro-American Folk Thought from Slavery to Freedom* (New York: Oxford University Press, 1977); Winifred K. Vass, *The Bantu Speaking Heritage of the United States* (Los Angeles: UCLA, Center for Afro-American Studies, 1979); Stuckey, *Slave Culture*; John K. Thornton, *Africa and Africans in the Making of the Atlantic World, 1400–1800*, 2nd ed. (New York: Cambridge University Press, 1998); Judith A. Carney, *Black Rice: The African Origins of Rice Cultivation in the Americas* (Cambridge, MA: Harvard University Press, 2001); Jessica Millward, *Finding Charity's Folk: Enslaved and Free Black Women in Maryland* (Athens: University of Georgia Press, 2015), 43.

19. Stuart Hall, "Negotiating Caribbean Identities," in *New Caribbean Thought: A Reader*, ed. Brian Meeks and Folke Lindahl (Kingston: University of West Indies Press, 2001), 24–39; Paul Gilroy, *The Black Atlantic: Modernity and Double Consciousness* (London: Verson, 1993); Philip D. Morgan, *Slave Counterpoint: Black Culture in the Eighteenth-Century Chesapeake and Lowcountry* (Chapel Hill: University of North Carolina Press, 1998); James Sidbury, *Becoming African in America: Race and Nation in the Early Black Atlantic* (New York: Oxford University Press, 2007); David Eltis, *The Rise of African Slavery in the Americas* (New York: Cambridge University Press, 2000).

20. Works that address the syncretic and diasporic nature of black culture include Morgan, *Slave Counterpoint*; Stuart Hall, "New Ethnicities," in *Black British Cultural Studies: A Reader*, ed. Houston A. Baker Jr., Manthia Diawara, and Ruth H. Lindeborg (Chicago: University of Chicago Press, 1996), 163–72; Paul Gilroy, *"There Ain't No Black in the Union Jack": The Cultural Politics of Race and Nation* (Chicago: University of Chicago Press, 1991); Michael Mullin, *Africa in America: Slave Acculturation and Resistance in the American

South and the British Caribbean, 1736–1831 (Bloomington: Indiana University Press, 1992), 269–70; Rosanne M. Adderley, *New Negroes from Africa: Slave Trade Abolition and Free African settlement in the Nineteenth-Century Caribbean* (Bloomington: Indiana University Press, 2006); James Sidbury, *Becoming African in America: Race and Nation in the Early Black Atlantic* (New York: Oxford University Press, 2007), see especially p. 6; Herbert S. Klein, *The Atlantic Slave Trade*, new ed. (New York: Cambridge, 2010).

21. Tunde Adeleke, *UnAfrican Americans: Nineteenth-Century Black Nationalists and the Civilizing Mission* (Lexington: University of Kentucky Press, 1998), 104.

22. On this point, see Sinha, *The Slave's Cause*.

23. On Phillis Wheatley's poetry and antislavery prose see John C. Shields, *Phillis Wheatley's Poetics of Liberation: Backgrounds and Contexts* (Knoxville: University of Tennessee Press, 2008); Peter P. Hinks, *David Walker's Appeal to the Colored Citizens of the World* (University Park: Pennsylvania State University Press, 2000), 40; Octavia V. Rogers, *The House of Bondage, or, Charlotte Brooks and Other Slaves* (New York: Hunt and Eaton, 1890).

24. Jacqueline Bacon, *Freedom's Journal: The First African-American Newspapers* (Lanham, MD: Rowan and Littlefield, 2007), 210. See also Herbert Aptheker, "The Negro in the Abolitionist Movement," *Science and Society* 5, no. 2 (Spring 1941): 148–72.

25. "The First Negro Newspaper's Opening Editorial, 1827," in *African American Political Thought: Integration vs. Separatism*, ed. Marcus D. Pohlmann (New York and London: Routledge, 2003), 2.

26. Tunde Adeleke, "Afro-Americans and Moral Suasion: The Debate in the 1830s," *Journal of Negro History* 83, no. 2 (1998): 127–42.

27. Patrick Rael, *Black Identity and Black Protest in the Antebellum North* (Chapel Hill: University of North Carolina Press, 2002), 200.

28. Sinha, *The Slave's Cause*, 213, 381, 419.

29. James McCune Smith, "Freedom and Slavery for the Afric-Americans (1844)," in *The Works of James McCune Smith: Black Intellectual and Abolitionist*, ed. John Stauffer (New York: Oxford University Press, 2006), 62–65; Gregory D. Smithers, *Science, Sexuality, and Race in the United States and Australia, 1780s–1940s*, rev. ed. (Lincoln: University of Nebraska Press, 2017), chap. 5.

30. James Oliver Horton, "Generations of Protest: Black Families and Social Reform in Ante-Bellum Boston," *The New England Quarterly* 49, no. 2 (June 1976): 242–56.

31. On Richard Allen and the AME Church see Richard Newman's insightful *Freedom's Prophet: Bishop Richard Allen, the AME Church, and the Black Founding Fathers* (New York: New York University Press, 2008). For the ABMS see Sandy D. Martin, *Black Baptists and African Missions: The Origins of a Movement, 1880–1915* (Macon: Mercer University Press, 1989), 1–40 ("Introduction: Laying the Foundations, 1815–1879"). On the American Moral Reform Society see Howard H. Bell, "The American Moral Reform Society, 1836–1841," *Journal of Negro Education* 27, no. 1 (Winter 1958): 34–40.

32. Hugh H. Smythe, "Changing Patterns in Negro Leadership," *Social Forces* 29, no. 2 (December 1950): 191–97; Leon F. Litwack, "The Abolitionist Dilemma: The Antislavery Movement and the Northern Negro," *The New England Quarterly* 34, no. 1 (March 1961): 50–73.

33. *Minutes of the Fifth Annual Convention of the Free People of Colour* (Philadelphia, 1835), 26.

34. Gregory D. Smithers, "Black Gentleman as Good as White": Comparing the Origins and Development of African-American and Australian Aboriginal Political Protest," *Journal of African American History* 93, no. 3 (Summer 2008): 315–36.

35. Patrick C. Kennicott, "Black Persuaders in the Antislavery Movement," *Journal of Black Studies* 1, no. 1 (September 1970): 5–20; Frederick Cooper, "Elevating the Race: The Social Thought of Black Leaders, 1827–50," *American Quarterly* 24 (December 1972): 604–25.

36. William Wells Brown, *Narrative of William Wells Brown, an American Slave: Written by Himself* (London: Charles Gilpin, 1849), iv.

37. *Narrative of the Life of Sojourner Truth, A Northern Slave, emancipated from Bodily Servitude by the State of New York, in 1828* (Boston: Printed for the author, 1850); Linda Brent (pseudonym), *Incidents in the Life of a Slave Girl* (Boston: Published by the author, 1861).

38. Henry Bibb, *Narrative of the Life and Adventures of Henry Bibb, an American Slave* (New York: Published by the author, 1849), 199. For further analysis of this point see Gregory D. Smithers, *Slave Breeding: Sex, Violence, and Memory in African American History* (Gainesville: University Press of Florida, 2012).

39. Allen quoted in *Constitution of the American Society of Free Persons of Colour, For Improving Their Condition in the United States; for Purchasing Lands; and for the Establishment of a Settlement in Upper Canada, Also The proceedings of the Convention, with Their Address to the Free Persons of Colour in the United States* (Philadelphia, 1831), 9, 11.

40. *Proceedings of the National Convention of Colored People, and Their Friends, Held in Troy, N.Y., on the 6th, 7th, 8th, and 9th October, 1847* (Troy, NY, 1847), 23, 27. See similarly *Minutes of the Fourth Annual Convention, for the Improvement of the Free People of Colour, in the United States, held by Adjournments in the Asbury Church, New-York, from the 2d to the 12th of June Inclusive, 1834* (New-York, 1834), 7; *Minutes of the Fifth Annual Convention of the Free People of Color, 1835*, 9; *Report of the Proceedings of the Colored National Convention, Held at Cleveland, Ohio, on Wednesday, September 6, 1848* (Rochester: John Dick, at the North Star Office, 1848), 17–18.

41. Douglass quoted in August Meier, *Negro Thought in America, 1880–1915: Racial Ideologies in the Age of Booker T. Washington* (1963; rpr. Ann Arbor: University of Michigan Press, 1988), 3.

42. Howard H. Bell, "National Negro Conventions of the Middle 1840s: Moral Suasion vs. Political Action," *Journal of Negro History* 42, no. 4 (October 1957): 247–60.

43. Benjamin Quarles, *Black Abolitionists* (1969; rpr. New York: Da Capo, 1991), 9, 15, 49, 70; Yee, *Black Women Abolitionists*, 86; Graham R. Hodges, *David Ruggles: A Radical Black Abolitionist and the Underground Railroad in New York City* (Chapel Hill: University of North Carolina Press, 2010), 4; Sinha, *The Slave's Cause*, 2.

44. William S. McFeely, *Frederick Douglass* (New York: W. W. Norton, 1991), 214.

45. Douglass quoted in Martin, *The Mind of Frederick Douglass*, 98.

46. Jane H. Pease and William H. Pease, "Negro Conventions and the Problem of Black Leadership," *Journal of Black Studies* 2, no. 1 (September 1971): 29–44.

47. Wilson J. Moses, *Alexander Crummell: A Study of Civilization and Its Discontents* (New York: Oxford University Press, 1989), 9.

48. See for example Martin R. Delany, *Principia of Ethnology: The Origin of Races and Color* (Philadelphia: Harper and Brothers, 1879). Historians continue to debate the significance of *Principia* to black intellectual history. See Robert S. Levine, *Martin Delany, Frederick Douglass, and the Politics of Representative Identity* (Chapel Hill: University of North Carolina Press, 1997), 234–35; Mia Bay, *The White Image in the Black Mind: African-American Ideas about White People* (New York: Oxford University Press, 2000), 96–97; Tunde Adeleke, *Without Regard to Race: The Other Martin Robison Delany* (Jackson: University Press of Mississippi, 2003), 167–70; Bruce D. Baum, *The Rise and Fall of the Caucasian Race: A Political History of Racial Identity* (New York: New York University Press, 2006), 152–53.

49. Howard H. Bell, "The Negro Emigration Movement, 1849–1854: A Phase of Negro Nationalism," *The Phylon Quarterly* 20, no. 2 (2nd Quarter, 1959): 132–42; Dexter B. Gordon, *Black Identity: Rhetoric, Ideology, and Nineteenth-Century Nationalism* (Carbondale: Southern Illinois University Press, 2003), 73; Rael, *Black Identity and Black Protest*, 254.

50. Martin R. Delany, *The Condition, Elevation, Emigration, and Destiny of the Colored People of the United States* (1852; rpr. Baltimore, MD: Black Classic, 1993), 171.

51. Ibid., 179.

52. Douglass quoted in Levine, *Martin Delany, Frederick Douglass, and the Politics of Representative Identity*, 12.

53. John Hope Franklin, *Reconstruction after the Civil War* (1961; rpr. Chicago: University of Chicago Press, 1994), 135; Leon F. Litwack, *Been in the Storm So Long: The Aftermath of Slavery* (New York: Vintage, 1980) 502–38; Eric Foner, *Reconstruction: America's Unfinished Revolution, 1863–1877* (New York: Harper and Row, 1988), 353–54, passim; Bruce A. Ragsdale and Joel D. Treese, *Black Americans in Congress, 1870–1989* (Washington, DC: Office of the Historian, U S House of Representatives, 1990); Edmund L. Drago, *Black Politicians and Reconstruction in Georgia: A Splendid Failure* (Athens: University of Georgia Press, 1992), 66–100; Nicholas Lemann, *Redemption: The Last Battle of the Civil War* (New York: Farrar, Straus and Giroux, 2006); Douglas R. Egerton, *The Wars of Reconstruction: The Brief, Violent History of America's Most Progressive Era* (New York: Bloomsbury, 2014).

54. Eric Foner, "Rights and the Constitution in Black Life During the Civil War and Reconstruction," *Journal of American History* 74, no. 3 (December 1987), 863–83; Michele Mitchell, *Righteous Propagation: African Americans and the Politics of Racial Destiny after Reconstruction* (Chapel Hill: University of North Carolina Press, 2004), 1–3.

55. William W. Freehling, *The Road to Disunion: Secessionists Triumphant, 1854–1861* (New York: Oxford University Press, 2007), 39; Stephen Middleton, ed., *Black Congressmen during Reconstruction: A Documentary Sourcebook* (Westport, CT: Greenwood, 2002),241; Eli Ginzberg and Alfred S. Eichner, *Troublesome Presence: Democracy and Black Americans* (New Brunswick, NJ: Transaction, 1993), 221.

56. Washington quoted in Louis R. Harlan, *Booker T. Washington: The Wizard of Tuskegee, 1901–1915* (New York: Oxford University Press, 1983), 176.

57. Kenneth J. King, *Pan-Africanism and Education* (New York: Oxford University Press, 1971), 21–50.

58. Harlan, *Booker T. Washington*, 175.

59. W. E. B. Du Bois, *The Souls of Black Folk* (1903; rpr. Rockville, MD: Manor, 2008), 119.

60. This was also a cause that transformed the philosophical foundation of Du Bois's thinking. From his liberal and integrationist scholarship and editorializing early in his career, Du Bois went on to embrace socialist ideas. See Adolph L. Reed, Jr., *W. E. B. Du Bois and American Political Thought: Fabianism and the Color Line* (New York: Oxford University Press, 1997).

61. W. E. B. Du Bois, *The Philadelphia Negro: A Social Study* (Philadelphia: University of Pennsylvania, 1899).

62. Peter Wallenstein, *Tell the Court I Love My Wife: Race, Marriage, and Law—An American History* (New York: Palgrave Macmillan, 2002); Phyl Newbeck, *Virginia Hasn't Always Been for Lovers: Interracial Marriage Bans and the Case of Richard and Mildred Loving* (Carbondale: Southern Illinois University Press, 2004); Peggy Pascoe, *What Comes Naturally: Miscegenation Law and the Making of Race in America* (New York: Oxford University Press, 2009); Jolie A. Sheffer, *The Romance of Race: Incest, Miscegenation, and Multiculturalism in the United states, 1880-1930* (New Brunswick: Rutgers University Press, 2013); Carlos Hiraldo, *Segregated Miscegenation: On the Treatment of Racial Hybridity in the U.S. and Latin American Literary Traditions* (New York: Routledge, 2014).

63. David Levering Lewis, *W. E. B. Du Bois: A Reader* (New York: Henry Holt, 1995), 372.

64. On this point see Pascoe, *What Comes Naturally*.

65. Jacqueline Jones Royster, ed. *Southern Horrors and Other Writings: The Anti-Lynching Campaign of Ida B. Wells* (Boston: Bedford Books, 1997); Walter F. White, *Rope and Faggot: A Biography of Judge Lynch* (New York: Alfred A. Knopf, 1929). See also Hazel V. Carby, "'On the Threshold of Woman's Era': Lynching, Empire, and Sexuality in Black Feminist Theory," *Critical Inquiry* 12, no. 1 (Autumn 1985): 262-77; Diane Miller Sommerville, "The Rape Myth in the Old South Reconsidered," *Journal of Southern History* 61, no. 3 (August 1995): 481–518.

66. Cooper quoted in Elizabeth Alexander, "'We Must be about our Father's Business': Anna Julia Cooper and the In-Corporation of the Nineteenth-Century African-American Woman Intellectual," *Signs* 20, no. 2 (Winter 1995): 351.

67. W. Montague Cobb, "The Physical Constitution of the American Negro," *The Journal of Negro Education* 3, no. 3 (July 1934): 340-88.

68. Du Bois quoted in Roger Sanjek, "Intermarriage and the Future of Races in the United States" in *Race*, ed. Steven Gregory and Roger Sanjek (New Brunswick: Rutgers University Press, 1994), 104.

69. On this point see Jeffrey P. Moran, "Reading Race into the Scopes Trial: African American Elites, Science, and Fundamentalism," *Journal of American History* 90, no. 3 (December 2003): 891–911; *American Genesis: The Antievolution Controversies from Scopes to Creation Science* (New York: Oxford University Press, 2012).

70. E. Franklin Frazier, *The Negro Family in the United States* (Chicago: University of Chicago Press, 1939).

71. U. S. Congress, House Committee on the District of Columbia, *Intermarriage of Whites and Negroes in the District of Columbia and Separate Accommodations in Street Cars*

for Whites and Negroes in the District of Columbia (House of Representatives, Sixty-Fourth Congress, First Session, 1916), 4, 8, 10.

72. George Washington Williams, *History of the Negro Race in America from 1619 to 1880: Negroes as Slaves, as Soldiers, and as Citizens* (New York: G. P. Putnam's Sons, 1883), 1:113.

73. Ibid., 113.

74. Anna Julia Cooper, *A Voice from the South* (New York: Oxford University Press, 1988), xl.

75. Banks, *Black Intellectuals*, 100–5; Mark I. Solomon, *The Cry Was Unity: Communists and African Americans, 1917–36* (Jackson: University Press of Mississippi, 1998), 4–5.

76. Harold Cruse, *The Crisis of the Negro Intellectual: A Historical Analysis of the Failure of Black Leadership* (1967; rpr. New York: New York Review Book, 2005), 451.

- CHAPTER TWO -

BLACK MARXISM

MINKAH MAKALANI

I don't know what Communists or communism have to do with my position, because this has been my position since 1912 before there was, as I understand it, a Communist Party in the United States.
CYRIL VALENTINE BRIGGS

The originality of the colonial context is that economic reality, inequality, and the immense difference of ways of life never come to mask the human realities. When you examine at close quarters the colonial context, it is evident that what parcels out the world is to begin with the fact of belonging to or not belonging to a given race, a given species. In the colonies the economic substructure is also a superstructure. The cause is the consequence; you are rich because you are white, you are white because you are rich. This is why Marxist analysis should always be slightly stretched every time we have to do with the colonial problem.
FRANTZ FANON

A striking feature of what one might call a black Marxist tradition is that many of those writing on the subject have pursued some manner of a Marxist (communist, socialist) political project. One benefit of this confluence is that the historiography itself provides insights into how black Marxists understand historical processes, social being, social change, political economy, philosophy, Marxist theory, the debates they engaged in, their motivations, and the seemingly idiosyncratic political twists and turns within organized Marxist formations.[1] Such accounts generally avoid the diminished returns of Cold War historiography that, to this day, views blacks in organized Marxism through what historian Mark Naison long ago described as "the dynamics of manipulation, disillusionment, and betrayal."[2] The historiography of black Marxism thus encompasses not only anticommunist, Cold War stalwarts and works by black Marxists plumbing their own history, but also ex-Communists and ex-socialists (though not necessarily ex-Marxists), offering criticism of the movements and organizations they had grown disillusioned with, at times in hope of charting an alternative politics form what was normally encompassed in formal American political parties.

It is not without irony, then, that much of the work on black Marxism is identified by a sort of historiographical bind, a limit on its range of inquiry born of the theoretical preoccupations of its subjects of study. Further, if one understands black Marxism in the United States simply as black radicals engaging Marxist theory and its organizational manifestations, then the proximity of that history to the history of the Communist Party of the United States of America (CPUSA) is understandable.

Scholarly histories of black Marxism generally take up questions centered on those issues that confronted the CPUSA, specifically its autonomy from the Soviet Union—whether its earliest efforts around race and organizing among African Americans grew from an assessment of the American political scene or issued form a Moscow directive. Cold War and anticommunist historians lean toward the latter and have spun narratives where black radicals appear as (alternatively willing, manipulated, and dubious) pawns of Kremlin intrigue.[3] In this telling, Lenin's Communist International (Comintern) dictated the American party's policy and imposed an approach to race designed to draw black people into its dastardly designs. The stress on "Moscow gold" looming behind every CPUSA policy and holding local parties in check ultimately has the effect, as historian Gerald Horne points out, of viewing "those to whom [the CPUSA] appealed as passive and incapable of having chosen their politics rationally."[4] Social historians of the left have shown a greater willingness to weigh how the American party responded to Comintern directives in light of local circumstances, identifying its emphasis on racial equality and its rhetorical linking of racial oppression to capitalism to explain the CPUSA's appeal to black radicals.[5]

A major concern for much of this scholarship has been the Comintern's 1928 "Resolution on the Negro Question," better known as the Black Belt Nation Thesis (BBNT), which declared African Americans in the US South an oppressed nation with the right to self-determination. For a time, this policy altered how Communists organized around race. As Gerald Horne points out, "the way the party posed the 'Negro national question'" together with how the BBNT "developed as an issue in the context of the African-American experience ... helps to explain the party's relative success among African-Americans."⁶ Not only did the BBNT mark a critical shift in Communist Party work and resources and help boost its image as staunchly antiracist, as Robin D. G. Kelley notes of the period following its adoption, but the CPUSA also became an organization that "offered African Americans a framework for understanding the roots of poverty and racism, linked local struggles to world politics, and created an atmosphere in which ordinary people could analyze, discuss, and criticize the society in which they lived." Read carefully, however, Kelley suggests that there remains a great deal to gain in attending to the intellectual pursuits, organizational endeavors, and practical experiences that black people engaged in, that led them to see in Marxism a theory of social revolution, and in the CPUSA and the Comintern an international organization that spoke to their concerns.⁷

What is at issue here, then, is not a debate between two historiographical schools, as it were, but the silences enacted in the intellectual questions asked and the series of methodological moves demanded by this debate and its available archive. Anthropologist Michel-Rolph Trouillot has implored historians to recognize how any history inaugurates a series of silences that are simultaneous and inherent in all narratives of the past. According to Trouillot, any event "enters history with some of its constituting parts missing. Something is always left out while something else is recorded." As a result, "there is no perfect closure of any event.... Thus whatever becomes fact does so with its own inborn absences, specific to its production."⁸ If any narrative, in the process of opening up an archive of inquiry, necessarily silences a part of its past, then the writing of a history involves a set of choices about what to include and what to leave out. However inevitable silences may be, Trouillot reminds us that the histories one silences are not always left out in order to judiciously tell a story. Rather than reflecting literary economy, silences often signal value judgements and power relationships that inhere in the creation of sources and the structures of archival holdings.

The imbrication of black Marxism and the CPUSA serving as the pivot of this history therefore neglects, leaves unexplored, silences black radicalism as a body of thought from which issues an engagement that alters or disforms the Marxism it encounters. If, following Cedric Robinson, we resist reducing black radicalism to "a variant of Western radicalism whose proponents happen to be Black," it becomes possible to see in this engagement the production a new theoretical current whose horizons rest well beyond the premises and assumptions guiding Marxism.⁹ Building on Trouillot, I want to argue that what has structured the range of inquiry into this history has been a black Marxist archive. Michel Foucault discussed an archive not as the physical repository of a culture's canon or the institutions that house the ephemera of historical scholarship, but the discursive structures that form a "law of what can be said" and constitutes the "system of its enunciability." For Foucault, any analysis of the archive occurs in a "privileged region" of analysis that is "at once close to us, and different from our present existence," that impinges on our current sense of possibility, and "is that which, outside ourselves, delimits us," whose "locus is the gap between our own discursive practices."[10]

That the scholarship on black Marxism has largely failed to address the engagement I am after here reflects the power of that archive. Largely taking the story of black Marxists as occurring within the histories of discrete national parties has limited what it was possible to say about a significant range of twentieth-century black radicalism. To be sure, the national party focus has grown equally from the structure of Comintern archival holdings available for the telling of such stories, as these are ordered around single national parties within given nation-states. Even when communist formations were oriented toward the seemingly capacious (gobal) "Negro problem," the Comintern archives still sequester the materials relating to the American Negro from the Caribbean, Africa, and Negro work in Europe. While newer works are beginning to cut against this archival grain, Comintern policy and national party responses continue to conceal the frazzled seams of such narratives, the uneven connections and broken lines that form a region where race and the colonial reveal the inadequacies of organized Marxism to the story of black Marxism. In other words, the black Marxist archive has foreclosed sustained attention to the insights of black Marxists whose political thought took up a different range of questions.

In breaking with dominant historiographical schools, I pursue here a genealogy of black Marxism that locates a body of thought that sat uneasily with its own sense of Marxism's efficacy. In facilitating attention to how black radicals engaged Marxism, I want to push back against Foucault's notion that any critique of an archive occurs in a privileged region of analysis so that we might take seriously Frantz Fanon's call to stretch Marxism "every time we have to do with the colonial problem." A Fanonian stretching entails what political theorist Anthony Bogues has called a black radical heretical practice of entering into "an engagement and dialogue with Western radical political ideas" that give way to "a critique of these ideas as their incompleteness [is] revealed" around race and colonialism.[11] We might therefore see Fanon pursuing a critique of the black Marxist archive, from a "privileged region" that is not defined by its proximity to (but nonetheless existence outside of) a given discourse, but a geographical locus of thought from which one can identify the decolonial coordinates of black Marxist thought.

This stretching, then, insists not merely on expanding the range of analysis, but also on altering the terms of analysis. Capital's need for expanding markets, and thus its imperial impulse, is refigured through an insistence on the coloniality of capital and empire. Indeed, the Peruvian theorist Aníbal Quijano draws on Fanon to locate race at the root of the "coloniality of power," the "key element of the social classification of colonized and colonizers" that simultaneously redefines gender, labor, and identity. Walter Mignolo has drawn on Quijano's insight to locate Fanon and many other black Marxists as operating within what he calls Marxism's colonial fracture. Mignolo observes of the corpus of Karl Marx that he "misses the colonial mechanism of power underlying the system he critiques." For nearly a century black radicals stepped into this fracture, attending to race and insisting on the centrality of anticolonial liberation to a socialist future, and thus "unfold[ed] the colonial matrix of power" within the capitalist world order and how within organized Marxism that matrix created "a fracture in the hegemonic imperial macro-narratives" that centered on a modern Europe and America whose advanced (read: white) proletariat would liberate a backward Africa and Asia.[12]

By invoking Fanon, I do not aim to reshape the US-centered history of black Marxists. Rather, I want to argue that a Fanonian stretching is generative of a decolonial project that has gone largely missed in studies of blacks and organized Marxism. Although proposing Marxism's colonial fracture as the region from which a black radical stretching is performed, I do not follow Mignolo's suggestion that such a fracture renders Marxism anemic to decoloniality—even though I agree with what I take to be his underlying claim:[13] in issuing from Enlightenment thought, Marxism (not simply its Western variant) is a modernist project rooted in the very coloniality of knowledge and power that decoloniality contests. Black Marxists pursuing a decolonial project thus confronted the limits of their own Enlightenment assumptions, modernist notions of advanced and backward, premodern and modern peoples and societies. Black Marxists also struggled with the limits of Hegelian markers of historical time that centered the nation-state as the locus of class struggle and rendered proletarian revolution the province of the advanced world, while nationalist struggles in backward Asia and Africa fulfill the function of bringing those societies into historical proximity with the West. The aim here, following Bogues, is to explore how a heretical practice disrupts proletarian revolution and a socialist state as the horizon of black Marxism. How has heresy, deviance enabled black Marxists to pursue decolonial liberation? Is it possible to see such impertinence to the strictures of received theory enabling and enabled by what Nelson Maldonado-Torres argues, in drawing on Fanon and Sylvia Wynter, is a politics that "generates epistemologies and politics which affirm the idea that 'another world is possible'"?[14] In short, of imagining an unimaginable world?

EARLY BLACK MARXIST HISTORIOGRAPHY

From its earliest iterations, black Marxism has been characterized by the dilemma captured in the question that black Socialists in 1910s Harlem routinely posed themselves before their public rallies: What shall we expound tonight, straight Socialism or Negro-ology? Betraying long-held frustrations with the white Left's tendency either to treat race as a façade masking class struggle, or to claim that as workers black people's liberation would issue seamlessly from socialist revolution, black Marxists refused the very dichotomy implicit in the question they asked. As early as the 1870s, Peter H. Clark, a Reconstruction-era educator and one of the first black Socialists in the United States, seized on the failure of white Socialists to address racial oppression as evidence that "the welfare of the Negro" was not among their guiding concerns. There was much to support this view. At its 1901 founding convention, the Socialist Party of America argued that blacks were merely exploited like all other workers. This seemingly innocuous claim often masked the explicitly racist views of white Socialists like Victor L. Berger, who in 1902 declared that "negroes and mulattoes constituted a lower race." Even antiracist Socialists like the iconic Eugene V. Debs, who opposed segregated unions and would not address segregated southern audiences, argued that since black people were workers, their oppression would end with socialism, which left the SPA "nothing special to offer the negro" and little need for special resolutions on race.[15] Those black radicals drawn into the Socialist Party in the 1910s—figures such as Hubert Harrison, A. Phillip Randolph, Grace Campbell, Richard B. Moore, and W. A. Domingo—understood they would have to develop for themselves an integrated approach to race and class—an approach they carried with them into the first American communist parties.

How black Marxism developed such an approach has until rather recently eluded historians of the Left. The anticommunist historian Wilson Record, in his *The Negro and the Communist Party* (1951) and *Race and Radicalism*

(1964), occluded any sense of black radicals' engagement with organized Marxism, while his contemporary Theodore Draper, in *The Roots of American Communism* (1957) and *American Communism and Soviet Russia* (1960), gave only slightly more attention to black intellectual activity in this milieu. Record and Draper established a practice of historical inquiry that used black Marxism largely to parcel a historiographical argument, glossing in the process how black radicals extended and innovated on Marxism in thinking about Africa, Asia, colonialism, and racial oppression as structures of the modern world.

Among the earliest to break with this historiographical mode, Philip Foner helped steer scholarly discussions toward what black radicals thought about and their actions upon encountering organized Marxist formations, in both socialist and communist parties. It is important to note, however, that Foner worked with and drew on the insights of James S. Allen, a longtime member of the CPUSA who wrote extensively since the 1930s on the Negro problem and the BBNT. Though Allen (born Sal Auerbach) was not black, he worked with Foner to coedit volume 1 of the document collection, *American Communism and Black Americans*, and more importantly stood alongside Harry Haywood as an early theorist of the BBNT. Writing on this resolution much of their lives, Allen and Haywood sought to advance what they (and many others) viewed as a critical theoretical tool in compelling intransigent white communists to take up the global struggle against racial oppression and colonialism. Both insisted on the political activity of black radicals in explaining the history of black activists in organized communism. But in seeking to substantiate the 1928 resolution, they often retrofitted history to theory, casting internecine struggles and debates and bending broader movement activities and social processes to substantiate the BBNT. In the 1930s Harry Haywood considered any disagreement with BBNT an "absolute desertion of the Marxian-Leninist position on this question" and called race a "super-historical concept" that had "no influence upon the social development of people in contemporary class society." In his 1948 pamphlet *Negro Liberation*, written as a defense of the BBNT after the CPUSA had abandoned it, Haywood largely emphasized what Joseph Stalin had identified in 1913 as the four characteristics of a nation (a common language, territory, economic life, and common psychological makeup), to which he attached a rout repetition of Lenin's position on the role of oppressed nations in proletarian revolution.[16]

Nell Painter's *The Narrative of Hosea Hudson*, which appeared in 1979, marked a turn in histories of black Marxism. Where previous studies had cast a much different light on the history of black encounters with organized Marxism, especially as those experiences involved the CPUSA's role in defending the Scottsboro Boys, Painter's introduction to Hudson's *Narrative* offered a sense of the Alabama branch of the CPUSA as "a southern, working-class black organization" that was quite distinct in its organizing and intellectual activities from other Communist Party branches. Painter noted that the Alabama branch focused on jobs, relief, and civil rights, and to the extent that the BBNT "translated into immediate goals like welfare and voting rights," it appealed to black Alabamans. Still, the cumbersome theory explained little about black life in the South and offered even less in practical terms about fighting racial oppression. Its appeal, Painter argued, was that it "focused attention on racial oppression as part of a wider economic system that victimized both black and white working classes in the South" and signaled the CPUSA's "concentration on the South and on Negroes that had not occurred in a national political organization since the middle of the nineteenth century."[17]

Mark Naison's *Communists in Harlem during the Depression* (1983) followed Painter's work, by proposing a model for carrying out "an in-depth study of [the CPUSA's] 'Negro work'" in a specific black community. Harlem offered an ideal setting, Naison argued, because it allowed him to track "the evolution of Party theory, the practical impact of its organizing," as well as "explore its changing relationships with black organizations, and assess the Party's impact on the diverse group of blacks who passed through its ranks or competed with it for leadership." Though concerned primarily with a political history of the CPUSA, "particularly the role of the Soviet Union in shaping Party policy," Naison also took as his concern "how the social and cultural atmosphere of Harlem gave a distinctive cast to Party activity, creating problems and opportunities which Party 'theory' did not always anticipate." Though subtle, Naison parted with the anticommunist Cold War trope of Kremlin intrigue to insist on the importance of local black social, cultural, and political institutions to understanding the history of organized communism in America, situating the party's Harlem branch within a matrix of independent black political formations, and in turn making Harlem the central public for a history of the US left.[18]

What remained unexplored was the consistency with which black radicals constantly sought to extend Marxism beyond its initial outline. For some doctrinaire Marxists, this betrayed a black radical deviation from historical materialism, or worse still, a tendency, when dealing with race, toward bourgeois liberalism. Yet, the more intriguing question remains: What insights might we gain if we see this theoretical deviance as productive of thoughtful practice? Following Bogues' notion of the black radical heretic, how might we see in the elaboration of an alternative framework the articulation of a different horizon of political possibility?

Such deviance or heresy was actually quite widespread in the early twentieth century. We could place alongside Fanon W. E. B. Du Bois, who in 1933 asked, "[W]hat shall we say of the Marxian philosophy and of its relation to the American Negro?" Rather than abandon or reject Marxism, Du Bois argued that the "Marxian philosophy is a true diagnosis of the situation in Europe in the middle of the 19th century despite some of its logical difficulties," yet he believed that "it must be modified in the United States of American and especially so far as the Negro group is concerned."[19]

Du Bois, Fanon, and scores of other black radicals took up issues and problems for which Marxism had no ready-made answers. This required that they cross what were often seen as distinct political fields, embrace seemingly contradictory concerns in an almost ecumenical manner, the fine grain of which often escapes serious scholarly attention. The Caribbean writer and theorist Sylvia Wynter, in describing the "pluri-conceptual" poiesis of the Trinidadian radical Marxist C. L. R. James, offers a way out of this bind by dwelling in those seeming tensions. She notes of James that he was, "a Negro yet British, a colonial native yet culturally a part of the public school code, attached to the cause of the proletariat yet a member of the middle class, a Marxian yet a Puritan, an intellectual who plays cricket, of African descent yet Western, a Trotskyist and Pan-Africanist, a Marxist yet a supporter of black studies, a West Indian majority black yet an American minority black." Most compelling about Wynter's anaphoric description of James's diverse qualities and concerns is her refusal to see these as contradictions or antagonisms, insisting instead on his complexity as an intellectual. She precludes any reading of James as open to an either/or logic where he (or one thinking about him) would choose between "either race or class, proletariat or bondsman labor, or *damnes de la terre*, Pan-African nationalism or labor internationalism. The quest for a frame to contain them all," Wynter alerts us, "came to constitute the Jamesian poiesis."[20] In announcing an analytical break that allows one to take the multiple interests of so complex an intellectual as James as parts of a whole, Wynter provides an analytic for approaching the habit among various black Marxists to build networks and institutions that inaugurated a process whereby in world revolution, to borrow from literary scholar Bill Mullen's felicitous description, African and Asian peoples "would often come to supplant the international (i.e., European) working class."[21]

BLACK STUDIES, BLACK MARXISM

Unlike the Cold War and "revisionist" debates about the autonomy of American communism, the intellectual preoccupations of black studies scholars took up another, though not entirely separate, set of questions. The earliest efforts to think through black radicals within organized Marxism focused on the storied but little-studied Harlem-based African Blood Brotherhood (ABB). For much of the last half-century, the overriding concern among those writing on the ABB has been gauging their authenticity to black politics and culture. In many respects this drew from the historical mythology that has long surrounded the ABB: a communist front organization that constituted the left wing of Marcus Garvey's Universal Negro Improvement Association (UNIA); communist moles boring from within the UNIA to divert its working-class membership to a white communist agenda.[22]

Harold Cruse first addressed the ABB in his classic tome *The Crisis of the Negro Intellectual* (1967), a wide-ranging work on the cultural politics of black life and the cultural nationalist imperative facing black intellectuals. Among the corps of black ex-communists writing on black Marxism, Cruse stands out for his especially acerbic barbs not so much against the Communist Party, with which he had grown disillusioned, but against the black communists he left behind.[23] Such animus cut across intradiasporic ethnic lines to indict the largely Caribbean ABB as culturally vacuous parrots of communist policies. Cruse's especially critical stance toward black intellectuals within the orbit of organized Marxism influenced how various scholars since have viewed the Brotherhood, in particular the ABB's perceived shift from nationalist separatism to class struggle, a shift that he believed was "predicated on a political strategy that had been directed from Moscow, that was remote from Harlem economic realities," and that transformed the ABB into communist infiltrators burdened with the unenviable charge to "influence, collaborate with, or undermine [Garvey's] movement" if all else failed.[24]

Several black studies scholars have followed suit. Tony Martin, in his history of the UNIA, takes up the ABB's conflict with Garvey in greater detail, similarly portraying them as foot soldiers in a communist plot to either weaken the UNIA or control its largely working-class membership. Robert A. Hill's introduction to the facsimile edition of the *Crusader* magazine that Cyril Briggs edited, and that was the ABB's publicity organ, offers what was at the time the most researched and balanced account of Briggs's political thought and the ABB's history, though Hill cast Briggs as a party functionary and located the ABB's origins in the machinations of communist officials rather than the political and cultural milieu of the New Negro movement. Despite suggesting that the Brotherhood's ideas and programs derived from the party rather than their own pursuits, Hill nonetheless discussed something of the organization's importance to the history of black radicalism. His tireless archival research and attention to Briggs as an intellectual opened up the ABB for further study. It is not without irony, then, that Hill's pioneering and indefatigable research on Briggs has helped displace the very trope of communist conspirators on which he writes.[25]

Rather than continue to trade in the same language of autonomy qua authenticity as Cold War historians, and thus insure that the ABB remained subjects more of mythology than scholarly study, recent works have shifted the focus of inquiry. Winston James and Mark Solomon each, in their turn, fleshed out the ABB's history and summoned an armada of evidence to construct narratives substantiating the organization's activities and the ideas of its members as more than the result of communist manipulations. Especially impressive is their demonstration that Briggs's connection to the Communist Party was not sui generis of his thinking on race, nationalism, and black liberation. Yet in arguing for the ABB's independence from white radical organizations, James and Solomon never addressed the implicit claim guiding the array of arguments described above—black figures and organizations emerging from or deeply engaged with white political institutions and thought are necessarily inauthentic and lack intellectual autonomy. As I have argued elsewhere, whatever the value in unraveling the ABB's independent origins, its legitimacy in the history of black political thought is hardly diminished by its ties to white radical movements.[26]

Bogues's notion of black radical heresy offers a way out of this argumentative bind by highlighting the critical character of black radical engagements with Western radicalism, an approach that echoes Cedric Robinson's in *Black Marxism*. Robinson describes black radicalism as the issue of a long historical process of black self-activity, its source being that very self-activity, and the institutions and internal developments in black communities that gave rise to it. One cannot therefore understand black radicalism as "a variant of Western radicalism whose proponents happen to be Black," but must see it as a "specifically African response to an oppression emergent from the immediate determinants of European development in the modern era and framed by orders of human exploitation woven into the interstices of European social life from the inception of Western civilization."[27] One of the "immediate determinants" Robinson identifies in Western civilization is racialism, "the legitimation and corroboration of social organization as natural by reference to the 'racial' components of its elements." Racialism existed elsewhere in the world, but its codification "into Western conceptions of society was to have important and enduring consequences."[28] Building on the work of sociologist Oliver Cox, especially *Capitalism as a System*, Robinson locates the emergence of racialism in the initial orderings of the West, which in turn "order[ed] the relations of European to non-European peoples" that "permeate[d] the social structures emergent from capitalism." It is important to note that part of Cox's project entailed challenging Karl Marx's labor theory of value; Cox situated the rise of capitalism, a central question in Marx's economic and philosophic corpus, several centuries before Marx did, in the Venetian maritime trading empire. For Cox, locating the rise of capitalism in the Venetian empire identified the source of value under capitalism in exchange, not labor exploitation.[29]

In shifting from Marx's labor theory of value to commerce, Cox sought to construct an account of racial oppression as constitutive of capitalism and, possibly more important, modernity. That many view his treatment of race as Marxist is owed to the materialist nature of his argument, as when he claims "racial antagonism is part and parcel of . . . class struggle, because it developed within the capitalist system as one of its fundamental traits." But in departing from Marx's notion of exploitation as only those production relations where a worker imparts to an exchangeable commodity a surplus value that reflects the difference between the worker's wages and the price that the commodity brings on the market, Cox allowed for a structure where the exchange of a commodity (e.g., a slave) realizes profit and could, too, be seen as a source of value outside the strict limits of the industrial workplace. Far from any sense of race-as-class, Cox offered a more nuanced approach to race, a social reality that he rather importantly pointed out "never existed in the world before about 1492." Far from reducing race to class or considering it the straightforward issue of capitalism, Cox approached a problem of the modern: "[P]robably a realization of no single fact is of such crucial significance for an understanding of racial antagonism as that the phenomenon had its rise only in modern times."[30]

Rather than take up this specific point in Cox's work, Robinson leaves it as a guiding framework as he summons a wealth of scholarship on the Venetian empire to sustain his own claim that racialism informed all European political, economic, social, and intellectual life in its earliest iterations. It would have therefore been "exceedingly difficult and most unlikely," Robinson maintains, "that such a civilization in its ascendancy . . . would produce a tradition of self-examination [Marxism] sufficiently critical to expose its most profound terms of order"—racialism.³¹ Since Marx developed historical materialism through an analysis of European societies, historical materialism's "analytical presumptions, its historical perspectives, its points of view" were equally informed by racialism.³² Robinson thus offers black radicalism as an African cosmological worldview, a negation of Western civilization that was not developed by twentieth-century black activist-intellectuals who operated in the orbit of organized Marxism, but something that, once they broke with Marxism, they discovered "first in their history, and finally all around them."³³

Robinson's work has informed how a new generation of scholars thinks about black radicalism, though the subtlety of his Coxian move has obscured the richness of that intervention, operating almost at a metatheoretical level that has left those working in Robinson's wake largely unfocused on the deep theoretical claims he made for rethinking a black radical history. Instead, the most suggestive aspect of *Black Marxism* has been Robinson's challenge to expand "the appearance of a world revolutionary Black intelligentsia" back before the twentieth century, to see it as "the issue of a longer process" of black resistance to Western civilization.³⁴ As compelling as this is, his central claim that black radicalism and Marxism are incongruent, that the former is an epistemic negation of Western civilization that is encapsulated in the character of black people's self-activity, and thus a critique of the latter, is difficult to follow. His detailed biographies of W. E. B. Du Bois, Richard Wright, and C. L. R. James conclude that all three broke with Marxism, which led them to "their eventual encounter with the Black radical tradition." Yet Du Bois and James at least never rejected Marxism, and James saw himself extending its theoretical contours and analyses—an intellectual biography mirroring that of several African diasporic activist-intellectuals such as Agostinho Neto, Amílcar Cabral, Claudia Jones, Louise Thompson Patterson, Aimé Césair, and Frantz Fanon.³⁵

What stands out in Robinson's analysis and deserves greater attention, however, is its framing of black radicalism around what today we might call coloniality. Whether Venice was a racialized society that exported racialism to the rest of Europe is doubtful. Yet Robinson does draw our attention to what political theorist Barnor Hesse describes in some detail as the process by which Europe, "*colonially* constituting itself and its designations of *non-Europeanness*," came to be defined through the logic of race. Hesse lays stress on that collection of processes through which "the modernity of social realities historically [is] brought into racialized being by colonial regimes of demarcations, designations and deployments." Rather than consider racialism the ordering logic of various relationships between the European and non-European, Hesse locates race *within* the colonially constituted assemblages of Europe/non-Europe, an *onto-coloniality* central to the modern/colonial world system. *Onto-coloniality*, unlike ontology, which is concerned with the nature of what already exists, brings into existence the racial being through the colonial practice of distinguishing the "European" from "non-European."[36] Although Robinson's argument is critically different than that of Hesse and other theorists of coloniality such as Wynter, Quijano, Enrique Dussel, and Linda Alcoff, his remains important for theorizing the racial structures (and thus the coloniality) of modernity. If Marx, Engles, and Lenin were unwilling to address or incapable of addressing the colonial, coloniality marks the terrain upon which African diasporic, Asian, and Latin American radicals perform a Fanonnian stretching required of decoloniality.[37]

BEYOND THE BLACK MARXIST ARCHIVE

Cedric Robinson's *Black Marxism* remains important for thinking through a genealogy of black Marxism that resists any neat, nation-centered narrative tethered to the CPUSA, Communist Party of Great Britain, or South African Communist Party. Departing from this frame allows greater attention to the international networks, exchanges, and formations that served as the spaces where black Marxists took up questions of coloniality—knowledge regimes, the constitution of the other, and the genocidal violence of modernity. By bringing in coloniality, I aim to amplify (if simultaneously modify) Robinson's more important interventions as a way to highlight Marxism's colonial fracture as the region where a black Marxist decolonial project emerges.

To take coloniality as a central concern for black Marxism is to suggest a different angle for considering the habit among black radicals of deforming the Marxism they encountered. C. L. R. James offers an interesting case. As someone who repeatedly insisted on the modernity of the Caribbean, what is intriguing is that one of his major concerns involved a critique of that modernity. His earliest gesture toward such a critique came in his classic history, *The Black Jacobins,* in his discussion of Toussaint Louverture's failures in Haiti. After locating Toussaint within a train of Enlightenment thought that ran from Thomas Payne to Karl Marx, he suggested something of the inherent limitations of this intellectual legacy for decolonization when, in an important passage, he called Toussaint's failures "the failure of enlightenment, not of darkness." Lest the point got lost, James drew it more finely by noting that Jean-Jacques Dessalines, the black general who ushered in

Haitian independence, could see more clearly what needed to be done than Toussaint because "the ties that bound this uneducated soldier to French civilization were of the slenderest."³⁸ It is important that James related Dessalines's success as the result of a way of seeing possible because of his distance from French culture. Though, as Bogues notes, James never considered the worldview of the Haitian slaves as possibly guiding the revolution, that Dessalines could see more clearly, that it was a consequence or product of what in Enlightenment thought would have been deemed "darkness," locates a necessary point of departure for decolonization outside Enlightenment thought by (possibly) tying it to African ways of knowing.

One way of reading James's insistence on the Caribbean as thoroughly modern, its centrality to Western civilization, to use his terms, is to see him insisting on the constitutive coloniality of modernity. In other words, rather than a mere declaration about Caribbean fitness for self-government that characterized his first major political work, *The Case for West Indian Self-Government*, I want to argue that James always focused attention on the need for a more thoroughgoing critique of the West that went beyond mere political independence or ending empire. From this perspective, it is possible to see James's attempt, elsewhere in *The Black Jacobins*, to reshape the Haitian masses into "the most modern proletariat" of the time, a claim that Robinson and others have rightly noted reflected his efforts to fit the Haitian revolution within a classic Marxian analysis of proletarian struggle, as a symptom of an incomplete decolonial turn in James's thought. Indeed, at the same time that James sought to stretch Marxism to account for the Saint Domingue slaves as a modern proletariat, he argued, "Voodoo was the medium of the conspiracy.... [T]he slaves travelled miles to sing and dance and practise the rites and talk; and now, since the revolution, to hear the political news and make their plans."³⁹ In turning to voodoo and African knowledge systems, instead of a consciousness born of the work regimen of the sugar plantation, or an encounter with a text of Enlightenment thought, one notices in James an incomplete turn, a gesture that takes Marxism's modernist critique of capital beyond the region of labor exploitation so that more than see slavery as constitutive, slave cultural practices and worldviews operate as a critique of modernity.

Put differently, even as early as *The Black Jacobins*, James pursued an array of questions and political concerns that lay beyond the horizon of Marxist theory. That James was at every turn critical of organized Marxism (the Comintern, Trotsky, British Trotskyism, and international socialism) and constantly articulated his intellectual engagement on theoretical terms unavailable within Marxist analytics reveals the frazzled seams in which black Marxist thought flourished. This point came across forcefully in 1958, with another black heretical Marxist. When seventy-year-old Cyril Briggs appeared, under subpoena, before the House Un-American Activities Committee to answer for his communist activities, he told the Committee that he did not "know what Communists or communism have to do with my position, because this has been my position since 1912 before there was, as I understand it, a Communist Party in the United States."[40] It was apparent as well when the Martinican radical Aimé Césaire resigned from the Parti Communiste Français (French Communist Party, PCF) in 1956, citing the PCF's subordination of anticolonial and antiracist problems to working-class struggles. Rather than continue with the French party's paternalism, which subordinated African and Asian concerns to those of the French working class, Césaire insisted that "Marxism and Communism be harnessed into the service of colored people, and not colored people into the service of Marxism and Communism." Envisioning a dynamic theory that one could bend and reshape to unique circumstances, a quality apparent in the rise to what he called a Chinese communism, he imagined an African communism capable of moving beyond the limitations of the European Marxism.[41]

Allowing for a black Marxism outside the corridors of organized Communism and the thought of Western Marxists brings into focus a genealogy that occasionally overlaps with but ultimately remains independent of what is generally presumed to be its history. This is indeed the kind of project that Césaire had in mind, that US black radicals set themselves to upon entering the Comintern, that challenged Caribbean radicals from the 1930s to the 1970s, and that African radicals on the continent took up in the latter half of the twentieth century. From this view, one can then attend to C. L. R. James's role in British Trotskyism in a way that privileges the anticolonial fervor of 1930s London: the International African Service Bureau (IASB), the collaborations between African diasporic and Asian radicals in the European metropole, and the resonances of this organizational work over the next several decades. James, Padmore, and others from the IASB typify a Fanonnian stretching that, by the 1970s, had a tremendous impact on black political discourse and organizing in Africa, the Caribbean, and the United States. As Bogues notes of James's time in the United States from 1938 through 1953 in the Johnson-Forest tendency, he developed "a modern, independent Marxism," and his "political activities and work were linked to the radical and progressive political currents" not easily explained by Marxism—"Black Power, Pan-Africanism and West Indian nationalism."[42]

THINKING THE HUMAN

The global dimensions of black Marxism, like those of black radical thought more generally, have travelled along the multiple routes of the African diaspora. To riff on Tiffany Patterson and Robin D. G. Kelley's observation that at times black internationalism "lives through or is integrally tied to other kinds of international movements—socialism, communism, feminism, surrealism," one might ask what happens when Marxism "lives through" or travels along the currents of black radical networks and movements.[43] As I have tried to show here, black Marxists who pursued a decolonial project broke with Marxism's historicist ordering of "advanced" and "backward" peoples to locate African and Asian liberation struggles, rather than the "advanced" proletariat, at the center of world revolution. When Marxism has lived through black radical currents, it has come under specific pressure, torqued between a commitment to its trenchant critique of the exploitative structures of capital and its imperialist orientations, and a set of circumstances, experiences, and ways of knowing that are seemingly incongruent with Marxism's Enlightenment precepts. C. L. R. James's pluri-conceptual approach offers a profitable point of departure for thinking about this aspect of the story, especially considering the work he carried out with the Johnson-Forrest tendency. In such a genealogy one finds an equally rich point of departure in the thought of Claudia Jones.

Claudia Jones immigrated to the United States from Trinidad as a young girl when her family settled in Harlem. Quite early in life, Jones became a political organizer and thrived in Harlem's rich intellectual and political culture, moving easily within its activist circle, and working for radical publications before joining the CPUSA in 1935—a membership that came in response to both the Scottsboro Case and Jones had emerged as a major thinker within the party, and as the only black woman on its National Committee, she focused on the lives and labors of black women. In this position, she grappled with gender oppression and the woman question within Marxism-Leninism, though her most imaginative work was easily the essay "An End to the Neglect of the Problem of Negro Women."[44]

Largely recognized as the earliest articulation of an intersectional analysis, Jones's theoretical discussions of black women and labor exploitation led to her elaboration of the concept of "triple-oppression," a single frame in which she theorized black women's experiences "as workers, as Negroes, and as women."[45] Breaking with organized Marxism's rhetorical habit of privileging (largely male) factory workers, "triple-oppression" located class alongside race and gender in pursuit of an alternative understanding of exploitation and value. Refusing the Left's class conceit thus allowed Jones, as Carole Boyce Davies notes, to stress that black women were not "remunerated in any way equivalent to their labor power."[46]

What stands out in Jones's work, though, her introduction of the concept "superexploitation" recognized the incongruence between domestic labor and that labor which Marx argued produced surplus value. If Marx's labor theory of value provided Jones the terms with which to limn black women's domestic labor—underpaid in white homes and unpaid in their own homes—the purchase of her efforts centered less on her ability to conceptualize such labor in strict Marxist terms than in insisting on a measure of black women's social value. Where Marx's labor theory of value conceived of labor exploitation as a worker imparting his or her labor power to a commodity in the production process, which when traded produces a profit that capitalists, in turn, realizes as capital, Jones focused instead on the gendered forms of racial oppression that structure capitalism in such a way as to render black women available to more than simply capitalists as exploitable labor and attended to the implication of such structures for the humanity of black people more generally. Elite white families, working-class (even communist) white women, and black men extract social (use) value from black women's domestic labor. Superexploitation thus indexed a measure of exploitation beyond unremunerated labor or capital extracted from labor power.

The move I want to argue that Jones made, then, was to take as her range of possibility a point beyond the normative limits to which organized Marxism demanded any theorizing confine itself. In one sense, this allowed Jones only enough room to pursue a rhetorical strategy whereby she could deploy the very terms of Marxism in order to move beyond the limits it imposed on how one could think the social. Yet, while couching her discussion of black women's domestic labor in the terms of analysis she found in Karl Marx's labor theory of value, Jones pursued a measure of value oriented toward a conception of the human for which Marxism proved inadequate.[47]

In moving beyond a mere question of class conflict, Jones elaborated what Davies has described as "a politics that . . . critiques Marxism-Leninism."[48] By insisting on other modes or regions of exploitation, Jones presents a concern with full human potential that is centered less on labor's alienation from itself than on the structures that forestall any sense of the black person as human. Erik McDuffie rightly notes that with "super-exploitation" Jones captured how black women were exploited "as mothers and as the breadwinners" in poor black communities.[49] In merging an orientation toward the varied ways in which black women's use value is exploited with an attention to how that exploitation gives rise to "conditions of ghetto-living" like low salaries, high rents, high-priced but poor-quality food, and unsanitary living conditions that limits the life, health, and spiritual well-being of black people, Jones brought into focus an array of social relationships and racialized, gendered practices that had produced a "maternity death rate for Negro women ... triple that of white women." This was thinking beyond, or perhaps before, the question of exploited labor power that Marx believed central to any concept of the political. For Jones, social reproduction was not some secondary question to be neatly cordoned off from the political, for this question stood at the heart of the reality that "one out of every ten Negro children born in the United States does not grow to manhood or womanhood!"[50]

Jones raised the question of black women's humanity through a discussion of their labor, though by invoking what Saidiya Hartman would call the afterlife of slavery, she notes that the very practices of domestic labor employment in 1940s Harlem (as elsewhere) often required that black women suffer "the additional indignity ... of having to seek work in virtual 'slave markets' on the streets where bids are made, as from a slave bloc, for the hardiest workers."[51] Alongside the psychic violence of virtual auction blocks came, as it did during slavery, the sexual violence visited upon black domestics that attended their superexploitation in white homes. Still, it is not coincidental that Jones also thought about how these black women often returned home to family structures and expectations that demanded they "begin housework anew to keep [their] own family together."[52] Triple oppression and superexploitation thus located black women at the center of any concern with black humanity and freedom, for in registering how white men and women extracted value from black women's bodies, as well as black men and families, drew on the full range of black women's value.

In this way, triple oppression and superexploitation index the coloniality of black domestic labor. For Jones, this required that black women assume leadership of leftist movements and unions, as they constituted the critical link "for the progressive women's movement" to realize a "heightened political consciousness." Her focus on black domestics called for new modes of thinking about value beyond the racialized limits of Marx's labor theory of value that centered European/white male worker as the universal agent, identifying a range of exploitative and oppressive relationships that confronted black women and rendered them essential to thinking about anticolonial, antifascist struggles and world revolution.[53] Her insistence on the centrality of black women and, by extension, black people's full human potential for a new world of human value was inconceivable within organized Marxism. By framing the experiences of black domestics through the imagery of the auction block, Jones registered the corresponding physical and sexual violence black women suffered more generally, as with the case of Rosa Lee Ingram, a forty-year-old widow, mother of fourteen, and Georgia sharecropper sentenced to life in prison for killing a white would-be rapist. Sexual violence and the judicial response to a black woman defending herself highlighted "the degradation of Negro women today under [an] American bourgeois democracy moving to fascism and war," the routine violations black women experience "in public places, no matter what their class, status, or position." If we consider Wynter's observation that slavery and debates about who could be a slave rendered race the guiding logic for other colonial assemblages like class and gender, man/nonhuman, advanced/backward, modern/premodern, it becomes possible to see in Jones's insistence that black women's oppression mandated their leadership of leftist movements a call for an alternative region of knowledge from which one might imagine new social relationships that enable a new humanity. The struggles of black women went beyond labor exploitation to address black humanity in its fullness, suggesting a political orientation for the future that was, within Marxist thought, inconceivable.[54]

COLONIALITY AND BLACK MARXISM

In opening his classic *Discourse on Colonialism,* Aimé Césaire offers a critique of the colonial underpinning of modernity when he declares the two central problems of Western civilization are "the problem of the proletariat and the colonial problem." Part of this claim involved articulating the proletarian to the colonial in a manner that rethinks Marxism so that the proletariat is no longer simply or even primarily European workers. To the extent that Césaire still trucked in universalisms, it was the colonized of the global south, those engaged in anticolonial and antiracist struggles who were best positioned to wage a thoroughgoing movement against Western civilization—modernity and capitalism. Importantly, then, it was also here that Césaire echoed earlier black radicals who closed the rhetorical distance that European powers sought to establish between empire and fascism. Describing the fascism of Hitler's Nazi regime as the "boomerang effect" of colonialism, Césaire argued that Europeans had tolerated "Nazism before it was inflicted on them," because until then "colonialist procedures . . . had been reserved exclusively for the Arabs of Algeria, the 'coolies' of India, and the 'niggers' of Africa."[55]

Fascism was not simply the product of an abhorrent mind, an aberration from modernity that required a special response. A case of colonial practices come home, Césaire brought into relief one of modernity's central features.[56]

As this suggests, the concern is not that black Marxist thought held colonialism as a central political concern, but that how those relationships, power dynamics, and knowledge regimes understood as colonialism represent rather an iteration, a particular set of practices available to coloniality.[57] Put differently, in taking up how black Marxists have approached colonialism within the privileged region of Marxism's colonial fracture, at issue is less an analysis of colonialism than one of coloniality—the structures of thought, knowledge, power, and valuation of certain life as human on which modernity crystallizes as those practices setting the European off from the non-European, human from nonhuman. Black Marxists thus take up precisely what Dussel calls the genocidal myth of modernity, where modern Europe engages in forms/practices of violence that constitute the non-European other as the premodern, uncivilized nonhuman in a state of nature that is available to violence in order to be civilized or brought into historical proximity with the West/modernity.[58]

Attending to the colonial constitutive elements of modernity remained a central feature of black Marxist thought for several decades. Perhaps its most important elaboration came from Césaire's former student in Martinique, Frantz Fanon, who brought into relief the centrality of violence to the colonial project, and the creation of a system that predetermines class and power based on the creation of the colonial other. This othering, as what Fanon calls racialization, which he approaches in *Black Skin, White Masks,* and which he more seriously pursues in *The Wretched of the Earth,* approaches Hesse's *onto-coloniality.* Importantly, in the latter work, especially in the chapters "The Pitfalls of National Consciousness" and "On National Culture," Fanon indicts nationalist projects ostensibly opposed to colonialism as bound up in the same racialized knowledge regimes as colonialism. Departing from a nationalist framework, he highlights the class cleavages among the colonized that would ultimately usher in a native ruling elite capable of sustaining colonial relationships. Possibly most suggestive, however, is his gesture towards a decolonial project in the closing pages of *Wretched of the Earth,* where he echoes Césaire's criticism of Europe's inability to resolve its own fundamental contradictions, urging that rather than follow Europe's example, "we must invent and we must make discoveries" that would allow an imaginative leap toward "turn[ing] over a new leaf . . . work[ing] out new concepts, and try[ing] to set afoot a new man."[59]

Tracing these points through Fanon helps tease out the contours for which we might consider his profound influence on US Black Power radicals who drew liberally on his work to think about the US context. One of the more general arguments to issue from US black radical reading, Fanon was to claim that black people constituted an internal (or domestic) colony. Among the more sustained efforts in this regard came from black Marxists who drew on Fanon, and to a lesser degree Kwame Nkrumah's *Neo-colonialism*, to break from the overly determined, mechanistic analysis found in the Comintern's BBNT. Theorizing US racial oppression in terms of colonialism, the internal colonialism argument signaled a departure from civil rights liberalism that, at a basic level, considered racial oppression a flaw in an otherwise sound liberal democratic project. Internal colonialism stressed the roots of the American national project in the continued colonial oppression of black people.

Jack O'Dell, a longtime communist and civil rights activist, as editor of the radical black periodical *Freedomways*, in 1967 noted that in failing to end slavery, the American revolution, itself an anticolonial revolution, ensured "that the African population in America remained a colonized people." While Malcolm X had long drawn links between black political struggles in the United States and anticolonial movements in Africa and Asia, figures as diverse as Harold Cruse and Huey Newton now discussed black people as an internal colony. In their classic work *Black Power*, Charles V. Hamilton and Kwame Touré (Stokely Carmichael) identified urban ghettos as the political and economic structures of internal colonialism's control in sustaining white supremacy. Touré had already drawn on Fanon to discuss institutional racism (or a system of racial oppression, as opposed to individual acts of racism) as a form of colonial violence. In *Black Power*, he and Hamilton extended the point to rethink black social movements as struggles that stood in opposition to realizing the American liberal democratic dream. Seeing America itself as an empire, they declared the only "place for black Americans in these struggles . . . is on the side of the Third World," where, they argued, one could approach "starting a new history of Man."[60]

Fanon's appeal to US black radicals and Marxists found possibly its most suggestive enunciation in Robert Allen's *Black Awakening in Capitalist America*. One of the more sustained analyses of the politics of the Black Power era, Allen's *Black Awakening* invoked the Communist International's BBNT, though at a different register. Allen's central claim concerned a shift in black America from an oppressed nation, its transformation "from a colonial nation into a neocolonial nation . . . subject to the will and domination of white America." Rather than the civil rights movement having granted black America full equality, Allen emphasized what today we might usefully see as the postcolonial condition of black America that, like many newly independent African colonies, incorrectly assumed "they were being granted equality and self-determination." Internal class cleavages in political leadership, the colonial administrative structures of urban ghettos, explicit attempts to destabilize black cultural practices and institutions, and a political economy structured around a cheap labor force, all reflected the "domestic colonial" condition that brought into focus the inability of a liberal democratic American political system to merely incorporate black people, and thus solve problems of race.[61]

In Allen's hands, internal colonialism reflected a sustained attempt to follow Fanon's stretching aphorism—in this case insisting on the colonial as the condition for such an undertaking. This entailed more than merely noting a colonial relationship. Taking the core of the internal colonialism thesis as collapsing the intellectual, rhetorical, and juridico-political distance between European empire and US freedom on which the logic of civil rights partially hinged, one can glean an indictment of the coloniality of the US nation-state as a modern political project, as constitutive of American democracy.[62] While one might argue that African Americans were not a colonialized people or part of a colony such as Jamaica, Trinidad, or Ghana, such positivism misses the critique offered by O'Dell that American anticolonial emancipation simultaneously maintained colonial institutions that ordered black life in North America, a view more recently put forward and expanded by Sylvia Wynter, who argues that modernity's colonial other was the biologized, racially inferior indigenous and, paradigmatically, African as "Man's" other. Allen and others thus were thinking through coloniality in black political discourse, which we might well read as not simply against the context of empire but a gesture beyond modernity. Locating black American political struggles as part of anticolonial struggles, which suffered from similar neocolonial or postcolonial fates as newly independent African and Caribbean nations, excavated the necessary theoretical space in which to chart new routes for globally oriented black struggles.

The shifting geography of black Marxism highlights a decolonial current within the United States that remains incomprehensible if one follows the national-state logic and structures to its historiography. We might usefully extend the genealogy that Mignolo and Nelson Maldonado-Torres anchor in the Caribbean and Latin America to also encompass Touré (Carmichael), Allen, O'Dell, and a score of other Black Power theorists of internal colonialism.

Black Marxism's shifting geography also underscores the critical postures toward the nation as a logical or normative result of black struggle. Where the Communist International's BBNT took as its premise the US nation, and thus raised the question of a seceding black nation (self-determination), Fanonian inspired discussions of internal colonialism inaugurated an as-of-yet-incomplete search for alternative forms of political association. Much of this theorizing flowed not only from critical readings of Fanon, but also from the intellectual production of C. L. R. James, as well as the work of the Guyanese radical Walter Rodney.

Between 1958 and 1962, C. L. R. James regularly returned to his native Trinidad,[63] where he worked in Eric Williams's People's National Movement (PNM), the ruling political party as Trinidad approached independence. In a series of lectures in August 1960 to the public library's Adult Education Program, which became the small book *Modern Politics,* James openly charted an independent thinking through of Marxism[64] and eschewed any pretense to a teleological political future. What remains remarkable about those lectures, however, was James's critique of liberal democratic structures of governance, Enlightenment thought, and possibly most revealing at the dawn of Caribbean independence, his efforts to think through a new form of democratic governance and political association beyond the nation-state. Indeed, he considered the nation-state an anachronism and "one cause of the degradation of modern society," a political structure that, "despite all its power and despite all the degradation to which it reduces the men who try to run it, never achieves its purpose."[65] This was the intellectual landscape upon which James held such hope in West Indies Federation—an archipelago formation that, while structured on the logics of the nation-state, nonetheless held the possibility, for James at least, of something beyond liberal democracy.

James left Trinidad for good in 1966 and settled again in London with his wife, Selma James, where they conducted in their Brixton flat a Marxist study group with Caribbean students that included Norman Girvan and Walter Rodney. For Rodney, who felt the British Left had little to offer and that "the political climate in Britain . . . was not conducive to the development of any independent Marxist thought," C. L. R. and Selma James offered a new way to think about engaging Marxism. Though forecasted in *The Black Jacobins* and elaborated further in the Johnson-Forrest tendency, it would take its most forceful form in Trinidad, where James's critique of modernity assumed its most fulsome articulation, and could be seen in his claim in the appendix to the 1963 edition of *The Black Jacobins,* where he argued that Caribbeans "were and had always been Western-educated," and consequently were confined "to a very narrow strip of social territory. The first step to freedom was to go abroad." The second, far more complex step involved getting "clear from [their] minds the stigma that anything African was inherently inferior and degraded. The road to West Indian national identity lay through Africa." Rather than see this as an essentialism, or a claim to some primordial unity between Africans and Caribbeans, James was gesturing at a break from the structures of thought issuing form the modern.[66]

In his London study group, James offered his most forceful iteration of a decolonial frame when he declared that "the origins of our nation are the Maroons who ran away from the plantations and hid in the mountains. Those are the real originators of the Haitian nation. Believe me!" Rather than point to a culturally modern Caribbean middle class, he located the origins of a Caribbean nation in maroonage, a slavery-era rejection of the West for the worldviews and social organization that issued from Africa and was reconstituted in the Americas. Far from modernity's conscripts, these were the earliest instantiations of a decolonial rejection that issued from the regions of coloniality. It bears pointing out, too, that in turning to Haitian maroons, James also looked beyond the normative limits of the nation-state—the Caribbean as a region, an archipelago, a social order capable of transcending the national form—and rooted his imagining of a Caribbean future in what was generally taken as the non- or premodern world of Africa, not the West. Reflecting such imaginative thinking was his inclusion of Cuba, Puerto Rico, and the Dominican Republic within this political body. This is also why James seriously considered Rastafari as a cultural and political movement that completely rejected British culture and Western civilization, a point that would not have been lost on Walter Rodney.[67]

In remarking on James's influence on his own political thinking and critical engagement with Marxism, Rodney recalled his mentor's time in Trinidad when, unlike so many others, James "seemed to be most complete in his acceptance of the necessity for the Trinidadian (and ultimately the West Indian) people to make a break with their past."[68] Seen in light of Rodney's own historical work, *How Europe Underdeveloped Africa,* but also *A History of the Upper Guinea Coast* (1970), and his essays in *The Grounding with My Brothers* (1969), we see Rodney making a corresponding decolonial gesture. As Anthony Bogues notes of his return to the Caribbean in 1968, "Rodney embodies a set of experiences that linked him to the past political experiences of early twentieth-century black radicalism, as well as the most radical segments of the African national liberation struggles," which allowed

Rodney to elaborate a conception of political affect that centered the human in terms of the concrete effects of colonialism and racial oppression.[69]

Thinking about James's influence on Rodney and those activist-intellectuals who formed the New World Group, we can locate a rather explicit decolonial bent among those who resisted a simple application of Marxism to the Caribbean, to pursue instead, following Césaire, a dynamic Caribbean Marxism. Several leaders of newly independent Caribbean nations were in some way influenced by Marxism—Norman Manley, and later Michael Manley in Jamaica; Forbes Burnham in Grenada; the West Indian Federal Labour Party's socialist orientation, to mention only a few—and James himself occupied a key place in both the West Indies Federation and Trinidad and Tobago. That many of these figures ushered in some of the more brutal Caribbean regimes, especially Burnham in Grenada, demonstrates the limits of such intellectual influences, their inability to eschew a condition of a postcolony. Nevertheless, this current conveyed to many radicals the possibility that they could in fact shape the Caribbean's future.[70]

That James repeatedly articulated the need for a dynamic Marxism and was unflinchingly critical of the prevailing articulations of Marxism and communist trends—Stalinist Soviet Russia, Maoist China, Trotskyism—resonated with the efforts of various African diasporic radicals to chart an alternative Marxist politics. Bogues's discussion of Rodney's experiences with African national liberation struggles, especially his encounter of Julius Nyerere's radical African humanism in Tanzania, reflects the possibility to be had in what Bogues describes as a project of producing an African political thought outside the confines of Marxism and socialism, which takes up a project centered on an ethical rather than economic motive. In this way, Bogues argues, Nyerere addressed a fundamental feature of colonialism and Western modernity, its "destr[uction] of the colonized as human." Modernity's inauguration of "man" or the "human" gave rise to a system of thought in which, as Césaire notes, at the "end of formal humanism and philosophic renunciation, there is Hitler." Nyerere's thought represents a more general effort of African anticolonial political thought to center the human, or following Fanon's discussion of resisting "History" in order to take "the real *leap* . . . of introducing invention into life," inventing a human occluded by modernity's "man."[71] Gary Wilder notes a similar attention to the human in Léopold Sedar Senghor's "epochal project for African decolonization," where Senghor's reading of Marx allows him to outline a "program for African socialism [that] would have redeemed humanity." In noting that Senghor considered socialism not simply a mode of production but, as Senghor put it, a world where "the development of the person's intellectual and spiritual life" could reach its full potential, Wilder reminds us that his sense of decolonization went beyond the normative conclusion of an independent nation-state to see decolonization as a process capable of transforming both Africa *and* Europe, the colonized *and* the colonizer. Whether or not Senghor's program would have proven transformative, Wilder argues that attention to such a redemptive vision offers "a more nuanced understanding of decolonization as a process and period of global restructuring rather than a dyadic story of national liberation or transfer of power."[72]

As part of this body of thought, I want to consider Amílcar Cabral, whose attention to culture proved a radical break with common Marxist approaches to national liberation. What echoes most closely with Nyerere and Senghor in Cabral is his attention to culture and his concept of the mode of production—"the level of productive forces and the system of ownership" within every society—as the motive force of history. He would put forward this approach more forcefully at the 1966 Tricontinental Conference in Cuba, where he rejected the Enlightenment notion of historical time that in Marxism considered class struggle the motive force of history, and thus located Africa, Asia, and Latin America outside history. What stands out in this address is the tension between Cabral's effort to deploy Marxism to theorize anticolonial movements and his resistance to the division within Marxism between "backward" non-Western and "advanced" Western nations. Postcolonial theorist Sanjay Seth observes that for Lenin, in whose train Cabral was thinking,[73] imperialism brought Asia and Africa into capitalism's orbit, in other words, into historical proximity with the West and thus available to "advanced" proletarian struggle.[74] But in arguing that imperialism had failed to fill this historical role, Cabral described imperialism as the "usurpation by violence of the freedom of the process of development of the dominated socio-economic whole." As such, national liberation was not liberating an indigenous bourgeoisie, which would set the stage for a subsequent proletarian struggle. It was a project to "free the process of development of the national productive forces."[75] As such, its "chief goal ... goes beyond the achievement of political independence to the superior level of complete liberation" of the means of production, in other words, a people's ability to control their history and culture. At stake for Cabral is not a return to a precolonial past, but the context that will allow for a new social being and new social relationships between people.[76] Indeed, as early as his Cuba address, Cabral considered it one of socialism's main goals to bring about "a higher level of ... appreciation of human values."[77]

It is in this context that the concept of "class suicide" as the main charge of the colonial elite or petty bourgeoisie in a national liberation struggle has its currency. Rather than see this as simply an insistence on the elite's allegiance to the interests of the colonial masses, it confronted the reality that upon ending formal colonial relationships with European powers, the petty bourgeoisie would be the "only stratum capable of controlling or even utilizing the instruments which the colonial state employed against our people." In a formulation that echoed James's claim that the path to a Caribbean national identity lay through Africa, Cabral argued that the colonial elite must undergo "reconversion—re-Africanization"—a return to the source, as he put it—where they would reject a colonial worldview in which Europe remains superior to African culture and society. National liberation therefore marked only the basis of revolution, not *the* revolution itself. "Class suicide" would thus cultivate "people with a mentality which could transcend the context of the national liberation struggle."[78]

Few have interrogated this point in Cabral's thinking to consider his sense that cultural revolution is a more thoroughgoing decolonial project that addresses more than merely ending imperialism. It seems ironic, then, that in his 1972 meeting with African American Black Power activists in New York during his final trip to the United States, he took up this very question. When asked what basis of law the PAIGC would use in Guinea-Bissau, Cabral made it clear they had no interest in preserving "any of the structures of the colonial state," insisting on the need to "totally destroy, to break, to reduce to ash all aspects of the colonial state in our country in order to make everything possible for our people."[79] That other independent African states retained colonial structures of governance and merely replaced white colonial administrators with black colonial administrators, who lived in the same houses and carried themselves in the same way as the old colonial authorities, facilitated the rise of neocolonies or postcolonies. Decolonization in Cape Verde-Guinea Bissau, in its refusal to replicate either the Portuguese colonial judicial system or the system in Portugal, would involve a new form of governance and a new cultural mood:

> If you really want to know the feelings of our people on this matter I can tell you that our government and all its institutions have to take another nature. For example, we must not use the houses occupied by the colonial power in the way they used them. I proposed to our party that the government palace in Bissau be transformed into a people's house for culture, not for our prime minister or something like this (I don't

believe we will have prime ministers anyway). This is to let the people realize that they conquered colonialism—it's finished this time—it's not only a question of a change of skin. *This is really very important. It is the most important problem in the liberation movement. The problem of the nature of the state created after independence is perhaps the secret of the failure of African independence.*[80]

Insisting on "another nature" for government institutions, turning a colonial government house into a people's cultural house, not having prime ministers, creating a context in which the masses realize that *they* conquered colonialism, rather than the party or the army emancipating them, Cabral centers not the question of the state per se, but what will be the nature of the new society, its form of governance, the structures of feeling and association that will facilitate the creation of a new social being.

There is an imaginative element to Cabral's thinking about how Cape Verde-Guinea Bissau might avoid a condition of the postcolony. His emphasis on taking another nature and not having prime ministers (or other forms of modern governance) should be read alongside his discussion of taking control of the means of production and thus one's culture. In his 1970 "National Liberation and Culture" lecture, given as the Eduardo Mondlane Memorial Lecture at Syracuse University, he seems to draw on Fanon's notion of the leap toward invention when he argues that the main tasks following national independence would include the "constant promotion of the *political and moral awareness* of the indigenous people (of all social groups)," and the "constant and generalized promotion of feelings of humanism, of solidarity, of respect and disinterested devotion to human beings." He saw these objectives as possible because the armed liberation struggle "in the concrete conditions of life of African peoples, confronted with the imperialist challenge, is an act of insemination upon history—the major expression of our culture and of our African essence."[81]

In other words, after national liberation would follow the revolution that, Cabral suggests, would not end at the borders of the new nation-state. In inseminating an "African essence" into history, he is describing a process whereby the cultural revolution can speak back to Europe. The revolution following liberation is not a proletarian one now possible because Africa has entered a stream of Western historical time, but one where a human beyond Western "man" is possible precisely because the revolution would translate "into a significant leap forward of the culture of the people who are liberating themselves."[82] It seems significant, then, that this decolonial program, even after Cabral's assassination in 1973, contributed to a process whereby a radicalized Portuguese military could launch its Carnation revolution, which overthrew fascism in Portugal, and inaugurate a process of decolonization in lusophone Africa.

THE SECTARIAN TURN IN US BLACK MARXISM

It is ironic that black Marxists in the Black Power era—many of whom met with Cabral; read and circulated the works of Rodney, Fanon, and James; and knew and celebrated the activism of the ABB and Claudia Jones—largely turned from the decolonial character of black Marxism. More startling is that the more serious theoretical and institutional efforts among US black Marxists after the 1960s entailed an insistence on a scientific Marxism, stressed its rational qualities against cultural nationalist notions of black spirituality, and rooted their emphasis on a universalizing class analysis to an assessment of "objective" conditions of capitalism that rendered racial oppression resoundingly secondary to class. US black Marxism was a complex intellectual current, and limning its intellectual contours in any manner risks obscuring important countercurrents. The work produced in *Freedomways* and *Black Scholar*, the activities of People's College and the Institute of the Black World, as well as the more recent work of scholars such as Angela Davis, Robin D. G. Kelley, Carole Boyce Davies, Fred Moten, Dayo Gore,[83] and a score of others would reveal an impressive range of interests informed by an engagement with Marxism (if not operating as Marxists themselves) that refuses its pretense to the certainty of scientific knowledge and its universalist class conceit. My concern here, rather, is with what, in the Black Power era, informed black Marxism's neglect of the decolonial arguments of earlier generations of diasporic radicals who considered culture an important realm of thought.

Part of the story lies in the wildly different political terrain on which US black Marxists struggled. The realities of Caribbean and African postcolonies[84] suggested the possibility of charting a new future in which one might, to borrow from Sylvia Wynter's useful amplification of Frantz Fanon, turn from man toward a history of the human. By the 1970s US black radicals drew more readily on an array of African and Asian Marxist influences. Along with the writings of Mao Tse-Tung and general support for Ho Chi Minh and the Vietcong, black radicals also drew on both the Cuban Revolution and a string of African Marxist intellectuals and anticolonial leaders, including Cabral and Rodney, who were traveling to the United States and speaking to African American audiences. Additionally, from the late 1960s to the early 1970s, the works of several thinkers became newly available: Kwame Nkrumah's *Consciencism* (1964), *Neo-Colonialism* (1965), and *Class Struggle in Africa* (1970), as well as Howard University Press's 1974 reprint of Walter Rodney's classic *How Europe Underdeveloped Africa*. The work of Julius Nyerere, Leopold Sédar Sénghor, and others on African Socialism and culture began to appear in the 1960s with increasing frequency.[85] So, too, did the work of C. L. R. James, when the Drum and Spear Collective republished his 1938 *A History of Negro Revolt* as *A History of Pan-African Revolt*, which was followed by a 1963 reprint of his classic *The Black Jacobins*.[86]

Alongside the growing popularity of African diasporic Marxists, various black nationalist organizations were beginning to articulate a Marxist politics. Maxwell Stanford (later Muhammad Ahmad) led the Philadephia-based Revolutionary Action Movement (RAM) in its embrace of "Marxism-Leninism Mao Tse-tung thought" in the early 1960s. For RAM, this entailed drawing on elements of black nationalism, Marxism, and Third World internationalism and reflected the tutelage of not only Malcolm X, but also longtime black Marxists and former communists Harry Haywood, Abner Berry, and the excommunist activist-intellectual Audley "Queen Mother" Moore. Similarly, black radicals in Detroit drew on the legacy of the Johnson-Forrest tendency, circulating C. L. R. James's articles and the writing of James Boggs (an auto worker) and Grace Lee (a Chinese American philosopher) in the local black community and among black workers, which informed that city's Revolutionary Union Movement and the formation of the League of Revolutionary Black Workers (LRBW) in June 1969 as an explicitly Marxist-Leninist formation. The LRBW went on to organize auto workers and the black community, publish a newspaper, produce political film,[87] and establish the Detroit branch of the Black Panther Party. Yet the problems it confronted—police repression, conflicts with other Black Power organizations, and internal sectarian struggles—foretold the general problems that would beset black Marxists in the 1970s.[88]

Black Power radicals suffered some political dissonance after they successfully helped elect black activists to public office, and those elected officials proved incapable of effecting meaningful change in black people's lives. These same radicals, like the iconic figure Amiri Baraka, were in contact with RAM and the LRBW and were drawn to the internal colonialism arguments that increasingly framed racial oppression in the United States in global terms. Though appealing to a wide cross-section of Black Power activists, internal colonialism proved critical for many to break with cultural nationalist politics for a traditional Marxist emphasis on class and capitalism as the basis of racial oppression. However, in their response to what they came to see as the limitations of Black Power and cultural nationalism, many lost sight of the decolonial gestures of the Caribbean and African thinkers to whom they were turning. In the 1960s, cultural politics tended to eschew material concerns and practical political engagements and in many cases advocated a return to what were overly romanticized, highly patriarchal visions of what they considered "traditional" African culture. Indeed, because part of the cultural nationalist project entailed pursuing alternative modes of knowing and human value, many Black Power Marxists felt that such decolonial gestures failed to address black life in the prevailing systems of oppression. Unfortunately, part of this reaction to cultural nationalism involved embracing the very Enlightenment notions of scientific investigation, reason, and progress that characterized some of the more sectarian variants of Marxist theory.

If in the 1970s various black cultural nationalists turned toward Marxism as a thoroughgoing critique of capitalism and imperialism as the bases for racial oppression and colonialism, 1974 marked a sectarian turn that foretold a significant decline in black radical organizing. Alongside Baraka's Congress of African Peoples (CAP), which by 1974 had adopted what it called "Marxism-Leninism-Mao Tse-Tung Thought," the emblematic example of this trend came in the major Black Power formation, the African Liberation Support Committee (ALSC). An outgrowth of a series of meetings and efforts in the early 1970s that culminated in the 1972 National Black Political Convention, the ALSC grew from the work of Owusu Sadaukai (born Howard Fuller), a North Carolina–based student activist and community organizer who had traveled throughout Africa. After meeting anticolonial leaders in Angola, Mozambique, and Guinea-Bissau, most importantly Amílcar Cabral, Sadaukai (with Baraka) led the formation of the African Liberation Day mobilization in the United States, which sought to raise awareness of continued African liberation struggles and build linkages between black people in Africa and the Americas and led to national organizational protests against US foreign policies. Following the 1973 assassination of Cabral, African Liberation Day became ALSC, a broad-based ad hoc alliance that included a range of black nationalists. By the summer of 1974, many within ALSC had moved toward Marxism, which struck many of their comrades who remained committed to cultural nationalism as a treasonous turn toward a white ideology.[89]

The concern over whether Marxism was suitable for black people and black movements gave rise to the "race vs. class" debate within Black Power circles. A central question in this debate concerned ideological purity, and an emblematic track in this regard was *The Black Scholar* article, "The Latest Purge," by Haki R. Madhubuti (Don L. Lee).[90] In this sweeping critique of black Marxists for emphasizing abstract systems over human action and ideas, Madhubuti also questioned the imposition of a white ideological/imperialist framework on black people. Far from an outgrowth of capitalism that would render white racists mere victims of false consciousness or crass economic actors, Madhubuti insisted on racism's independence from class and its prehistory to capitalism. More stridently, he and many others saw the turn toward Marxism as marking a supplication to white ideas/thinkers, culture, and organizations. In possibly the most substantial response to Madhubuti, Mark Smith, a long-time activists and ALSC organizer, criticized Madhubuti for failing to actually address the arguments that ALSC Marxists had made, his view of race as *the* ordering principle of history, and his explicit contempt for black people as "mentally . . . just above animals."[91] Remarkably, neither Madhubuti nor Smith (or the scores of others to weigh in on this debate) spoke in the decolonial registers of Cabral, Nyerere, or Rodney. Though Smith exhibited a more nuanced approach to a Marxist program that would shape its politics to the contemporary conditions, little of this was actually reflected in the thinking of black Marxists. Still, both based their claims on a notion of ideological purity that drew increasingly less on actual political struggles.

The sectarian wrangling reflected in the Madhubuti/Smith debate actually signaled a more general sectarianism among ALSC activists. As Cedric Johnson notes, the "doctrinaire ideology and ad hominem attacks versus reflexive political theory and constructive engagement" weakened black radical circles in the mid-1970s. The sectarian turn inflected more than just the black nationalist/Marxist debate, but organizing among black Marxists themselves. By 1973, black Marxists within ALSC were split into three competing groups: Sadaukai's North Carolina group and Abdul Alkalimat's People's College; the Houston ALSC; and the Atlanta and New Orleans ALSC chapters. Regardless of their particular focus, they shared a retreat from mass political organizing tactics that "served to buttress their privileged status" as intellectuals. Johnson points out that both "leftists' and cultural nationalists' advocacy of ideological education rather than populist political strategies" stressed programs of study that emphasized a radical, at times esoteric cannon that privileged intellectuals over working-class black people. As a result, "Marxist and cultural nationalist activists became mired in esoteric debates that rarely had anything to do with issues of immediate concern to the broader black citizenry." For many ALSC Marxists, the turn from cultural nationalism to "scientific socialism" signaled an important political shift, but one that nonetheless came with rather strong variants of economic determinism, stilted theorizing to squarely within the given parameters of Marxist theory, offered overly simplistic conceptions of racism as an elite super-structural façade, and thus came with a "corresponding loss of popular resonance."[92]

CONCLUSION

Manning Marable is perhaps one of the more intriguing black Marxist intellectuals of the post–Black Power era. His work with a range of other black radicals to form the Black Radical Congress (BRC) in 1998 signaled an effort to reboot a broadly cast, wide-ranging political movement capable of capturing the potential of the 1970s, in the hopes of avoiding many of its ideological and sectarian pitfalls. If the BRC proved unable to avoid sectarian splits and an emphasis on elite leadership, at a minimum it marked a conscious effort to come to terms both with the history of Black-Power-era black Marxism and with those questions and concerns that one might think about as a form of decolonial thought. I turn to Marable here, not to venerate him politically or intellectually, but because in one of his earlier works, *How Capitalism Underdeveloped Black America,* itself an invocation of Walter Rodney's classic text, Marable limned the racial structures of capitalism and insisted on a black Left revolutionary solution to racial oppression. Yet far more compelling, however, was possibly its most underdeveloped part—its concluding embrace of a politically unknown future. In its final two pages, Marable invokes C. L. R. James to argue that "the transition to socialism, will not be fixed or predetermined," leading him to implore that we "consciously learn from other people's revolutionary experiences without reifying them into a pseudo-revolutionary catechism."[93] He was drawing on James's 1960 lectures in Trinidad that became his *Modern Politics,* where James examined democratic forms of governance from the Greeks to the Russian Revolution in an effort to envision a political future beyond available forms of parliamentarian and liberal democracy. Thus, when Marable claims "a workers' democracy in America will not look precisely like anything we can ever imagine at this moment," he was, if unconsciously, invoking the very radical imaginary that James pursued, as a mode of decolonial critique of modernity and the nation-state. Though Marable never fully developed this point, it suggests a range of possibility for a renewed engagement with black Marxism, not as a rehabilitative project, but as a project that can draw from those engagements over the span of the twentieth century in pursuit of a new approach to black liberatory thought.

Although far more complex than the distillation offered here, and despite black Marxism's emphasis on ideological education and its corresponding tendency to constrict political organizing, efforts by black feminists to theorize racial and gender oppression along the lines of someone like Claudia Jones, in many ways were the era's most suggestive modes of decolonial thinking. Within CAP, the Black Women's United Front critiqued the sexism and nationalists' calls for patriarchal traditional African gender relations, insisting instead on greater attention to working-class women's issues.[94] The Black Women's United Front took up issues more immediately related to the practical concerns of black women and forecast a range of black feminist decolonial thought over the last twenty-five years. As Michelle Wright reveals in his work on black subject making in black thought, Audre Lorde, a former labor activist and excommunist, offered critical approaches to the question of the human through her thinking about black women's sexuality, gender roles, and modes of political deviance around her notion of mother-blood. Indeed, in Lorde's insistence at the beginning of her autobiography, *Zami*, that many black women were dykes, meaning that they occupied a third designation outside women and men, Lorde drew on a marginalized notion of humanity issuing from margins of black life and thought. Even Angela Davis's work, which in *Women, Race, and Class,* reflected a crass economic determinism, when it turned to the prison industrial complex, broached a whole range of other questions than those normally taken up in Marxism or even liberal political discourse.

NOTES

1. I use "organized Marxism" for a range of communist and socialist formations that considered themselves Marxist. "Organized Left" more broadly includes formations that pushed a leftist politics but were not Marxists (e.g., labor unions and anarchists).

2. Mark Naison, *Communists in Harlem during the Depression* (New York: Grove, 1985), xv.

3. Theodore Draper, *The Roots of American Communism* (New York: Viking, 1957) and *American Communism and Soviet Russia: The Formative Period* (New York: Viking, 1960); Wilson Record, *The Negro and the Communist Party* (Chapel Hill: University of North Carolina Press, 1951) and *Race and Radicalism: The NAACP and the Communist Party in Conflict* (Ithaca, NY: Cornell University Press, 1964); Nathan Glazer, *The Social Basis of American Communism* (New York: Harcourt, Brace: 1961); David A. Shannon, *The Decline of American Communism: A History of the Communist Party in the United States since 1945*

(New York: Harcourt, Brace, 1959); Harvey Klehr, *The Heyday of American Communism: The Depression Decade* (New York: Basic Books, 1984); Harvey Klehr and William Tompson; "Self-Determination in the Black Belt: Origins of a Communist Policy," *Labor History* 30, no. 3 (1989): 354–66; Harvey Klehr and John Earl Haynes, *American Communist Movement: Storming Heaven Itself* (New York: Twayne, 1992).

4. Gerald Horne, "The Red and the Black: The Communist Party and African Americans in Historical Perspective," in *New Studies in the Politics and Culture of U.S. Communism*, ed. Michael E. Brown, Randy Martin, Frank Rosengarten, and George Snedeker (New York: Monthly Review, 1993), 202.

5. To say that the label "revisionist" is something of a misnomer is to equally misstate the intent of those who have applied the label. It is more a play on nominal historiographical politics that would argue for the accuracy of such earlier works as those by Record and Draper, and to indict social historians writing since the 1980s who have sought to supplant those works, the suggestion being that they have been given to overstatement, willful ignorance, or even malicious misrepresentation that, some Cold War historians would argue, boils down to plain old sloppy history. The positivist assumptions backing these claims have seemingly been strengthened by the opening of Soviet archives, which have appeared to substantiate many of the claims of Cold War historians. Yet what is at issue is less the evidence now available—which hardly supports the Cold War positivism as those historians would suggest—than the emplotment of the story being told, the critical choices involved in how historians narrate this history, rather than a question of who has best represented what really happened, as if it is some verifiable scientific truth, a set of hypotheses for which the archive serves as a kind of lab allowing for scientific verification of certain hypotheses, and the necessary disproving of others. See Harvey Klehr, John Earl Haynes, and Fridrikh Igorevich Firsov, *The Secret World of American Communism* (New Haven: Yale University Press, 1995); Harvey Klehr, John Earl Haynes, and K. M. Anderson, *The Soviet World of American Communism* (New Haven: Yale University Press, 1998); and John Earl Haynes and Harvey Klehr, *Venona: Decoding Soviet Espionage in America* (New Haven: Yale University Press, 1999). Especially dismissive, mean-spirited, and wrong-headed is John Earl Haynes and Harvey Klehr's more recent effort to discredit social historians writing about the Left. See John Earl Haynes and Harvey Klehr, *In Denial: Historians, Communism, and Espionage* (San Francisco: Encounter Books, 2003).

6. Horne, "The Red and the Black," 208.

7. The body of work in this vein is massive and far more diverse in its subject matter, theoretical frameworks, and historical claims than either the Cold War historiography or what I have suggested here. For works that treat black radicals with an eye to the debate with Cold War historians, see Philip S. Foner, *American Socialism and Black Americans: From the Age of Jackson to World War II* (Westport, CT: Greenwood, 1977), and *Organized Labor and the Black Worker: 1619–1994*, 2nd ed.(New York: International, 1981); Philip S. Foner and James S. Allen, eds., *American Communism and Black Americans: A Documentary History, 1919–1929* (Philadelphia: Temple University Press, 1987); Leslie G. Carr, "The Origins of the Communist Party's Theory of Black Self-Determination: Draper vs. Haywood," *The Insurgent Sociologist* 10, no. 3 (Winter 1981): 35–49; Naison, *Communist in Harlem*; Paul

Buhle, *Marxism in the United States: A History of the American Left*, rev. ed.(New York: Verso, 2013); Maurice Isserman, *Which Side Were You On? The American Communist Party during the Second World War* (Middletown, CT: Wesleyan University Press, 1982) and *If I Had a Hammer: The Death of the Old Left and the Birth of the New Left* (New York: Basic Books, 1987); Horne, "The Red and the Black," 199-237; Gerald Horne, *Black Liberation/ Red Scare: Ben Davis and the Communist Party* (Newark: University of Delaware Press, 1994); Andor Skotnes, "The Communist Party, Anti-Racism, and the Freedom Movement: Baltimore, 1930-1934," *Science and Society* 60, no. 2 (Summer 1996): 164-94; Barbara Foley, *Radical Representations: Politics and Form in U.S. Proletarian Fiction, 1929-1941* (Durham: Duke University Press, 1993); Barbara Foley, *Spectres of 1919: Class and Nation in the Making of the New Negro* (Urbana: Univsersity of Illinois Press, 2003); Oscar Berland, "The Emergence of the Communist Perspective on the 'Negro Question' in America: Part One," *Science and Society* 63, no. 4 (Winter 1999/2000): 411-32 and "The Emergence of the Communist Perspective on the 'Negro Question' in America: Part Two," *Science and Society* 64, no. 2 (Summer 2000): 194-217.

For those works focused more directly on black radicals in organized Marxism but that are not as expressly concerned with this debate, see Sally M. Miller, "The Socialist Party and the Negro, 1901-1920," *The Journal of Negro History* 56, no. 3 (July 1971): 220-29; Nell Painter and Hosea Hudson, "Hosea Hudson: A Negro Communist in the Deep South," *Radical America* 11, no. 4 (July-August 1977): 7-23; Nell Irvin Painter, *The Narrative of the Life of Hosea Hudson: His Life as a Negro Communist in the South* (Cambridge: Harvard University Press, 1979); Jeff Henderson, "A. Philip Randolph and the Dilemmas of Socialism and Black Nationalism in the United States, 1917-1941," *Race and Class* 20, no. 2 (October 1978): 143-60; Robin D. G. Kelley, "The Third International and the Struggle for National Liberation in South Africa," *Ufahamu: A Journal of African Studies* 15, no. 1-2 (1986): 99-120 and *Hammer and Hoe: Alabama Communists during the Great Depression* (Chapel Hill: University of North Carolina Press, 1990); Richard B. Moore, *Richard B. Moore, Caribbean Militant in Harlem: Collected Writing, 1920-1974*, ed. W. Burghardt Turner and Joyce Moore Turner(Bloomington: Indiana University Press, 1988); Susan Campbell, "'Black Bolsheviks' and the Recognition of African-America's Right to Self-Determination by the Communist Party USA," *Science and Society* 58, no. 4 (Winter 1994): 440-70; Marika Sherwood, "The Comintern, The CPGB, Colonies, and Black Britons, 1920-1938," *Science and Society* 60, no. 2 (Summer 1996): 137-63; Rosemary Feurer, "The Nutpickers' Union, 1933-34: Cross the Boundaries of Community and Workplace," in *"We Are All Leaders": The Alternative Unionism of the Early 1930s*, ed. Staughton Lynd(Urbana: University of Illinois Press, 1996), 27-50; Paul Buhle and Robin D. G. Kelley, "Allies of a Different Sort: Jews and Blacks in the American Left," in *Struggles in the Promised Land: Towards a History of Black-Jewish Relations in the United States*, ed. Jack Salzman and Cornel West (New York: Oxford University Press, 1997): 197-229; Rebecca Hill, "Fosterites and Feminists, or 1950s Ultra-Leftists and the Invention of AmeriKKKa," *New Left Review* 228 (March 1998): 67-90; Bill Mullen, *Popular Fronts: Chicago and African-American Cultural Politics, 1935-46* (Urbana: University of Illinois Press, 1999); Winston James, "Being Black and Red in Jim Crow America," *Souls* 1, no. 4 (1999): 45-63; William J. Maxwell, *New Negro, Old Left: African-American Writing and*

Communism between the Wars (New York: Columbia University Press, 1999); Katherine Anne Baldwin, *Beyond the Color Line and the Iron Curtain: Reading Encounters between Black and Red, 1922–1963* (Durham: Duke University Press, 2002).

8. Michel-Rolph Trouillot, *Silencing the Past: Power and the Production of History* (Boston: Beacon, 1995), 49.

9. Cedric Robinson, *Black Marxism: The Making of the Black Radical Tradition* (Chapel Hill: University of North Carolina Press, 2000), 73.

10. Michel Foucault, *The Archaeology of Knowledge and the Discourse of Language* (New York: Basic Books, 1982), 129. Foucault warrants a full quotation on this point: "The analysis of the archive, then, involves a privileged region: at once close to us, and different from our present existence, it is the border of time that surrounds our presence, which overhangs it, and which indicates it in its otherness; it is that which, outside ourselves, delimits us. The description of the archive deploys its possibilities (and the mastery of its possibilities) on the basis of the very discourses that have just ceased to be ours, its threshold of existence is established by the discontinuity that separates us from what we can no longer say, and from that which falls outside our discursive practice; it begins with the outside of our own language (*langage*); its locus is the gap between our own discursive practices" (ibid., 130–31).

11. Anthony Bogues, *Black Heretics, Black Prophets: Radical Political Intellectuals* (New York: Routledge, 2003), 13.

12. Aníbal Quijano, "Coloniality and Modernity/Rationality," *Cultural Studies* 21, nos. 2–3 (March/May 2007): 171. For an engagement with Quijano through Fanon, see also Sylvia Wynter, "Unsettling the Coloniality of Being/Power/Truth/Freedom," *CR: The New Centennial Review* 3, no. 3 (Fall 2003): 265–68. Barnor Hesse, too, engages the question of the coloniality of race, though to much different effect, which I take up below. See Barnor Hesse, "Racialized Modernity: An Analytics of White Mythologies," *Ethnic and Racial Studies* 30 no. 4 (July 2007): 643–63.

13. Walter D. Mignolo, "Delinking: The Rhetoric of Modernity, the Logic of Coloniality and the Grammar of De-Coloniality," *Cultural Studies* 21 nos. 2–3 (April 2007): 483.

14. Nelson Maldonado-Torres, "Enrique Dussel's Liberation Thought in the Decolonial Turn," *Transmodernity* 1, no. 1 (2011): 17, 18. See also Walter Mignolo, *The Darker Side of Western Modernity: Global Futures, Decolonial Options* (Durham, NC: Duke University Press, 2011), especially his introduction and chapter 1, "The Road to the Future: Rewesternization, Dewesternization, and Decoloniality."

15. Foner, *American Socialism*, 59–62, 94–100; James, "Being Red and Black," 338–49; Mari Jo Buhle, Paul Buhle, and Dan Georgakas, eds., *Encyclopedia of the American Left* (Urbana: University of Illinois Press, 1992), 711; Eugene V. Debs, "The Negro in the Class Struggle," *International Socialist Review* 4, no. 5 (November 1903): 260.

16. Harry Haywood, "Against Bourgeois-Liberal Distortions of Leninism on the Negro Question in the United States," *The Communist* 9, no. 8 (August 1930): 694–712; Harry Haywood, *Negro Liberation* (New York: International, 1948).

17. Painter, *Narrative of Hosea Hudson*, 16–17.

18. Naison, *Communists in Harlem*, xvii.

19. W. E. B. Du Bois, "Marxism and the Negro Problem," *Crisis*, May 1933, reprint in *W. E. B. Du Bois: A Reader*, ed. David Levering Lewis (New York: Henry Holt, 1995), 543.

20. Sylvia Wynter, "Beyond the Categories of the Master Conception: The Counterdoctrine of the Jamesian Poiesis," in *C. L. R. James's Caribbean*, ed. Paget Henry and Paul Buhle (Chapel Hill: Duke University Press, 1992), 69.

21. Bill Mullen, *Afro-Orientalism* (Minneapolis: University of Minnesota Press, 2004), xxiv–xxv.

22. Tony Martin, *Race First: The Ideological and Organizational Struggles of Marcus Garvey and the Universal Negro Improvement Association* (Westport, CT: Greenwood, 1976); Rupert Lewis, *Marcus Garvey: Anti-colonial Champion* (Trenton, NJ: Africa World Press, 1988); Robert Smith, *We Have No Leaders: African Americans in the Post–Civil Rights Era* (Albany: State University of New York Press, 1996); Harold Cruse, *The Crisis of the Negro Intellectual* (New York: Morrow, 1967).

23. Notable black excommunists include George Padmore, Richard Wright, Audre Lorde, Richard B. Moore, and Audley "Queen Mother" Moore. Whatever animus any of these held, none took such caustic aim at other blacks who remained communists.

24. Cruse, *The Crisis of the Negro Intellectual*, 46, 76. Winston James discusses the conceptual and empirical problems in Cruse's arguments in a thoroughly argued postscript to his *Holding Aloft the Banner of Ethiopia*. See Winston James, *Holding Aloft the Banner of Ethiopia: Caribbean Radicalism in America, 1900–1932* (New York: Verso, 1999), 262–91.

25. Martin, *Race First*; Robert Hill, "Racial and Radical: Cyril V. Briggs, *The Crusader* Magazine, and the African Blood Brotherhood, 1918–1922," in *The Crusader*, ed. Robert A. Hill (New York: Garland, 1987), v–lxx.

26. James, *Holding Aloft the Banner of Ethiopia*; Mark Solomon, *The Cry Was Unity: Communism and African Americans, 1917–1936* (Jackson: University Press of Mississippi, 1998); Minkah Makalani, *In the Cause of Freedom: Radical Black Internationalism from Harlem to London, 1917–1939* (Chapel Hill: University of North Carolina Press, 2011).

27. Bogues, *Black Heretics, Black Prophets*; Robinson, *Black Marxism*, 73.

28. Robinson, *Black Marxism*, 2, 66, 72–73, 168, 175, 309, 316.

29. Oliver C. Cox, *Capitalism as a System* (New York: Monthly Review, 1964); Robinson, *Black Marxism*, 110; Cedric Robinson, "Oliver Cromwell Cox and the Historiography of the West," *Cultural Critique* no. 17 (Winter 1990–1991): 5–20.

30. Oliver C. Cox, *Caste, Class, and Race: A Study in Social Dynamics* (1948; rpr., New York, Modern Reader Paperbacks, 1970), xxx, 322.

31. Robinson, *Black Marxism*, 66–68. Robinson's discussion of Western civilization never pinpoints its origins, and he never identifies the presence of racialism in what is generally considered its origins. Thus, it is unclear how Marxism emerged during the "ascendancy" of Western civilization.

32. Robinson, *Black Marxism*, 2.

33. Ibid., 170.

34. Ibid., 175–76.

35. Ibid., 68. See Amilcar Cabral, *Unity and Struggle: Speeches and Writings* (New York: Monthly Review, 1979); Ronald H. Chilcote, *Amilcar Cabral's Revolutionary Theory and Practice: A Critical Guide* (Boulder, CO: Lynne Rienner, 1991); Ntongela Masilela, "Pan-Africanism or Classical African Marxism?" in *Imagining Home: Class, Culture, and Nationalism in the African Diaspora*, ed. Sidney Lemelle and Robin D. G. Kelley (New

York: Verso, 1994), 308–30; Kwame Nkrumah, *Consciencism: Philosophy and Ideology for Decolonization and Development with Particular Reference to the African Revolution* (New York: Monthly Review, 1965); Abdul Rahman Mohamed Babu, *African Socialism or Socialist Africa?* (London: Zed, 1981).

36. Hesse, "Racialized Modernity," 646, 659.

37. Mignolo, "Delinking," 452, 483. For an insightful discussion of African intellectuals "stretching" Marxist analysis in the colonial context, see Masilela, "Pan-Africanism or Classical African Marxism?"

38. C. L. R. James, *The Black Jacobins: Toussaint L'Ouverture and the San Domingue Revolution* (New York: Vintage Books, 1989), 288. I would, however gently, disagree with David Scott's illuminating reading of James's treatment of Toussaint's tragic failure. On my reading, James broached a critique of the modern that, although it never came fully into view, nevertheless led him to pose important questions that only a few have followed up on. Scott offers his reading of this passage in *Conscripts of Modernity: The Tragedy of Colonial Enlightenment* (Durham, NC: Duke University Press, 2004), chap. 5. See also Bogues, *Black Heretics*; Wynter, "Beyond the Categories of the Master Conception"; Hesse, "Racial Modernity"; Richard Iton, *In Search of the Black Fantastic: Politics and Popular Culture in the Post–Civil Rights Era* (New York: Oxford University Press, 2008); Deborah Thomas, *Black Exceptionalism: Embodied Citizenship in Transnational Jamaica* (Durham, NC: Duke University Press, 2011).

39. Robinson, *Black Marxism*, 241–86; Bogues, *Black Heretics, Black Prophets*, 69–94; Pagent Henry, "C. L. R. James, African, and Afro-Caribbean Philosophy," in *Caliban's Reason: Introducing Afro-Caribbean Philosophy* (New York: Routledge, 2000), 47–67.

40. Testimony of Cyril Valentine Briggs, *Hearing before the Committee on Un-American Activities, House of Representatives*, 86th Cong., 1st sess., September 3, 1958, pt. 1: 75–81.

41. Césaire, *Letter to Maurice Thorez* (Paris, France: Présence Africaine, 1957), 6, 12–13.

42. Anthony Bogues, *Caliban's Freedom: The Early Political Thought of C. L. R. James* (London: Pluto, 1997), 3.

43. Tiffany Ruby Patterson and Robin D. G. Kelley, "Unfinished Migrations: Reflections on the African Diaspora and the Making of the Modern World," *African Studies Review* 43, no. 1 (April 2000): 27.

44. Claudia Jones, "An End to the Neglect of the Problems of Negro Women," *Political Affairs* (June 1949), in *Claudia Jones: Beyond Containment*, ed. Carole Boyce Davies (Oxfordshire, UK: Ayebia Clarke, 2011), 74–86; Carole Boyce Davies, *Left of Karl Marx: The Political Life of Black Communist Claudia Jones* (Durham: Duke University Press, 2007), 43; Erik McDuffie, *Sojourning for Freedom: Black Women, American Communism, and the Making of Black Left Feminism* (Durham: Duke University Press, 2011), 138, 167–69.

45. Jones, "An End to the Neglect," 85.

46. Davies, *Left of Karl Marx*, 43; McDuffie, *Sojourning for Freedom*, 138, 167–69.

47. A less generous reading might argue that Jones could not imagine an alternative frame for her argument beyond those terms already enunciated within Marxism, what Michel Foucault describes, in talking about a sort of anti-Stalinist Stalinism in the French Communist Party, as delimiting possible analyses to a nervous repetition of the already said. See Michel Foucault, "Truth and Power," in *The Foucault Reader*, ed. Paul Rabinow

(New York: Pantheon Books, 1984), 52–53. Whatever one might determine as the "historical" accuracy of such a reading, it forecloses precisely the kind of critique I want to see Jones and other black Marxists making of the theoretical archive they operated within, which requires excavating the very heretical, disciplinary deviance that I identify as the productive terrain, the privileged region on which black Marxists pursued a practice of analyzing and criticizing the archive they operated within.

48. Davies, *Left of Karl Marx*, 27.

49. McDuffie, *Sojourning for Freedom*, 167.

50. Jones, "An End to the Neglect," 76.

51. Farah Jasmine Griffin, *Harlem Nocturne: Women Artists and Progressive Politics during World War II* (New York: Basic Civitas, 2013); Saidiya Hartman, *Lose Your Mother: A Journey along the Atlantic Slave Route* (New York: Farrar, Straus and Giroux, 2008), 6; Jones, "An End to the Neglect," 79.

52. Jones, "An End to the Neglect," 79.

53. Ibid., 83. It is important to keep in mind that Jones was writing in the context of a factional CP struggle between those aligned with Browder and the Fosterites (the faction of which she was a part); see Hill, "Fosterites and Feminists," 67–90.

54. Jones, "An End to the Neglect," 74–86. On the Rosa Lee Ingram case, see Martha Biondi, *To Stand and Fight: The Struggle for Civil Rights in Postwar New York City* (Cambridge: Harvard University Press, 2003), 198–200; Charles H. Martin, "Race, Gender, and Southern Justice: The Rosa Lee Ingram Case," *The American Journal of Legal History* 29, no. 3 (July 1958): 251–68. On Jones's thinking about the Ingram case, see Davies, *Left of Karl Marx*; McDuffie, *Sojourning for Freedom*, 165–68.

55. Amié Césaire, *Discourse on Colonialism* (1955; rpr. New York: Monthly Review, 2000), 31, 36.

56. For a discussion of this thinking by Ashwood, James, and Padmore in London, see Makalani, *In the Cause of Freedom*, 203–207. See also Robinson, "Fascism and the Intersection of Capitalism, Racialism, and Historical Consciousness," *Humanities in Society* 3 (Autumn 1983): 325–49; Robin D. G. Kelley, "A Poetics of Anticolonialism: Introduction," in Césaire, *Discourse on Colonialism*, 19–21. One notes, too, a corresponding argument by Hannah Arendt about the colonial practices that served as the basis of fascism more recently, though in a certain respect missing the (admittedly fleeting) references to the colonial in Arendt's and Foucault's work. Giorgio Agamben theorizes a link between democracy and totalitarianism through the camp, reading it as a moment arrived at which permits a totalitarian turn. I take issue with Agamben's framing, however, to argue that the state of nature he identifies as a critical feature of the structure and logic of the camp is already always present in the structures and discourses of coloniality/modernity. See Hannah Arendt, *The Origins of Totalitarianism* (New York: Harcourt, Brace, 1951); Giorgio Agamben, *Homo Sacer: Sovereign Power and Bare Life* (Standford, CA: Stanford University Press, 1998) and *State of Exception* (Chicago: University of Chicago Press, 2005); Christopher Lee, "Locating Hannah Arerndt within Postcolonial Thought: A Prospectus," *College Literature* 38, no. 1 (Winter 2011): 95–114. My thinking along these lines has been aided by a similar discussion by Anthony Bogues in *Empire of Liberty: Power Desire and Freedom* (Lebanon, NH: Dartmouth College Press, 2010).

57. Richard Iton makes a similar observation in discussing black public political debate in *In Search of the Black Fantastic*.

58. Enrique Dussel, "Eurocentrism and Modernity (Introduction to the Frankfurt Lectures)," *boundary 2* 20, no. 3 (Autumn 1993): 65–76. See also Michelle Wright's discussion of Hegel in "The European and American Invention of the Black Other," in *Becoming Black: Creating Identity in the African Diaspora* (Durham: Duke University Press, 2004), 27–65.

59. Frantz Fanon, *The Wretched of the Earth* (New York: Grove Weidenfeld, 1963), 312–16. Fanon mentions such a leap in *Black Skins, White Masks*, and bringing invention into life.

60. Harold Cruse, *Rebellion or Revolution?* (New York: William Morrow, 1968), 76–77; Jack H. O'Dell, *Climbin' Jacob's Ladder: The Black Freedom Movement Writings of Jack O'Dell*, edited by Nikhil Pal Singh (Berkeley: University of California Press, 2010), 129; Stokely Carmichael and Charles V. Hamilton, *Black Power: The Politics of Liberation* (1967; rpr. New York: Vintage Books, 1992), xix, 2–32. For an illuminating treatment of the influence of Fanon's discussion of colonial violence on Carmichael's distinction between individual and institutional racism, see Priscilla Wald, "American Studies and the Politics of Life," *America Quarterly* 64 (June 2012): 190–91.

61. Robert L. Allen, *Black Awakening in Capitalist America: An Analytic History* (1967; rpr. Trenton, NJ: Africa World, 1990), 2, 14.

62. For a discussion of the declining appeal of internal colonialism in black political/public discourse, see Iton, *In Search of the Black Fantastic*. On American freedom as a project of empire, see Bogues, *Empire of Liberty*.

63. James left Trinidad in 1962 and returned briefly in 1965 as a cricket correspondent for the *London Times* to cover the British test match tour of the Caribbean. He arrived in Trinidad during a sugar workers strike, which led Eric Williams's government to place him under house arrest. James returned again in 1965 to run for public office in his home province of Tunapuna and left in 1966 after his Workers and Farmers Party lost to Williams's PNM.

64. In his second lecture, James declared, "I am very hostile to the particular brand of Marxism that is dominant today." See C. L. R. James, *Modern Politics* (Port-of-Spain, Trinidad: P.N.M., 1960; rpr. Detroit: Bewick/ed, 1973), 32.

65. James, *Modern Politics*, 84.

66. James, *The Black Jacobins*, 402. George Lamming makes a somewhat similar claim in *The Pleasures of Exile* (Ann Arbor: University of Michigan Press, 2004), 164–65.

67. C. L. R. James, "Rastafari at Home and Abroad," *New Left Review* (1964), reprinted in James, *At the Rendezvous of Victory* (London: Allison and Busby, 1984), 163–65. For James's statement about Haitian Maroons, see the documentary *W. A. R.: Walter Anthony Rodney* (2011), at the minute mark 10:38.

68. Walter Rodney, *Walter Rodney Speaks: The Making of an African Intellectual* (Trenton, NJ: Africa World, 1990), 16.

69. Anthony Bogues, "Black Power, Decolonization, and Caribbean Politics: Walter Rodney and the Politics of *The Groundings with My Brothers*," *boundary 2* 36, no. 1 (2009): 134, 141.

70. Achille Mbembe, *On the Postcolony* (Berkeley: University of California Press, 2001); David Scott, *Omens of Adversity: Tragedy, Time, Memory, Justice* (Durham, NC: Duke University Press, 2014).

71. See Bogues, *Black Heretics, Black Prophets*, 120; Césaire, *Discourse on Colonialism*, 37; Fanon, *Black Skin, White Mask*, trans. Richard Philcox (1952; rpr. New York: Grove, 2008), 204. See also, Wynter, "Unsettling," 331. It should be noted that Bogues specifically engages the quotes from Césaire and Fanon and references Wynter as well.

72. Gary Wilder, "Decolonizing France: L. S. Senghor's Redemptive Program for African Socialism," in *Endless Empire: Spain's Retreat, Europe's Eclipse, America's Decline*, ed. Alfred W. McCoy, Josep M. Fradera, and Stephen Jacobson (Madison: University of Wisconsin Press, 2012), 234. It bears pointing out that Senghor's African socialism resonated with Césaire's own sense of the redemptive possibilities of decolonization for Europe that he offers in the closing paragraph of his *Discourse*. While one might reasonably read Césaire's claim that the proletariat would liberate Europe centers European workers as the historical agents of such revolutionary or redemptive change, I have argued elsewhere for a reading that takes as part of Césaire's revision of Marxism a reconceptualization of the proletariat as not simply European workers, but as those engaged in anticolonial and antiracist struggles in the global South. See Minkah Makalani, "Internationalizing the Third International: The African Blood Brotherhood, Asian Radicals, and Race in the Communist International, 1919-1922," *Journal of African American History* 96, no. 2 (Spring 2011): 175.

73. To think about or approach Cabral only in terms of whether he was what one might call a Marxist-Leninist how closely his ideas aligned with Marxism-Leninism, or stress whether he was an original thinker who articulated a singular body of thought seems to me such an obviously supercilious concern as to warrant little commentary, other than to note, by way of departure, that Cabral's real importance was as an anticolonial activist-intellectual whose thinking reflected his engagement with anticolonial organizing and revolutionary struggles, rather than any fealty to a political theory. See Ronald Chilcote's treatment of "The Political Thought of Amílcar Cabral," *Journal of Modern African Studies* 6, no. 3 (1968): 373-88, and Patrick Chabal's criticism that would reject a view of Cabral as a thinker, in "The Social and Political Thought of Amilcra Cabral: A Reassessment," *Journal of Modern African Studies* 19, 1 (March 1981): 31-56; and *Amílcar Cabral: Revolutionary Leadership and People's War* (Trenton, NJ: Africa World, 2003).

74. Sanjay Seth, *Marxist Theory and Nationalist Politics: The Case of Colonial India* (Delhi: Sage, 1995), 11-12 34-44, 61-66. Dipesh Chakrabarty augments Seth's discussion through an analysis of the structures of historical time permeating Marxist historiography through such terms as "precapitalist," "real," and "abstract" labor and "commodity," which more generally exist within a sense of the disciplining and modernizing function of industrial labor. See Dipesh Chakrabarty, *Provincializing Europe: Postcolonial Thought and Historical Difference* (Princeton: Princeton University Press, 2000), 6-16, 47-50, 90-96.

75. Amílcar Cabral, "The Weapon of Theory: Presuppositions and Objectives of National Liberation in Relation to Social Structure," in *Unity and Struggle*, 124-25, 130.

76. Amílcar Cabral, "National Liberation and Culture," in *Return to the Source: Selected Speeches of Amílcar Cabral* (New York: Monthly Review, 1973), 52.

77. Cabral, "Weapon of Theory," in *Unity and Struggle*, 126.

78. Amílar Cabral, "Brief Analysis of the Social Structure in Guinea," in *Revolution in Guinea: An African People's Struggles* (New York: Monthly Review, 1970), 55–58.

79. Amílcar Cabral, "Connecting the Struggles: An Informal Talk with Black Americans," in *Return to the Source*, 83.

80. Ibid., 84.

81. Cabral, "National Liberation and Culture," in *Return to the Source*, 55–56.

82. Ibid.

83. Angela Davis, *Women, Race, and Class* (New York: Vintage Books, 1983); Robin D. G. Kelley, *Freedom Dreams: The Black Radical Imagination* (Boston: Beacon, 2003); Carole Boyce Davis, *Left of Karl Marx: The Political Life of Black Communist Claudia Jones* (Durham, NC: Duke University Press, 2008); Fred Moten, *In the Break: The Aesthetics of the Black Radical Tradition* (Minneapolis: University of Minnesota Press, 2003); Dayo Gore, *Radicalism at the Crossroads: African American Women Activists in the Cold War* (New York: New York University Press, 2011).

84. This is an obvious allusion to Achille Mbembe's argument in *On the Postcolony*, which, on my reading, makes a claim for the continued colonial existence of former colonies. See Achille Mbembe, *On the Postcolony* (Berkeley: University of California Press, 2001).

85. Nkrumah, *Consciencism*; Kwame Nkrumah, *Neo-Colonialism: The Last Stage of Imperialism* (London: Nelson, 1965); Kwame Nkrumah, *Class Struggle in Africa* (London: Panaf Books, 1970); Walter Rodney, *How Europe Underdeveloped Africa* (Washington: Howard University Press, 1974); Julius K. Nyerere, *Ujamaa—Essays on Socialism* (Dar es Salaam: Oxford University Press, 1968); Leopold Sédar Sénghor, *On African Socialism: Leopold Sédar Sénghor*, trans. Mercer Cook (New York: Praeger, 1964).

86. C. L. R. James, *A History of Pan-African Revolt* (1937; rpr. Chicago: Kerr, 1995); James, *Black Jacobins*.

87. See the film *Finally Got the News*, produced by Stewart Bird et al., with cooperation of the League of Revolutionary Black Workers (Cinema Guild, 1970), DVD (Icarus Films, 2003).

88. On the Revolutionary Action Movement, see Robin D. G. Kelley, "Stormy Weather: Reconstructing Black (Inter)Nationalism in the Cold War Era," in *Is It Nation Time? Contemporary Essays on Black Power and Black Nationalism*, ed. Eddie S. Glaude Jr. (Chicago: University of Chicago Press, 2002), 67–90; Muhammad Ahmad (Maxwell Stanford Jr.), *We Will Return in the Whirlwind: Black Radical Organizations, 1960–1975* (Chicago: Charles H. Kerr, 2007). On the League of Revolutionary Black Workers, see James A. Geschwender, *Class, Race, and Worker Insurgency: The League of Revolutionary Black Workers* (New York: Cambridge University Press, 1977), 80–89, 121, 160, 177–87; Dan Georgakas and Marvin Surkin, *Detroit: I Do Mind Dying* (Cambridge, MA: South End, 1998), 13–22, 69–70.

89. For a brilliant discussion of the ALSC Marxist turn, see Cedric Johnson, *Revolutionaries to Race Leaders: Black Power and the Making of African American Politics* (Minneapolis: University of Minnesota Press, 2007), 131–72. See also Komozi Woodard, *A Nation within a Nation: Amiri Baraka (LeRoi Jones) and Black Power Politics* (Chapel Hill: University of North Carolina Press, 1999), 161–80.

90. Haki R. Madhubuti, "The Latest Purge: The Attack on Black Nationalism and Pan-Afrikanism by the New Left, The Sons and Daughters of the Old Left," *The Black Scholar* 6, no. 1 (September 1974): 43–56.

91. Mark Smith, "A Response to Madhubuti," *The Black Scholar* 6, no. 5 (January-February 1975):44–53.

92. Johnson, *Revolutionaries to Race Leaders*, 148, 151, 155–61, 163, 166–70.

93. Manning Marable, *How Capitalism Underdeveloped Black America*, rev. ed. (Cambridge, MA: South End, 2000), 262.

94. Kimberly Spring, "Black Feminists Respond to Black Power Masculinism," in *The Black Power Movement: Rethinking the Civil Rights–Black Power Era*, ed. Peniel E. Joseph (New York: Routledge, 2006), 116.

- CHAPTER THREE -

THE QUEST FOR RACIAL CHANGE

African American Intellectuals and the Black Liberal Tradition

BRIAN D. BEHNKEN

In his influential book *Stride toward Freedom*, Dr. Martin Luther King Jr. argued that the United States had displayed "a schizophrenic personality on the question of race." In making this statement, he linked the double consciousness that black people experienced on a daily basis to the broader American body politic.[1] The United States, King wrote, "has been torn between two selves—a self in which she has proudly professed democracy and a self in which she has sadly practiced the antithesis of democracy." This bipolarity had plagued the United States since the birth of the Republic. King recognized in the civil rights movement, and in the federal government's and some white people's responses to it, the awakening of America to its finest and democratic self. For many blacks, the willingness of the Supreme Court to begin dismantling Jim Crow, the readiness of the Congress to debate new civil rights legislation, and the ability of local governments to address civil rights issues represented the coming victory of black liberal reform over American racism.[2]

Dr. King's description of the United States, and his belief in local, state, and national governmental institutions to bring about racial change, spoke to generations of black liberals. While his words and ideas made sense to black liberals, and especially African American intellectuals, other Americans fundamentally misunderstood his elucidation of the black liberal tradition. Too often, black liberalism was lumped with white liberalism, distorting the differences between the two. Scholars and laypeople continue to misconstrue black liberalism today. African American intellectual thought has traditionally been viewed as either conservative or liberal, nationalistic or integrationist. Such binaries obscure a great deal about what black liberalism entails. Black liberalism remains in many ways distinct and apart from its white liberal cousin.

This chapter offers an overview of the history of the African American intellectual liberal tradition in the United States. I define black liberalism as a belief system based on conceptions of American democracy, equality, and capitalism designed to bring African American structural incorporation into US society. Black liberals, generally speaking, believe in the power and integrity of the Constitution, the role of government in bringing about reform, and the power of black activism to eradicate racism. For black intellectual liberals—those individuals who attained advanced degrees and pursued an academic or scholarly life—and for liberals more generally, racism, segregation, and discrimination ran counter to American democratic traditions. To overcome these obstacles black liberals argued for something broader than integration or equality: they argued for racial change. If black intellectual liberals had a single goal, racial change was it. That term, like black liberalism itself, encapsulated a host of ideas and assumptions. Most important, racial change symbolized a transformation of black and white society. For black intellectuals, it connoted an elevation of African American status in the United States, the opening of American education and the workforce, access to quality jobs and affordable homes, and social integration, among other things. For whites, racial change meant the acknowledgment of the roles and accomplishments of black people throughout American history, the discarding of racial prejudices and stereotypes, and the recognition of blacks as the equals of whites. For both, it represented improved race relations, open communication, and cooperation.

EARLY BLACK LIBERALISM

Black intellectual leaders concentrated primarily on scholarship and philosophical thought to counter and correct the racist and stereotypical opinions white people had about blacks.[3] For intellectuals, research and scholarly activism provided the best means for changing the white mind. This intellectual tradition stretches back to the nineteenth century. For example, abolitionist and intellectual James W. C. Pennington understood that in order for both blacks and whites to understand the black past, someone had to write an accurate history. Pennington was born a slave but escaped to the North, where he experienced a world as deeply racist as the one he had recently left. Much of this racism was muddled by a poor understanding of history. Whites tended to view blacks as trapped in some kind of historical time warp—a forever backward, uncivilized, and tribal people. Pennington hoped to argue against this viewpoint. He took classes at Yale University (the first black person to do so) and eventually published the first historical text on people of African descent.

Pennington's *A Text Book on the Origin and History, of the Colored People* actually went far beyond a standard history of black people. He began his study of the black experience with African kingdoms, arguing that the ancient Kemetic and Kushite civilizations had far exceeded European standards of "civilization." He further asserted that Africa was the root of European civilization, not vice versa. Unlike Afrocentrist scholars who tended to concentrate solely on ancient Egypt, Pennington also examined Africa's west coast, the region from which most black slaves in the Western Hemisphere originated. Pennington hoped to turn much of America's historical understanding of black people on its head. His goal in doing so was twofold: uplift the historical image of American blacks and diminish white perceptions of their own grandiose history. But *A Text Book on the Origin and History, of the Colored People* was more than just an account of early black history. It was also a historical ethnology of race and blackness. He evaluated the biblical and historical "branches" of humanity, ultimately concluding that race had made no difference in the evolution of the human species and that blackness, therefore, did not connote deficiency when compared to whiteness. Rather, the two were equal and the same. Thus Pennington concluded that race was a socially constructed category that had no basis in history or biology.[4]

James Pennington also published an important slave narrative about his experiences entitled *The Fugitive Blacksmith; or, Events in the History of James W. C. Pennington*. His account remains important because it involves more than just a recollection of his experiences as a slave. As he did in *A Text Book on the Origin and History, of the Colored People*, Pennington went beyond a simple narrative retelling to include analysis of the master-slave relationship, of social relations among the slaves, and of slave culture. As did other escaped slaves who offered narratives of their bondage and escape, Pennington concentrated on the brutality and immorality of slavery. In so doing, he castigated whites who condoned slavery, saw it as beneficial for blacks, or sanctioned it due to the perceived inferiority of black people. In his telling, black slaves come off as superior to whites for withstanding the horrors of southern slave life. This was a necessary corrective for many of the common misconceptions about slavery.[5]

Like Pennington, Ida B. Wells saw the potential of sound scholarship and intellectual liberalism to right wrongs. Wells firmly believed in the power of the Constitution and American democracy to eradicate social and racial ills, but her detailed study would expose problems in black society. In the late nineteenth and early twentieth centuries there proved no greater social threat to black life than lynching. African Americans had experienced death at the hands of lynch mobs since before the founding of the Republic, but in the post–Civil War era, white people came to use lynching as a method of keeping blacks in their place. Whites meted out lynch "justice" primarily against black men for alleged sexual violations, most often false claims of rape made by white women. Below this veneer of chivalry, however, lay a deeper truth. Whites did not lynch blacks for sexual crimes; they lynched black people for standing up for their civil rights, for becoming successful business people, for getting a good education, and for voting.[6]

Wells had firsthand experience with lynch "justice" in Memphis. In 1891, a white mob lynched three of her good friends. They were three black men who ran a successful grocery store that took business away from a local white-owned store. The local press implied that they had harassed and possibly had sexual relations with several white women. Wells knew the allegation of sexual impropriety was false. More important, she understood that such accusations removed blame from the white store owners and hid the more mundane, profit-oriented reasons for the lynching.[7]

Wells traveled abroad to speak about the horror of lynching and published accounts of the deaths—including those of her three friends—in works such as *Southern Horrors: Lynch Law in All Its Phases* (1892) and *The Red Record* (1895). In these texts, Wells forcefully articulated an intellectual vision regarding how the government could work to end lynching.

In *The Red Record*, Wells asserted that black people "demand a fair trial by law for those accused of a crime, and punishment by law after honest conviction." In short, she wanted to see the law exercised freely and equally for black and white Americans. Wells went further, however. In explaining what she hoped would be "the remedy" for lynching, she encouraged her readers to call upon state and federal representatives to pass laws making lynch justice illegal. "Congressman [Henry W.] Blair offered a resolution in the House of Representatives, August, 1894," Wells wrote. "[T]he organized life of the country can speedily make this a law by sending resolutions to Congress indorsing Mr. Blair's bill.... In no better way can the question be settled."[8] Here, Wells uttered what became a mantra for her and other black liberals; the use of scholarship to push federal laws that would help secure rights and destroy lynching.

The congressional campaign against lynching, one inspired by Ida B. Wells, continued for the next several decades. The National Association for the Advancement of Colored People (NAACP), which Wells helped found, made antilynching one of its most important aims. Like Wells, many of the leaders of the NAACP considered themselves political and intellectual liberals. NAACP leaders regularly published accounts of lynching in their influential magazine *The Crisis*. In 1916 the organization founded its Antilynching Committee to develop a legislative agenda and appeal to sympathetic members of the Congress to pass laws that would end lynching.[9] The debate over antilynching legislation continued until the 1950s. Bills similar to Blair's appeared with some frequency, but none ever passed. Still, it is fair to say that the NAACP's efforts, and those of intellectual black liberals like Ida Wells, caused a significant decline in the number of black people murdered at the hands of lynch mobs.[10]

The NAACP became the organization most associated with black activism and liberalism in the twentieth century. The group concentrated not only on lynching, but also on eradicating obstacles to the franchise; destroying housing, school, and social segregation; and providing minorities better job opportunities. When the NAACP was founded in 1909 it had only one black member, William Edward Burghardt Du Bois, the most important black intellectual of the early twentieth century.[11] Du Bois served as the NAACP's director of publicity and research and edited *The Crisis*. While his leadership style overall might best be described as black nationalistic, his scholarship clearly reflected the liberal intellectual paradigm of leadership. Du Bois was born and raised in Massachusetts, attended Fisk University, and completed a PhD at Harvard University in history in 1895, the first black person to do so. Du Bois soon embarked on a career of letters, settling first at the University of Pennsylvania and then moving on to Atlanta University. Like other black liberals, he hoped to bring about racial change through his scholarship and scholar activism. His most profound works pushing such an agenda in the early twentieth century were *The Philadelphia Negro* and *The Negro Artisan*.

The Philadelphia Negro, published in 1899 and distributed in 1900, was one of the first sociological studies of black people in a major American city. Philadelphia's black population totaled nearly forty thousand at the time, was historically poor, and was segregated into a small ghetto in the city's seventh ward. Most white Americans viewed blacks as ghettoized because of race:

black people were racially inferior, and that inferiority manifested itself in cities in the form of poor, overcrowded, and dilapidated black communities. As Du Bois biographer David Levering Lewis noted, Du Bois felt "'the world was thinking wrong about race, because it did not know.' He would teach it to think right."[12] In Philadelphia, he concluded that poverty, crime, despair, and living conditions did not derive from race, but rather from the racism blacks experienced. Whites forced blacks to live in the seventh ward. The city spent less on the education of blacks than whites. Social services were nonexistent. Black men and women found themselves denied a higher education, excluded from high-paying jobs, and as a result burdened by poverty. As Du Bois noted, the difference between blacks and other Americans was "the ancestors of the English and the Irish and the Italians were felt to be worth educating, helping[,] and guiding because they were men and brothers, while in America a census which gives a slight indication of the utter disappearance of the American Negro from the earth is greeted with ill-concealed delight." Racism infected the United States, rendering white people incapable of seeing the real causes of black social inequalities.[13]

Du Bois went in a different direction with *The Negro Artisan*. Instead of looking at a city, he chose to examine a particular class of people. He surveyed thirteen hundred skilled craftsmen, as well as a host of other data, to create an impressive picture of race and race relations in labor. Once again, he sought to challenge prevailing, racist viewpoints that argued that blacks could not excel at skilled trades because they were inferior. He showed instead that racism kept blacks out of trade schools, out of unions, and hence seemingly out of the skilled trades. But Du Bois also discovered a great number of black skilled craftsmen, noting that while organized labor generally excluded African Americans, there were more than forty thousand unionized blacks. Moreover, blacks often worked as skilled craftsmen below the radar of many white people, operating in segregated communities where only black people knew or saw them. Du Bois, as such, concluded simply, "The Negro evinces considerable mechanical ingenuity."[14] And there it was—the use of scholarship to specifically refute American racism and prejudicial perceptions about black people.

Du Bois's scholarship at the turn of the century was important, as was his scholarship after he left academia, especially his monumental *Black Reconstruction in America* and his work as editor of *The Crisis*. Indeed, his editorship of *The Crisis* allowed him to continue his intellectual pursuit of racial change in a venue that gave him a considerably wider audience than his other publications generated. In 1915, for instance, he discussed how *The*

Crisis advanced research on black people that, like his *The Philadelphia Negro* and *The Negro Artisan*, challenged American racism. Above all, *The Crisis* gave Du Bois and the NAACP "publicity . . . to carry on the propaganda for equal rights in the United States and, to a degree, to inform, guide and entertain thousands of readers."[15] The following year, Du Bois added what came to be a regular feature of *The Crisis*: criticism of scholarly works that denigrated black people. In the January 1916 edition, for example, Du Bois took aim at John Todd, who had recently published an account of southern cotton agriculture that regurgitated standard notions of black "laziness" and "immorality" popular at the time. Du Bois sharply rebuked Todd, asserting sarcastically that such "'laziness' had succeeded in raising the rate of wages and the standard of living of black men" and wished that Todd would "soon get 'lazy' enough to raise his wage to some dim resemblance of decency."[16]

Where W. E. B. Du Bois chose to focus on sociological studies of distinct communities, Alaine LeRoy Locke explored the world of black artistic contributions. Locke was one of the leading intellectual figures of the early twentieth century. He became the first African American Rhodes Scholar, and he earned a PhD in philosophy from Harvard in 1918. Locke's doctoral dissertation demonstrated a keen intellect, one able to analyze concepts beyond traditional academic disciplines. In "The Problem of Classification in the Theory of Value," he critically analyzed the developing field of value theory and the classification of values by human beings. Locke argued that understanding values was not the first step in value classification. Instead, philosophers had to discern what values were important, why they were important, and how they impacted human emotions. More importantly, he questioned whether human beings shaped the theory of value or if such developing theorems shaped people. Values, like opinions or biases, were malleable, Locke observed, and always subject to change.[17]

Locke had no explicit discussion of race in "The Problem of Classification in the Theory of Value." Reading between the lines, one can easily discern the core of his intellectual liberalism and his understanding of race, which were woven throughout the text. For example, by tying value theory to human biases, he underscored the ways in which both can reinforce and undermine prejudices. More importantly, in seeing values as malleable, he attributed the creation of values and their classification to human beings. This was a profound explication at the time, one that would become important for the study of race in the coming years as scholars began to understand race and racism as socially constructed. He also discussed value and the arts, which showed Locke's developing sense of the importance of artistic creation.

Indeed, Locke is best known for his cataloging and analysis of black art, especially the literature and fine art coming out of the Harlem Renaissance.[18]

A number of other black liberal intellectuals chose to focus on the impact that segregation had on the African American community. By scrutinizing Jim Crow, these scholars could, like Du Bois, demonstrate the inequalities of the American racial caste system. The study of history offered the best avenue for explaining the myriad problems generated by racial segregation. By examining the black past, not only could historians set the record straight as to the accomplishments of African Americans, but they could also counter the prevailing racist climate that pigeonholed black people as racially inferior. The most important black historian of the twentieth century, Carter G. Woodson, did exactly this. He is widely and correctly regarded as the "Father of Black History." Woodson was largely denied an education growing up in rural Virginia and West Virginia. At the turn of the century, he enrolled in Berea College, where he achieved a bachelor's degree in literature. He then entered the University of Chicago, where he earned a master's degree. He then went to Harvard University, earning his PhD in history in 1912; he was the second African American after Du Bois to achieve such a distinction. Like other black liberal intellectuals, Woodson remained convinced that Americans fundamentally misunderstood the role of black people in US history. Only sound scholarship, he believed, could correct this historical amnesia and bring about racial change.

Woodson's first book on black history set the stage for his broader role in the study of black history, especially the education of African Americans. In *The Education of the Negro Prior to 1861*, published in 1915, he presented a detailed accounting of the history of black education, primarily concentrating on the slave South. Woodson chose to focus on southern states because most Americans believed either that masters did not educate their slaves or that slaves were not able to be educated. He showed that for philanthropic, economic, and/or industrial reasons, numerous whites found it necessary to educate slaves. For example, slave owners frequently had to contract with skilled craftsmen for blacksmithing or mechanical repair work. Those who hoped to centralize production on plantations trained slaves as blacksmiths, coopers, or mechanics and thereby saved a great deal of money. While Woodson noted the capitalistic aspects of this type of education, he also demonstrated how slaves excelled at this training, something which frequently surprised white observers who believed them incapable of such education. Thus, Woodson refuted those who viewed black people as racially inferior and lacking the capacity to learn. As he acknowledged,

Intelligent colored men proved to be useful and trustworthy servants; they became much better laborers and artisans, and many of them showed administrative ability adequate to the management of business establishments and large plantations. Moreover, better rudimentary education served many ambitious persons of color as a stepping-stone to higher attainments. Negroes learned to appreciate and write poetry and contributed something to mathematics, science, and philosophy. Furthermore, having disproved the theories of their mental inferiority, some of the race, in conformity with the suggestion of Cotton Mather, were employed to teach white children.[19]

Woodson's other major study on black education went further than *The Education of the Negro Prior to 1861*. In 1933, he published *The Mis-Education of the Negro*, a searing indictment of black education in the twentieth century. Woodson explored both the history and the sociological aspects of black schooling, interjecting his own experiences and opinions throughout. He articulated the black liberal intellectual theory that only through sound teaching and scholarship could African Americans inaugurate racial change in the United States. "Only by careful study of the Negro himself and the life which he is forced to lead can we arrive at the proper procedure in this crisis [of black education]," he argued.[20] Woodson criticized a system which either viewed blacks as unable to learn or more often simply indoctrinated them into the US body politic as second-class citizens. To overcome problems with the education system, he contended that black people had to develop a new educational model that would not only educate them but also reform whites. "The program for the uplift of the Negro in this country," he concluded, "must be based upon a scientific study of the Negro from within to develop in him the power to do for himself what his oppressors will never do to elevate him to the level of others." As such, he rearticulated the basic formula for racial change in America—black people would reform themselves and in the process reform whites.[21]

Carter Woodson was a pioneer beyond his scholarship. He also created one of the most important vehicles for the study of black Americans, the Association for the Study of Negro Life and History (ASNLH), founded in 1915. The ASNLH proved an important step in the work of intellectuals to uplift the status and image of black people. Even more important, however, was the ASNLH's publication, the *Journal of Negro History*, which was published continually for nearly one hundred years and renamed the *Journal of African American History* in 2002. The journal not only helped advance the message of black intellectuals; it served as a clearinghouse for scholarly knowledge on African Americans. Woodson also established Negro History Week in 1926, now Black History Month, for the acknowledgment and appreciation of black contributions to the United States.

Like Carter Woodson, Marion Thompson Wright took school segregation as her area of focus. One of the pioneering female intellectuals of the twentieth century, Wright initially cast a wide net by examining segregated schooling in sixteen different states for her master's thesis at Howard University. In 1938, she earned her doctorate from Columbia University, becoming the first black historian to graduate from the Teachers College. Wright's dissertation "The Education of Negroes in New Jersey" condensed her work on several states into an exhaustive study of one state. By examining New Jersey, she chose a state that many Americans might not have considered a hardcore, segregated locale. Her choice was masterful. As a northern state, New Jersey's system of segregated schools demonstrated that racism and school segregation were not simply southern issues. Rather, as she noted, they were national issues. As Wright demonstrated, New Jersey schools operated along the southern model. Most districts reserved a pittance for the education of black children, black children attended classes in dilapidated buildings, and black teachers received on average half the pay of white teachers. More importantly, Wright expanded her focus to examine the social consequences of these inferior schools. She tied school segregation to crime, juvenile delinquency, joblessness, and poverty. Her analysis echoed Du Bois, as well as numerous later studies that analyzed the deleterious effects segregation had on black people.[22]

The most influential black historian of the twentieth century was John Hope Franklin. He attended Fisk University and earned his doctorate from Harvard in 1941. A master of the historian's craft, Franklin, like James Pennington, sought to write the first definitive history of black people in the United States. As he noted in his 2005 autobiography, American racism and southern segregation laws unfairly burdened black people. "I became a student and eventually a scholar," he wrote, "and it was armed with the tools of scholarship that I strove to dismantle those laws, level those obstacles and disadvantages, and replace superstitions with humane dignity." Capturing the spirit of black intellectual liberalism, Franklin noted, "I thought [of black history] ... from the outset, as a corrective or as a supplementary revision of United States history."[23] In 1947 he published that corrective, the monumental *From Slavery to Freedom: A History of African Americans*, which has been continually expanded and updated since it was first written.

From Slavery to Freedom did what no history text had done before: it accurately and honestly surveyed African American history from its African origins to the present day. Franklin chose to begin in Africa, but he focused not on Egypt, as other scholars had done, but instead on the great West Coast African kingdoms of Ghana, Songhai, and Mali. When he moved on to discuss the slave trade, he included a frank discussion of the African role in the trade. Unlike numerous other scholars before him, Franklin distinguished between colonial era slavery and slavery in the nineteenth century. His discussion of nineteenth-century slavery excoriated slave masters and the ideological underpinnings of the institution. He also discussed the abuses slaves endured and their resiliency. Most importantly, he recorded aspects of the black experience that most Americans knew nothing about: the black migration westward, the African American role in the military, the Harlem Renaissance, and the developing civil rights movement.[24]

Franklin was an excellent scholar. Over his career he wrote more than a dozen books, while constantly updating *From Slavery to Freedom*. His intellectual prowess encouraged numerous others interested in the black past to make their careers studying African American history. As a liberal, he was also an activist. He served on the NAACP team that fought *Brown v. Board*, providing crucial information on the history and legacy of school segregation. He joined Dr. King during the Selma campaign and marched in support of voting rights. In the late 1960s he joined other scholars in denouncing the war in Vietnam. Franklin was a model of black intellectual liberalism who used his scholarship in an attempt to better the lives of black Americans and bring about racial change. As an activist-scholar he also joined the black freedom struggle to achieve the same goal.

Finally, E. Franklin Frazier also fit into the liberal model of black intellectualism. Frazier was educated at the University of Chicago, where he earned his doctorate in sociology in 1932. While his research interests were broad, Frazier primarily concentrated on African American social relationships, especially those of the black church and black family, his work fusing black history and sociology seamlessly. In *The Negro Church in America*, for example, Frazier not only synthesized African American religious traditions going back to their African origin, but he also detailed the ways in which post–Civil War church organizations and activities bound black people together. The black church thus became an incubator of sorts for the maintenance of African American people and communities, one that helped to give rise to the civil rights era of the 1960s. For Frazier, like other black liberal intellectuals, African Americans had a fundamental right to full citizenship in the United States.[25]

BLACK LIBERAL INTELLECTUALISM
IN THE CIVIL RIGHTS ERA

John Hope Franklin, Marion Wright, Carter Woodson, E. Franklin Frazier, and numerous other black liberals combined scholarship with many of the broader strands of black liberal thought. For example, they argued that segregation violated American values and that quality schooling was a right due to all Americans. In the 1950s, their research, especially Wright's "The Education of Negroes in New Jersey" and Franklin's vast knowledge of African American history, became a part of the body of evidence presented in the *Brown v. Board* case.[26] That case and the members of the NAACP's Legal Defense and Education Fund (LDF) who fought it marked an important evolution in black intellectual liberal thinking. The LDF had originally been founded by Charles Hamilton Houston as the NAACP's Legal Redress Committee. Houston was an intellectual giant in his own right. He received his law degree from Harvard Law School in 1919, became the NAACP's litigation director, and served as professor and later dean of Howard Law School. He educated generations of black attorneys for the sole purpose of destroying Jim Crow.[27]

While a firm believer in integration, Houston originally promoted the legal strategy of equalization. Like numerous other black leaders, he knew that in the South separate was not equal. The NAACP could sue local governments and school districts by arguing that they did not comply with the law since separate black and white facilities were not the same. It may appear that Houston and other attorneys attempted to make segregation more palatable—that they embraced the system and simply wanted separate to be equal. But this would miss the broader point. Houston knew that southern governments and businesses, if made to equalize facilities, would go bankrupt. In forcing them to equalize facilities, he would actually bring about the end of Jim Crow because communities would choose to integrate rather than face the cost of equalization.

Houston's greatest acolyte, one who would succeed him as head of the LDF and as the preeminent black legal mind of the twentieth century, was Thurgood Marshall. A student of Houston at Howard, Marshall graduated at the top of his class and soon embarked on a legal career with the NAACP's LDF. One of his first cases, *Murray v. Pearson*, which Houston and Marshall fought together in 1936, forcefully communicated Houston's equalization strategy. Donald Gaines Murray had been denied admittance to the University of Maryland Law School because he was black. He sued with the assistance Marshall and Houston, who argued in state court that the lack of equal facilities (Maryland had no law school for African Americans) violated segregation laws. The Maryland court agreed, handing Murray, Marshall, and Houston a victory, but one confined to Maryland.[28]

The problem with *Murray v. Pearson* and the equalization strategy was that the benefits were restricted to Maryland. To benefit blacks across the United States, Marshall would have to break with his mentor and develop a new strategy. He did so in two important cases—*Sweatt v. Painter* and *Brown v. Board*. *Sweatt* was in many ways an important evolution in Marshall's legal thinking and one that laid the groundwork for *Brown*. In 1946, University of Texas president Theophilus Painter had rejected Heman Sweatt as an applicant to the UT Law School because of his race. Texas had no Negro law school, so Sweatt sued. When the *Sweatt* case reached the Supreme Court in 1950, Marshall argued—as he had in *Murray*—that the lack of equal facilities violated the law. But he also asserted that other intangible factors marked segregation as harmful to black people. The Court agreed, asserting that the Texas situation violated Sweatt's Fourteenth Amendment rights while simultaneously arguing that separation harmed African Americans and damaged their ability to compete fairly in the legal field.[29]

Brown v. Board took Marshall's legal thinking one step further. In that case, he abandoned Houston's equalization strategy and attempted instead to eradicate the basis for segregation, the 1896 *Plessy v. Ferguson* case. Marshall presented an array of statistical and sociological data that demonstrated that segregation had a harmful effect on black children. Instead of arguing that facilities were unequal and hence violated the law, he asserted that the law itself was wrong and that segregation must end. The Supreme Court agreed. It stated that since schools formed the foundation of good citizenship, and that the children who emerged from American schools would form the basis of the American democratic order, segregation was deeply problematic and constitutionally indefensible. *Brown* reversed generations of constitutional law and effectively overturned *Plessy*. The case represented one of the great victories of the black intellectual tradition and vindicated the goals of black liberals going back to the nineteenth century.[30]

Where the law had the potential to eradicate the political system that buttressed segregation, black faith traditions offered a different kind of redress.[31] Black religious liberals knew the Bible made no specific demand for the separation of the races. In fact, the Bible mandated the exact opposite of segregation—brotherly love, Christian compassion, and the love of one's neighbor. They also took specific inspiration from numerous biblical stories that they regarded as liberal: the call to action of Jeremiah, the story of Moses, the trials of Job, and the teachings of Jesus all inspired black religious liberalism. As such, religious liberals knew that Jim Crow was not only wrong; they saw it as a violation of the spiritual tenets of Christianity. As Christians, black liberal ministers had to fight against segregation and racism.

Perhaps no one better represents the combination of religious and intellectual liberalism than Martin Luther King Jr. His religious leadership is well understood, but his intellectual accomplishments are often forgotten. King attended Morehouse College and Crozer Theological Seminary before earning his PhD from Boston University in 1955. His doctoral dissertation, "A Comparison of the Conception of God in the Thinking of Paul Tillich and Henry Nelson Wieman," while an important academic accomplishment and an important marker of his intellectual gifts, has relatively little to say about black liberalism and civil rights. In his dissertation, King explored the differing perceptions of God as held by two of the preeminent religious minds of the time, Tillich and Wiemen. He began by discussing Tillich's thinking on God. Tillich, King wrote, viewed God as omnipresent and omniscient, as a god of love but also justice. Wieman, King noted, viewed God as more finite. Still, King concluded that the thinking of the two men was more similar than different. His siding with Tillich represented in some ways King's thinking not only on God but also in the biblical aspects of the civil rights movement. Since Tillich and King's god was a god of justice, faith in a righteous cause would ultimately be victorious. That success would come from faith and God's assistance. As historian David Chappell has shown, this type of theological and intellectual thinking was common among black ministers at the time.[32]

King's sermons and published works offer more insight into his intellectual liberalism than does his dissertation. As noted above, *Stride toward Freedom* does a good job of elucidating King's liberal thinking on the United States. His book *Where Do We Go from Here: Chaos or Community?* is even more important. This was King's last attempt to elucidate his intellectual liberalism. He was assassinated several months after its publication. In the book, King expands upon his views of American society and the course of the civil rights movement. "When a people are mired in oppression," he wrote, "they realize deliverance only when they have accumulated the power to enforce change.... Our nettlesome task is to discover how to organize our strength into compelling power so that government cannot elude our demands." Such had been the challenge of the black liberal tradition for more than one hundred years. "It is enormously difficult," King continued, "for any oppressed people even to arrive at an awareness of their latent strengths.... Only when they break out of the fog of self-denigration can they begin to discover the forms of action that influence events.... This is where the civil rights movement stands today."[33] King once again reminds his readers about the overarching goal of racial change. The civil rights movement and black intellectual liberalism had to reform American society as a whole and not just its constituent elements.

King's sermons were perhaps even more important pieces of his intellectual thought than his published works. One of his last sermons, "Remaining Awake through a Great Revolution," delivered at the National Cathedral shortly before his assassination in 1968, is a classic elucidation of King's liberal vision. King stated:

> One day we will have to stand before the God of history and we will talk in terms of things we've done. Yes, we will be able to say we built gargantuan bridges to span the seas, we built gigantic buildings to kiss the skies....It seems that I can hear the God of history saying, "That was not enough! But I was hungry, and ye fed me not. I was naked, and ye clothed me not. I was devoid of a decent sanitary house to live in, and ye provided no shelter for me. And consequently, you cannot enter the kingdom of greatness. If ye do it unto the least of these, my brethren, ye do it unto me." That's the question facing America today.

Here King shows once again his intellectual dexterity, combining biting social commentary with theology. As other liberal intellectuals had done, he raised the question about what the United States had done for the black community and found in the answer the United States wanting. He borrowed from Matthew 25:35–36 and 42–43 to allow "the God of history" to assess the value of the things America had done. For King, as for his "God of history," without correction, without answering "the question facing America today," America would not enter the "kingdom of greatness." Yet King ended his sermon on a positive note, stating, "I can still sing 'We Shall Overcome.'... With this faith we will be able to hew out of the mountain of despair the stone of hope. With this faith we will be able to transform the jangling discords of our nation into a beautiful symphony of brotherhood."[34]

It would seem that with all the words spoken, sermons given, and books written by the likes of W. E. B. Du Bois, Carter Woodson, or Martin Luther King, all that needed to be said about black intellectual liberalism had been said. But as King had noted, without programs and actions their words meant very little. While direct action demonstrations themselves are neither liberal nor conservative, the widespread usage of protests and the dissemination of philosophical nonviolence fit in well with the broader liberal agenda. Black liberal intellectuals, as King, Shuttlesworth, and numerous others had done, debated the merits of nonviolent protest activism and found within protest not only a key feature of their ideals, but also concrete action. More importantly, their elucidation of nonviolent direct action inspired and appealed to individuals across the United States. These individuals frequently called on leaders such as Dr. King, but even more often they took the ideals of nonviolent protest as their own and engaged in their own local freedom movements.[35]

Legal victories and legislation helped mark the success of intellectual liberalism and protest activism. Black liberals had their most important legislative victories with the passage of the Civil Rights Act of 1964 and the Voting Rights Act of 1965. The Civil Rights Act satisfied many of the goals that African Americans had fought for since Reconstruction. These included bans on almost every form of racial segregation and protection for voting. The voting provisions in the Civil Rights Act were generally weak, so the Congress passed the Voting Rights Act to shore up protection of black voting. The Civil Rights Act justified the activism of black liberals going back at least four generations. The Voting Rights Act, while certainly another vindication, did something more. It allowed for a revolutionary expansion of the black electorate and the election of hundreds of black politicians to local, state, and national offices.

Barbara Jordan of Texas is a good example of the political evolution of black liberalism. Jordan was born in 1936 in Houston. She attended Texas Southern University and then went to Boston University Law School. She returned to Texas in 1960, passed the state bar, and practiced law for several years before contemplating running for political office. Jordan's initial campaigns demonstrate the overall power of the Voting Rights Act on the local level. She ran for the Texas House in 1962 and 1964, both times losing resoundingly. But after the passage of the Voting Rights Act, she ran for a seat in the Texas Senate in 1966. She won, becoming the first black woman ever elected to that body. In the Texas legislature, Jordan fought for a state minimum wage, increased voting protection via redistricting and greater statewide acceptance of labor unions. In 1973, she ran for a seat in the US House and won easily. She was the first black woman from a southern state to serve in the House and one of the first two blacks (she and Andrew Young both won seats in 1973) to win election from the South in the twentieth century.[36]

Once in Congress, Jordan quickly made her intellectual prowess evident. She became an outspoken critic of President Nixon and testified before the House Judiciary Committee during the Watergate hearings. Jordan told the committee, "My faith in the Constitution is whole, it is complete, it is total and I am not going to sit here and be an idle spectator to the diminution, the subversion, the destruction of the Constitution."[37] Black political liberals stretching back to the nineteenth century probably could not have spoken of their faith in the Constitution with such eloquence. Jordan gave her most profound speech at the 1976 Democratic National Convention. In her address, she linked many of the principles of black liberal thought to the overarching ideals of the Democratic Party. For example, she emphasized freedom and fair play. "We believe in equality for all and privileges for none," she intoned, "This is a belief that each American regardless of background has equal standing in the public forum, all of us." In regards to the role of the government in racial change, she stated, "We believe that the government . . . has an obligation to actively underscore, actively seek to remove those obstacles which would block individual achievement . . . obstacles emanating from race, sex, economic condition." Finally, Jordan emphasized the benefits of America's constitutional democracy, one of the key elements of black liberalism. "We believe that the people are the source of all governmental power; that the authority of the people is to be extended, not restricted. This can be accomplished only by providing each citizen with every opportunity to participate in the management of the government," Jordan declared. Throughout this speech, she tied the Democratic Party to the long history of black liberalism. Her constant use of the personal pronoun "we" not only demonstrated shared ideals; it represented a coupling of black and white liberalism for a united purpose.[38]

Jordan represents the pairing of black political liberalism and black intellectual liberalism. After the Voting Rights Act of 1965, thousands of black liberals have won election to local, state, and national office, continuing the trend of securing racial change through the electoral process. Political liberalism has perhaps won most of the goals that African Americans have fought for since the nineteenth century, but black liberal politicians still fight for the betterment of the black community and the alleviation of historical inequalities.

BLACK LIBERALISM TODAY

The black liberal intellectual tradition has continued beyond the civil rights movement and black politics. Today, numerous black liberals occupy positions of importance in America's top institutions of higher learning. One of the recent and most important black liberal intellectuals is Henry Louis Gates Jr. Like other black liberals, Gates has expressed a consistent and profound belief in American democracy and the power of scholarly thinking to right wrongs. He received his doctorate in literature from Yale University in 1979. He currently directs Harvard's W. E. B. Du Bois Institute for African and African American Research. Gates is an expert on African and African American literature. His major scholarly work in this field, *The Signifying Monkey*, explores the African American cultural practice of "signifying." Signifying is akin to the double consciousness discussed by Du Bois and King. It relates to a practice, traceable back to Africa, of doubletalk or code speech in which blacks employ a culturally understood vocabulary that white people do not understand. Slaves called this "puttin' on ole massa" or using deception to trick the slave owner (perhaps best exemplified in the countless retellings of the Br'er Rabbit story). For Gates, signifying is something more than just a literary trope. It is the foundation for an entirely overlooked and in some cases maligned genre of literature. Not only does he resurrect the history of signifying, but he traces that history back to Africa and then incorporates it into American literary traditions.[39]

The Signifying Monkey in many ways continues the trends of black intellectual liberals going back to Pennington and Du Bois. Gates uses a concept familiar to most black people and analyzes it methodically. He notes that signifying serves as an authentic part of the black voice, and in analyzing it in many ways he reauthenticates it. More importantly, he exposes the concept of signifying to the broader American public in general, and white people in particular, and thereby brings it into the broader scope of American literature. As such, Gates went far both in studying an important element of black culture and in reforming white people's understanding of blacks.

Perhaps even more along the lines of the black liberal intellectual traditions discussed thus far was Gates's PBS show *African American Lives*. The show traces the genetic descent of a handful of prominent black celebrities. It purported to move our understanding from the broader undiscovered past of the black community to examine the unknown past of distinct black people. In so doing, Gates reminds us that not only have Americans ignored the history of the black community, but our own familial histories are often forgotten or unknown. For example, Gates tested the DNA of comedian Chris Rock and determined that one of Rock's relatives, his great-great-grandfather Julius Tingman, won election to the South Carolina legislature in the nineteenth century. When asked if he ever dreamed that he had an elected official, a politician, in his family, Rock responded, "Never in a million years." The surprise Rock displayed is understandable, but the point was not to shock. Rather, Gates hoped to reveal the past to those who do not know it. And by displaying this search for discovery on television, a broad swath of the public witnessed this revelation. As the promotional material for the show asserted, "by the end of their journey, guests know more about their family, and themselves."[40]

William Julius Wilson has also experienced a great deal of public recognition as a black liberal intellectual in the past few decades. A sociologist and professor at Harvard University, Wilson has written and frequently commented on the black community. His earliest work, *The Declining Significance of Race*, explores the black inner-city community and attempts to explain the social class positions of African Americans. Despite the title (and many critical observations of Wilson's work), he did not argue that race was no longer important or that we live in a postracial society. Instead, he asserted that as the black middle class grew it began to be affected more by class or economic issues as opposed to racism. The black underclass, on the flipside, continued to experience significant problems both with their economic status and with racial issues. What Wilson ultimately demonstrated was that while the Great Society was at least partially successful in elevating the economic position of some black people, it also worked to create rifts between African Americans who escaped to the middle class and those who remained behind in the inner city.[41]

Wilson followed *The Declining Significance of Race* with *The Truly Disadvantaged*, which focuses exclusively on poverty and joblessness in black inner-city communities. He once again tied racial and economic issues together to show their detriment to blacks, but he further asserted that the loss of good-paying factory jobs in the inner core of cities such as Chicago had dealt poor blacks their most devastating blow. He averred that instead of promoting an end to racist hiring practices, the government would be better served by promoting job opportunities and business growth for black Americans. He explores similar themes in his book *When Work Disappears*.[42] Wilson's most recent, and boldest, attempt to explain the relationship between race and poverty is *More than Just Race*. He shows, for example, that while some black men (particularly those who deal drugs) are seen by society as shunning hard work, they are in fact working within the confines of what is available to them and most lucrative within the inner city. As opposed to being averse to hard work, Wilson argues, they actually work hard at being good drug dealers. More importantly, lack of opportunity and resources molds the lives of these young men, not societal pressures or a lack of expectations. He also shows that some of the problems in the black inner city, especially crime and poverty, are the result of cultural factors within the black community. While this stance earned him a good deal of criticism, Wilson took culture seriously and explored how a sense of anti-intellectualism and a lack of opportunity could explain social ills in the inner city.[43]

Wilson's work fits in well with the liberal intellectual paradigm of black leadership. His scholarship was both cutting edge and incredibly timely. By concentrating on the immediate post–civil rights period and also on many of the ideas of the civil rights generation, he offers a persuasive series of explanations for the continuation of black poverty and inequality. Most importantly, by commenting on the legacy of the civil rights movement, Wilson was able to probe the successes and failures of the black freedom struggle and explore the progress of racial change in America. As he noted in a 1997 interview commemorating the *Brown v. Board* decision, "a lot of people back then felt that we would be free by '93 or '83 or '73 just by removing racial barriers. But the problem is that a system of racial discrimination over a long period of time can create racial inequality, a system of racial inequality that will linger on even after racial barriers come down." Some of his solutions to this continuing inequality remain in sync with many of the historical ideas with other black intellectual leaders. For example, he argued that "black leaders [need] to broaden their vision and their imagination in the public policy arena. To continue to push for very specific policies, affirmative action, these things are necessary and important and we need them. But they're also going to have to join with other forces and call for some sort of economic reform." The black intellectual leaders who called for affirmative action and War on Poverty programs in the 1960s would have clearly understood his ideas.[44]

Former *New York Times* columnist Robert Herbert is another good example of a modern, and very critical, black liberal intellectual. He frequently attacks conservative American ideals and those who continue to view black people as deficient or pathological. Like Wilson, he examines social and racial inequalities. For example, in a recent column on segregated schools and the *Brown* decision, Herbert opined that "long years of evidence show that poor kids of all ethnic backgrounds do better academically when they go to school with their more affluent—that is, middle class—peers. But when the poor kids are black or Hispanic, that means racial and ethnic integration in the schools. Despite all the babble about a postracial America, that has been off the table for a long time." Herbert ties the issue of school segregation with recent attacks on educators in Wisconsin. He ends with one of the dogmas of black intellectual liberalism: "I favor integration for integration's sake. This society should be far more integrated in almost every way than it is now."[45]

Robert Herbert's final op-ed with the *New York Times* in 2011 was perhaps his most poignant defense of the black liberal intellectual position. He reacted to the broad array of problems facing the United States, from the recession to the war on terror. Herbert found the maldistribution of wealth in the United States particularly problematic. "This inequality, in which an enormous segment of the population struggles while the fortunate few ride the gravy train, is a world-class recipe for social unrest. Downward mobility is an ever-shortening fuse leading to profound consequences." Like Du Bois and several other black liberals before him, Herbert found great contradictions in a society that claims to protect liberties and fight for equality while simultaneously politicians cozy up to big businesses and the rich seemingly get richer. As he had done in previous columns, he called on the United States to renew the vision of a prosperous and equalitarian American for all people.[46]

CONCLUSIONS

Black intellectual liberalism remains distinct from other aspects of black thought. On perhaps the polar opposite from black liberals are the black conservatives.[47] Most black conservative intellectuals emphasize cultural conservatism, patriotism, and the ability of free market capitalism to right black America's wrongs. One of the best examples of this line of thinking is economist Thomas Sowell. A professor at the Hoover Institute at Stanford, Sowell emerged as a scholar at roughly the same time as William Julius Wilson. Their scholarship could hardly be more different. Take for example Sowell's *The Economics and Politics of Race*, in which he criticizes liberal viewpoints, especially those that hold that government aid and social programs can remedy social problems and bring about racial change. Sowell compares the experiences of American blacks with minority groups in other nations and finds that racism and economics cannot alone explain the position of African Americans in US society. Instead, he finds cultural patterns among black people and white liberal paternalism at fault. African Americans have not advanced in American society because they have not stressed hard work and education as cultural norms. At the same time, black and white liberal elites have coddled the black community, Sowell argues, reinforcing a culture of laziness. His critique of black culture and his belief in the power of the free market to redress historical wrongs is what marks Sowell as a conservative. His other publications follow similar arguments and lines of reasoning.[48]

Other black intellectuals do not fit neatly into a mold or model of scholarly thought. Take John McWhorter, a trained linguist who specializes in the creole language. Like Gates he resurrects a forgotten aspect of the black past. Like Wilson, McWhorter frequently offers very stinging intellectual indictments of the African American community. But McWhorter does not fit neatly into any category. He is neither a liberal nor a conservative, and if he fits any label it is perhaps "middle course."[49] In *Losing the Race*, for example, McWhorter not only criticized the United States, he laid the blame for some problems in the black community at the feet of black people. He explored what he viewed as a "disease of defeatism" and a "cult of victimology" that plagues African Americans. He further asserted that the failure of integration rests at least in part on black people.[50] He followed *Losing the Race* with the appropriately titled *Winning the Race*. In this book he continued to criticize African Americans for problems in the black community, and he called for a new focus on black achievement. He further argued that racism alone cannot explain problems in the black community. He suggested going back in time to claim some of the "family values" of black folks in the 1940s or 1950s, while simultaneously using those values to move past race. Both *Losing the Race* and *Winning the Race* offer an analysis that is at the same time liberal and conservative, that produces a moderate course line of reasoning. McWhorter has been criticized by both liberals and conservatives for his work, as sure a sign as any that he fits into neither category.[51]

Numerous black intellectuals have commented on the African American experience and focused on race and culture. It is not really that surprising that liberals, conservatives, radicals, and moderates have come to different conclusions about the black past and the black future. Black liberals and conservatives, for instance, both have a profound and fundamental belief in the power of American ideals and the Constitution to remedy social problems, but they differ in how those ideals should be viewed and how the Constitution should be used. For liberals, the power of the federal government can be used as a wedge against racism, and the Constitution can be employed as a weapon to correct social ills and bring about racial change. For conservatives, government aid is corrupting, and only free market capitalism can help black people. Using the Constitution as a weapon, conservatives hold, runs counter to the ideas of the founders and is an abuse of government power. Black liberals and conservatives—as well as moderates, radicals, and Afrocentrists—also comment on culture. For many liberals black culture has many positive attributes. It has reinforced the black psyche and imbued African Americans with pride. For conservatives, black culture is often viewed as moribund, lacking positive features and reinforcing social problems that harm black people. Again, black intellectuals look at a similar subject but from widely varying points of view and modes of analysis.

Black liberalism clearly has had a long history in the United States. The black liberal intellectual tradition extends back in time to the late eighteenth century and continues today. While it has gone through many evolutions, the basic tenets of black liberalism have remained consistent for more than one hundred years: the need for a fair society, the exercising of democratic freedoms, the fundamental belief in the Constitution, the elevation of black status in the United States, and the eradication of racism. Most importantly, black intellectual liberals firmly believed in and fought for racial change. The idea of racial change remains the most consistent aspect of black liberalism because it connoted a transformation not only of black society, but of white society as well. African American leaders knew that for black people to make real progress, they not only had to improve the lives of blacks, but they also had to change the opinions of whites. For black intellectual liberals, scholarship and study provided the most effective method for redressing wrongs. By studying black people seriously, these scholars could counter much of the basis for American racism. And by including black people in the long history of the United States, these scholars could bring about racial change by reforming the identity of black people and the ideas white people had about blacks.

While it has accomplished much, black liberalism has also tended to be slow and its victories only partial. We can give black liberals credit, for example, for bringing about racial change during the civil rights movement, African Americans still have to deal with many problems related to race and racism. Black political liberals tried for generations to achieve legislative victories banning lynching, but they never succeeded. While the election of Barack Obama and other black politicians has certainly vindicated black liberal ideals, the racism Obama has faced signals that much work remains to be done.[52]

NOTES

1. W. E. B. Du Bois originally crafted the idea of "double consciousness" in *The Souls of Black Folk* (New York: Signet Classic, 1995), 45.

2. Martin Luther King Jr., *Stride toward Freedom: The Montgomery Story* (New York: HarperSanFrancisco, 1958), 190, 191–224.

3. On black intellectual leadership, see Gaines, *Uplifting the Race*; Manning Marable, *Black Leadership* (New York: Columbia University Press, 1998); Joy James, *Transcending the Talented Tenth: Black Leaders and American Intellectuals* (New York: Routledge, 1997); William M. Banks, *Black Intellectuals: Race and Responsibility in American Life* (New York: W. W. Norton, 1998); Gordon, *Black Leadership for Social Change*; John T. Barber, *The Black Digital Elite: African American Leaders of the Information Revolution* (Westport, CT: Praeger, 2006).

4. Reverend James W. C. Pennington, *A Text Book on the Origin and History, of the Colored People* (Hartford: L. Skinner, printer, 1841).

5. James W. C. Pennington, *The Fugitive Blacksmith; or, Events in the History of James W. C. Pennington, Pastor of a Presbyterian Church, New York, Formerly a Slave in the State of Maryland, United States* (London: Charles Gilpin and Bishopsgate Without, 1849).

6. Jonathan Markovitz, *Legacies of Lynching: Racial Violence and Memory* (Minneapolis: University of Minnesota Press, 2004), xv–xvi; Amy Louise Wood, *Lynching and Spectacle: Witnessing Racial Violence in America, 1890–1940* (Chapel Hill: University of North Carolina Press, 2009), 1–9; Christopher Waldrep, *The Many Faces of Judge Lynch: Extralegal Violence and Punishment in America* (New York: Palgrave Macmillan, 2002), 4, 6–9, 67–80, 85–95, 103–26.

7. See Ida B. Wells, *Southern Horrors: Lynch Law in All Its Phases*, available online at http://www.gutenberg.org/files/14975/14975-h/14975-h.htm (accessed July 27, 2010), chap. 1 "The Offense" and chap. 2 "The Black and White Of It."

8. Ida B. Wells, *The Red Record: Tabulated Statistics and Alleged Causes of Lynching in the United States*, available online at http://www.gutenberg.org/etext/14977 (accessed July 8, 2010). See also Wells, *Southern Horrors*; Paula J. Giddings, *Ida: A Sword among Lions: Ida B. Wells and the Campaign against Lynching* (New York: Harper Paperbacks, 2009); Mia Bay, *To Tell the Truth Freely: The Life of Ida B. Wells* (New York: Hill and Wang, 2010).

9. On various aspects of the antilynching campaign, see Kimberly Johnson, *Reforming Jim Crow: Southern Politics and State in the Age before Brown* (New York: Oxford University Press, 2010), 43–65; Crystal N. Feimster, *Southern Horrors: Women and the Politics of Rape and Lynching* (Cambridge: Harvard University Press, 2009), 212–34; Christopher Waldrep, *African Americans Confront Lynching: Strategies of Resistance from the Civil War to the Civil Rights Era* (New York: Rowman and Littlefield, 2009), passim.

10. The number of lynchings in the United States declined precipitously in the 1930s. See Waldrep, *African Americans Confront Lynching*, chap. 4.

11. On Du Bois, see David Levering Lewis, *W. E. B. Du Bois: Biography of a Race, 1868–1919* (New York: Henry Holt, 1993); Lewis, *W. E. B. Du Bois, 1919–1963: The Fight for Equality and the American Century* (New York: Henry Holt, 2001).

12. Lewis, *W. E. B. Du Bois*, 188.

13. W. E. Burghardt Du Bois, *The Philadelphia Negro: A Social Study* (Philadelphia: University of Pennsylvania, 1899), 387. (quotation), and passim.

14. W. E. Burghardt Du Bois, ed., *The Negro Artisan: A Social Study* (Atlanta: Atlanta University Press, 1902), 188.

15. "Editorial: The Result," *The Crisis*, November 1915.

16. "Editorial: Lazy Labor," *The Crisis*, January 1916.

17. Leonard Harris and Charles Molesworth, *Alain L. Locke: Biography of a Philosopher* (Chicago: University of Chicago Press, 2010), 130–32.

18. See Alaine LeRoy Locke, *The New Negro: Voices of the Harlem Renaissance* (New York: Touchstone, 1997); David L. Lewis, *When Harlem Was in Vogue* (New York: Penguin, 1997); Cary D. Wintz, *Harlem Speaks: A Living History of the Harlem Renaissance* (Naperville, IL: Sourcebooks, 2006).

19. Carter Godwin Woodson, *The Education of the Negro Prior to 1861: A History of The Education of the Colored People of the United States from the Beginning of Slavery to the Civil War* (New York: Putnam, 1915), 14.

20. Carter Godwin Woodson, *The Mis-Education of the Negro* (CreateSpace, 2010), xvi.

21. Ibid., 144.

22. Marion Thompson Wright, "The Education of Negroes in New Jersey" (PhD dissertation, Columbia University, 1938); Marion Thompson Wright, "New Jersey Laws and the Negro," *Journal of Negro History* 28, no. 2 (April 1943): 156–59.

23. John Hope Franklin, *Mirror to America: The Autobiography of John Hope Franklin* (New York: Farrar, Straus and Giroux, 2005), 3, 122.

24. John Hope Franklin, *From Slavery to Freedom: A History of African Americans* (New York: Knopf, 2000).

25. E. Franklin Frazier, *The Negro Church in America* (New York: Schocken Books, 1964).

26. Margaret Smith Crocco and Ozro Luke Davis, eds., *"Bending the Future to Their Will": Civic Women, Social Education, and Democracy* (Lanham, MD: Rowman and Littlefield, 1999); Pero Gaglo Dagbovie, "Black Women Historians from the Late 19th Century to the Dawning of the Civil Rights Movement," *The Journal of African American History* 89, no. 3 (Summer 2004): 241–61; Stephanie Y. Evans, *Black Women in the Ivory Tower, 1850–1954: An Intellectual History* (Gainesville: University Press of Florida, 2008).

27. On Houston, see Genna Rae McNeil, *Groundwork: Charles Hamilton Houston and the Struggle for Civil Rights* (Philadelphia: University of Pennsylvania Press, 1983); Rawn James, *Root and Branch: Charles Hamilton Houston, Thurgood Marshall, and the Struggle to End Segregation* (New York: Bloomsbury 2010).

28. James, *Root and Branch*, 65–78.

29. Gary M. Lavergne, *Before* Brown: *Heman Marion Sweatt, Thurgood Marshall, and the Long Road to Justice* (Austin: University of Texas Press, 2010).

30. *Brown v. Board*, 347 US 483 (1954); Richard Kluger, *Simple Justice: The History of* Brown v. Board of Education *and Black America's Struggle for Equality* (New York: Vintage Books, 2004).

31. On black religious leadership, see White, *Black Leadership in America*; E. Franklin Frazier and C. Eric Lincoln, *The Negro Church in America: The Black Church Since Frazier*

(New York, Schocken, 1977); Peter J. Paris, *Black Religious Leaders: Conflict in Unity* (Louisville, KY: Westminster, John Knox, 1991); Andrew Billingsley, *Mighty like a River: The Black Church and Social Reform* (New York: Oxford University Press, 1999); Johnson and Stanford, eds., *Black Political Organizations in the Post–Civil Rights Era*; Gordon, *Black Leadership for Social Change.*

32. For a copy of King's dissertation, see http://mlk-kpp01.stanford.edu/primarydocu ments/Vol2/550415AComparisonOfTheConceptionsOfGod.pdf (accessed May 10, 2011). This draft of the dissertation also has an explanation of the plagiarized portions of the text. See also David L. Chappell, *A Stone of Hope: Prophetic Religion and the Death of Jim Crow* (Chapel Hill, 2004).

33. Martin Luther King Jr., *Where Do We Go from Here: Chaos or Community?* (Boston: Beacon, 1967), 136–38.

34. Martin Luther King, Jr. "Remaining Awake through a Great Revolution," http://mlk -kpp01.stanford.edu/index.php/kingpapers/article/remaining_awake_through_a_great_ revolution/ (accessed on May 10, 2011).

35. This is a point that has been widely studied by historians. See, for example, William H. Chafe, *Civilities and Civil Rights: Greensboro, North Carolina, and the Black Struggle for Freedom* (New York: Oxford University Press, 1981); Aldon Morris, *The Origins of the Civil Rights Movement: Black Communities Organizing for Change* (New York: Free, 1984); John Dittmer, *Local People: The Struggle for Civil Rights in Mississippi* (Chicago: University of Illinois Press, 1994); Clayborne Carson, *In Struggle: SNCC and the Black Awakening of the 1960s* (Cambridge: Harvard University Press, 1995); David L. Chappell, *A Stone of Hope: Prophetic Religion and the Death of Jim Crow* (Chapel Hill: University of North Carolina Press, 2004).

36. See Mary Beth Rogers, *Barbara Jordan: American Hero* (New York: Bantam Books, 1998); Barbara Jordan, *Barbara Jordan: Speaking the Truth with Eloquent Thunder* (Austin: University of Texas Press, 2007).

37. Barbara Jordan, *Testimony before the House Judiciary Committee, July 25, 1974,* available online at http://www.watergate.info/impeachment/74-07-25_barbara-jordan.shtml.

38. Barbara Jordan, "Who Then Will Speak for the Common Good?" July 12, 1976, Democratic Convention Keynote Address, available online at http://gos.sbc.edu/j/jordan1 .html.

39. Henry Louis Gates Jr., *The Signifying Monkey: A Theory of African-American Literary Criticism* (New York: Oxford University Press, 1988).

40. See http://www.pbs.org/wnet/aalives/ (accessed July 27, 2010).

41. William Julius Wilson, *The Declining Significance of Race: Blacks and Changing American Institutions* (Chicago: University of Chicago Press, 1980).

42. William Julius Wilson, *The Truly Disadvantaged: The Inner City, the Underclass, and Public Policy* (Chicago: University of Chicago Press, 1990); William Julius Wilson, *When Work Disappears: The World of the New Urban Poor* (New York: Vintage Books, 1997).

43. William Julius Wilson, *More than Just Race: Being Black and Poor in the Inner City* (New York: W. W. Norton, 2010).

44. Interview with William Julius Wilson, available online at http://www.pbs.org/ wgbh/pages/frontline/shows/race/interviews/wilson.html (accessed May 20, 2011).

45. Robert Herbert, "Separate and Unequal," March 21, 2001, http://www.nytimes.com/2011/03/22/opinion/22herbert.html?_r=1&ref=bobherbert (accessed May 18, 2011).

46. Robert Herbert, "Losing Our Way," March 25, 2001, http://www.nytimes.com/2011/03/26/opinion/26herbert.html?_r=1&ref=bobherbert (accessed May 25, 2011).

47. For a good discussion of black conservatives, see Michael L. Ondaatje, *Black Conservative Intellectuals in America* (Philadelphia: University of Pennsylvania Press, 2010).

48. Thomas Sowell, *The Economics and Politics of Race: An International Perspective* (New York: Quill, 1985).

49. On the history of middle-course leadership, see Brian D. Behnken, "'Count on Me': Reverend M. L. Price of Texas, a Case Study in Civil Rights Leadership," *Journal of American Ethnic History* 25, no. 1 (Fall 2005).

50. See John McWhorter, *Losing the Race: Self-Sabotage in Black America* (New York: Harper-Perennial, 2001).

51. See John McWhorter, *Winning the Race: Beyond the Crisis in Black America* (New York: Gotham, 2005).

52. On the future of black leadership, see Stephen J. Herzog, *Minority Group Politics: A Reader* (New York: Holt, Rinehart, and Winston, 1971); Robert C. Smith, *We Have No Leaders: African Americans in the Post–Civil Rights Era* (Albany: State University of New York Press, 1996); Andrea Y. Simpson, *The Ties That Bind: Identity and Political Attitudes in the Post–Civil Rights Generation* (New York: New York University Press, 1998); Andra Gillespie, ed., *Whose Black Politics? Cases in Post-Racial Black Leadership* (New York: Routledge, 2010).

- CHAPTER FOUR -

BLACK CONSERVATIVE THOUGHT IN THE POST–CIVIL RIGHTS ERA

DANIELLE L. WIGGINS

In a 1991 issue of *Policy Review*, Clarence Thomas lamented "the loneliness of the black conservative." The former chairman of the Equal Employment Opportunity Commission detailed his isolation as a black conservative in a world in which seemingly all conservatives were white.[1] Thomas, however, was actually not alone in his liminal position as a black conservative. He was a member of a vanguard of new black conservatives, or "neoconservatives," who rose to prominence in the post–civil rights era. Thomas, along with fellow Reagan appointee Clarence Pendleton; economists Thomas Sowell, Walter Williams, and Glenn Loury; and other public intellectuals such as Anne Wortham and Shelby Steele gained widespread publicity in the 1980s and 1990s with their iconoclastic critiques of the "civil rights establishment" and the "plantation mentality" of black liberals.[2]

To many, the very idea of a black conservative seems rather paradoxical. Could African Americans, whose political engagement has been inherently radical in its persistent assault on the limitations of the American political system, ever truly be conservative? Since the civil rights era, a substantial minority of African Americans—45 percent in 2008—have self-identified as conservative.[3] Yet, conservative policies have relatively little support within the black community, and fewer than 12 percent of blacks align their politics with the conservative Republican Party.[4] Journalist Clarence Page explicated this critical disconnect between ideology and partisan identity by distinguishing between "black conservatives" and "conservative blacks." He wrote, "The former (black conservatives) is a relatively small, if high profile movement in avowed conservatives who happen to be black. The latter (conservative blacks) best describes the black masses who harbor many conservative attitudes, but part company with traditional conservative party lines, especially the line that says black people make too much of racism."[5] While there are many conservative blacks, there are far fewer black conservatives. Given the slippery nature of black conservatism, what do black conservatives actually believe? What are they trying to "conserve"?

Scholars have posited several definitions of black conservatism. Peter Eisenstadt outlined five broad characteristics of black conservative ideology: an abiding respect for American culture and Western institutions, an enduring optimism, "anti-Utopian" accomodationism, a devotion to capitalism and the free market, and adherence to the "African American Protest Ethic" or Christian moralism and hierarchy.[6] Other scholars have taken into account the diversity in black conservative thought and have outlined categories of black conservatives. Gayle T. Lewis and Lewis A. Randolph describe three main camps of black conservatism in the post–civil rights era: antistatists, organic conservatives, and neoconservatives. Antistatists advocated for the free market and a limited government, believing interventionist government programs like affirmative action and minority set-aside programs harm more than they help. Organic conservatives believed in traditionalism, patriarchy and family values, and Christian morality. Neoconservatives were former liberals, black nationalists, socialists, and progressives of other kinds who came to critique the liberal agenda and the expansion of the welfare state. Angela Lewis traced out four camps of black conservatism in the post–civil rights era similar to Lewis and Randolph's categories, with the addition of Afrocentric conservatives. Afrocentric conservatives shared with other conservatives a belief in family values, self-help, and morality but differed from other black conservatives in their belief that blacks should embrace their racial identity and reject assimilation into the mainstream American.[7] Historian Angela Dillard also emphasizes the diversity within black conservative thought but contends that all black conservatives "shared [a] style of thought."[8] Dillard outlined the contours of post–civil rights era black conservative thought by examining the ways in which black conservatives have defined themselves through the construction of a black conservative canon. They claimed to draw their political and intellectual lineage from a variety of black figures, including Booker T. Washington, whom they considered the "father of black conservatism"; Marcus Garvey; Malcolm X; Martin Luther King Jr.; and Ralph Ellison.

The roots of black conservatism are deeper and more organic in the black intellectual tradition than the black conservatives of the post–civil rights era insinuated. A conservative impulse has remained a vital, tempering force in black politics since the era of American slavery. This conservative tradition has emphasized self-help, antistatism, pragmatism, a faith in Western institutions such as free market capitalism, and Protestant-influenced moralism. Figures as diverse as enslaved poet Jupiter Hammon, educator Booker T. Washington, novelist Zora Neale Hurston, satirist George Schuyler, Senator Edward Brooke, and former communist Manning Johnson voiced conservative critiques of African American politics and culture in the public sphere before the new black conservatives of the post–civil rights era came to prominence. Nevertheless, black conservative ideology gained unprecedented attention with the ascendance of the black conservatives during that era. These new black conservatives believed that the federal government had mismanaged the amelioration of racial discrimination and inequality in the years following the passage of the Civil Rights Act of 1964 and the Voting Rights Act of 1965. They also assailed interventionist policies such as affirmative action and government assistance programs such as welfare, which they argued made blacks dependent on government largesse and overemphasized the significance of race.

The black conservatives of the post–civil rights era made appeals to conservative traditions in African American political culture, seeking to position themselves in a lineage of black conservatism.[9] However, they differed from their forebears, as their politics were informed by the rhetoric and ideology of the New Right. In the postwar period, the New Right emerged from a diverse group of conservative intellectuals and activists most often associated with the Republican Party, who developed a sustained critique of American liberalism. They challenged the excesses and limitations of Keynesianism, the growth in the size and influence of "special-interest" groups, and the moral breakdown of American society.[10] The new black conservatives were active participants in the construction of the politics of the New Right, using race to lend an air of authenticity to conservative critiques of welfare and affirmative action. Thus, black conservative ideology of the post–civil rights era emerged from a confluence of the rhetoric and ideology of the predominantly white New Right of the 1970s and 1980s and the intellectual and cultural traditions of conservatism within the African American political culture.

The triumphs and shortcomings of the civil rights movement along with the concomitant decline of liberalism and the rightward shift of the American political climate fostered the proliferation of black conservative thought. Black conservatives sought to present conservatism as a viable political alternative and an ideology more organic to the African American political tradition than liberalism. Their rhetoric evolved as they responded to social issues as diverse as welfare and rap music and the broader shifts in the American political landscape. Nonetheless, their attacks on liberalism and the debilitating dependency they believed the state had fostered among African Americans remained consistent throughout the last quarter of the twentieth century. However, black conservative thought struggled to gain widespread acceptance among African Americans, and black conservatives themselves were often unpopular. Critics charged that black conservatives blamed the victims of racism and diminished the continuing significance of race and discrimination in the post–civil rights era. Black conservatives were often alienated from the broader black community and instead found much of their support in predominantly white institutions. However, in white conservative institutions, black conservatives were often tokenized and limited to discussions of race and civil rights. As Clarence Thomas suggested in his discussion of the loneliness of the black conservative, they occupied a liminal and marginalized space in the American political landscape. Nonetheless, black conservatism still became an important component of both American and African American political culture, as black conservative thought informed discourses concerning race, rights, and responsibility. Black conservatives forced black Americans—left, right, and center—to refine their conceptions of racial identity, citizenship, and liberty in the post–civil rights era.

THE HISTORY OF BLACK CONSERVATISM

The history of black conservatism begins with the seventeenth-century "cosmopolitan" slaves who were entrenched in the colonial society, adopting the names, language, religion, and economic practices of the European colonizers.[11] The most successful of the creoles were the first black capitalists, purchasing land (and sometimes slaves) and adopting the protocapitalist practices of the European colonizers.[12] Black Christians of the slavery era also developed the African-American Protestant Ethic, which emphasized acceptance of contemporary circumstances in the hope of redemption in the afterlife. One of the most prominent black conservative thinkers of this era was Jupiter Hammon, an enslaved poet from Long Island, New York, who urged enslaved blacks to accept their position as slaves.[13] In his poetry, Hammon asserted that through righteous, Christian behavior slaves could make the best of their situation and assure their salvation in the afterlife.[14] In the nineteenth century, conservatism was also prevalent among black elites such as the Philadelphia-based business owner James Forten and the freeborn abolitionist Martin Delaney, who were radical in their critiques of the institution of American slavery and the denial of black citizenship but quite conservative in their acquiescence to Protestant moralism, exploitative capitalism, and elitism.[15] Forten and Delaney detested the institution of slavery but were also critical of what they perceived as the idle and immoral behavior of slaves and working-class free blacks. Furthermore, many black elites were committed integrationists, who respected and believed in American institutions and ideals. Forten was a businessman who appreciated the privileges of property ownership and believed that blacks must be taught American economic practices. Forten also supported black emigration to Africa, an idea advocated by groups such as the American Colonization Society, insisting like several other black abolitionists that African Americans' place was in the United States.[16] This paradoxical "conservative radicalism" characterized the political ideology and rhetoric of elites into the Reconstruction period.[17] The black political leaders during Reconstruction were at once radical and deeply conservative. They demanded equal protection, the franchise, and the protection of blacks from racial terrorism, yet they were incredibly disparaging of poor blacks who did not conform to the behavioral standards of middle-class decorum.

The period following Reconstruction, which historian Rayford Logan referred to the as the nadir in African American history, was actually a pinnacle for black conservative thought. As African Americans' citizenship rights were restricted, black conservatives, particularly in the South, came to the forefront as negotiators for the black community. The quintessential black conservative of this period was Booker T. Washington. Washington advocated a gradual approach to improving the situation of African Americans in the post-emancipation era. He argued that former slaves should focus on developing agricultural skills that would enable them to find steady employment in the rural economy of the postbellum South. He stressed self-improvement, arguing that African Americans must prove their suitability for citizenship by adopting Victorian standards of respectability, thrift, and diligence.[18] Washington also famously spoke of segregation in his famous speech at the 1895 Atlanta Cotton Exposition. He urged blacks to "cast down their buckets" and improve themselves from within the increasingly segregated Jim Crow South.[19] He insisted blacks should focus on gaining economic security and independence within their own communities, rather than demanding full political participation and integration in the mainstream. W. E. B. Du Bois famously referred to Booker T. Washington's Atlanta speech as the "Atlanta Compromise." Scholars have often positioned Du Bois as a radical rival to Washington, yet Du Bois was an elitist who, like Washington, assailed the poor behavior of lower-class blacks.[20] Washington and Du Bois, as well as many prominent black elite leaders in the women's club movement and other reform movements, sought to uplift blacks so that they could meet the standards of citizenship, as defined by white Americans. Respectability, the adoption of Victorian ideals of decorum and behavior, was central to black elites' class-based conservative politics.[21]

Black conservatism remained a prominent ideology in the early twentieth century. After his death in 1915, Washington's ideals lived on through the many institutions he founded and supported, such as the Tuskegee Institute and the National Negro Business League (NNBL).[22] The most prominent black conservative of this era was Marcus Garvey. In many ways, Garvey's politics were radical—he championed black nationalism and pan-Africanism. Through his organization, the Universal Negro Improvement Association, he advocated a rejection of American nationalism and asserted that blacks in the United States, the Caribbean, and South America needed to redeem the continent of Africa from European colonizers. Yet, he was heavily influenced by Washington's emphasis on self-help, economic independence through business success, and advancement through bourgeois decorum and a strict moral code.[23] Though Garvey's power faded after he was convicted of mail fraud in 1923 and eventually deported to his native country of Jamaica in 1927, Garvey's ideals of black pride, self-help, business success, religious conviction, and strong patriarchal households would influence later generations of Afrocentric black conservatives.[24]

The New Deal era witnessed the beginning of a decline in black conservative thought. Many African Americans welcomed the relief and reform of the New Deal and the increasing federal and state intervention into issues of black civil and political rights. Nonetheless, the New Deal found a harsh critic in George Schuyler, the most vocal black conservative of the midtwentieth century. Schuyler, a satirist and journalist, was one of the first black neoconservatives. A former socialist, Schuyler abandoned his radical politics during the New Deal era. He questioned the effectiveness of New Deal initiatives and what he perceived as an impulse toward collectivism. In the 1950s, Schuyler became a staunch anticommunist and "reinvented himself as African American patriot."[25] He gained access to the political circles of the burgeoning conservative movement of the 1950s. Schuyler also became the most vocal black critic of the civil rights movement. He opposed the *Brown v.*

Board of Education decision and the Montgomery bus boycott, claiming that the NAACP and Martin Luther King were "prematurely" seeking integration. Echoing Booker T. Washington, Schuyler argued that African Americans should instead seek economic independence through entrepreneurship and capitalism.[26] Perhaps unsurprisingly, Schuyler had few champions within the black community and instead was supported by right-wing institutions such as the John Birch Society.

Peter Eisenstadt has argued that the civil rights and Black Power eras of the 1960s were a "nadir" for black conservatism.[27] However, conservative strains of thought persisted throughout the supposedly radical period. As Leah Wright-Rigueur illustrates, African American Republicans during the civil rights era sought to employ a "pragmatic conservatism" to expand the rights and liberties of black Americans.[28] The most prominent black Republican of the civil rights era was Massachusetts senator Edward Brooke. Brooke was a moderate Republican who advocated what he called, quite paradoxically, "progressive conservatism." Brooke's politics were informed by traditional conservative beliefs like self-help, personal responsibility, free enterprise, limited government, and traditionalism. Yet, he was progressive in that he supported the use of the state's power to ensure that American ideals were inclusive.[29] Brooke and the other "progressive conservative" black Republicans of the civil rights era thought of themselves as protectors of the American ideals of liberty and equality. Conservatism remained a motivating political ideology for many black Democrats as well. Legal historian Tomiko Brown-Nagin argues that middle-class civil rights activists in Atlanta, who by the mid-1960s were predominantly Democrats, were driven by a conservative impulse that she deems "pragmatic civil rights." "Pragmatism," she argues "privileged politics of litigation, placed a high value on economic security, and rejected the idea that integration (or even desegregation) and equality were one and the same."[30] An abiding conservatism and commitment to gradualism tempered the radical politics of civil rights activists in Atlanta and in other cities. Many prominent civic leaders were often property owners and business owners, whose financial success depended on the upholding of some aspects of Jim Crow segregation.[31] Many in the black middle class during the civil rights era were also committed to property rights, capitalism, and law and order, the same principles driving the politics of the developing New Right.[32]

Conservatism also existed among Black Power advocates. Organizations such as the Nation of Islam, Malcolm X's Organization of Afro-American Unity, and Ron Karenga's Us followed in the tradition of Garvey, espousing a distinctly Afrocentric conservatism. Like Garvey, they championed black pride, community self-help, a strict moral code, strong male-headed households, and antistatism. Though many aspects of their politics were radical—particularly their nationalism—their social conservatism overlapped with many of the conservative groups of the growing New Right. Furthermore, "black capitalism" became a buzzword among Black Power activists who rejected the liberal integrationism of the traditional civil rights leaders and advocated for black control over black communities, particularly businesses and municipal governments. Floyd McKissick, the former chairman of the Congress of Racial Equality, assailed welfare and other government "handouts," claiming that they "do violence to a man, strip him of dignity, and breed in him a hate of the system."[33] McKissick instead advocated free enterprise, small business ownership, and community control over schools. Several conservative black nationalists, including McKissick's successor, Roy Innis, became prominent black neoconservatives in subsequent decades.

The 1970s and 1980s witnessed the genesis of what historian Christopher Bracey calls "a new breed of black leadership" with a "new vision of black conservatism."[34] Bracey argues these new black conservatives "were less concerned about self-identity than about transcending race through the adoption of what they generally perceived as the 'raceless' values of success" such as capitalism and individualism.[35] Though conservative thought persisted throughout African American history, the post–civil rights period saw a rightward shift of black conservatism, which began to overlap more with the conservatism of the New Right than the conservative traditions within the African American political development. The New Right emerged from a coalescence of several conservative camps: traditional antistatists who had been ardent anticommunists; proponents of free enterprise particularly from the business community; white suburbanites who evoked property rights to critique taxation, busing, and other extensions of state power; and evangelical Christians who decried the permissiveness of liberalism and decline of America's moral order. The politics of the New Right were incubated in a number of institutions, think tanks, foundations, and, eventually, the Republican Party. In the Heritage Foundation, the American Enterprise Institute, the University of Chicago's Department of Economics, Stanford University's Hoover Institution, Jerry Falwell's Moral Majority, and other institutions, conservatives formed a well-funded and well-organized network that ushered in a conservative ascendancy in the 1980s. Black conservatives found a platform in these mainstream conservative institutions and in offshoot organizations they founded themselves such as the Lincoln Institute, the National Center for Neighborhood Enterprise, the Black Alternatives Association, and the National Black Republican Council.³⁶

One of the New Right's preferred black conservatives was Thomas Sowell. Called the father of new black conservatism and the Reagan administration's "favored black spokesman," Sowell became one of the most well known black intellectuals of the post–civil rights era.³⁷ He had an archetypal biography for a black conservative, rising up from the poverty of Gastonia, North Carolina to the halls of Stanford University. After serving in the Korean War, the high school dropout attended Howard University before graduating *magna cum laude* from Harvard University with an honor's thesis on Marx. He quickly followed up with a master's degree from Columbia, where his politics shifted rightward. He then began doctoral work in economics at the University of Chicago where he studied with George Stigler and Milton Friedman, who championed free market principles. In 1980, he became a senior fellow at the Hoover Institution, the conservative think tank based at Stanford University. That December, he also organized the Black Alternatives Conference at the Fairmont Hotel in San Francisco. Many prominent black conservatives of the post–civil rights era attended the summit, including fellow economist Walter Williams and future Reagan appointees Clarence Pendleton and Clarence Thomas. In his opening speech, Sowell announced the objective of the conference—"to explore alternatives" with "people who have challenged the conventional wisdom on one or more issues."³⁸ At the conference, black conservatives addressed issues such as affirmative action, the minimum wage, unemployment welfare, black poverty, and black education, and they previewed many of the arguments they would maintain throughout the subsequent decades. They confidently positioned themselves as iconoclasts, renegades, and independent thinkers, seeking to challenge the hegemonic power of the "liberal civil rights establishment," to free blacks from Democratic liberalism, and to provide alternative solutions to secure the liberty that African Americans had sought since the era of slavery.

MAJOR ISSUES IN BLACK CONSERVATIVE THOUGHT IN THE POST–CIVIL RIGHTS ERA

The new black conservatives were united in a shared critique of American liberalism and the active role of the state in the lives of African Americans. Until the 1980s, the new black conservatives were relatively unknown outside of the intellectual and political circles of the New Right. However, during and after the Reagan Era, black "neoconservatives," as they were most often called in the press, came to the mainstream as they engaged in public policy debates concerning African Americans, particularly welfare and affirmative action. Black conservatives were often the most vociferous critics of these policies. In debates over welfare, the crisis of black poverty, affirmative action, and significance of race and racism, black conservatives imparted their political philosophies and offered solutions for the problems of black America.

Welfare and black poverty were primary targets of New Right black conservatives. "Welfare" was a catchall term for a number of federal programs that assisted people living in poverty, people with disabilities, and the unemployed. The welfare state had expanded since Franklin Roosevelt's New Deal had created social protection programs, such as Social Security. However, in Lyndon B. Johnson's Great Society and more specifically, the War on Poverty, federal social spending increased, funding a host of job training programs such as Job Corps, improvements in public education and housing such as Head Start and the Model Cities Program, health care initiatives such as Medicare and Medicaid, and means-tested cash assistance such as Aid to Families with Dependent Children (AFDC).[39] However, following the downward turn of the American economy in 1973 and the rightward shift of the American political culture, the attitude toward the poor became disparaging. Conservatives on the New Right attacked the "wasteful" Great Society programs that coddled the "undeserving" poor. They argued that the federal "handouts" eroded the poor's incentive to work and fostered a culture of dependency within urban ghettos.[40] Though there were many social welfare programs, the term "welfare" came to refer to the AFDC, and the archetypal and fictitious welfare recipient was a single black mother. Ronald Reagan famously employed the image of the pink Cadillac–driving "welfare queen" who had "eighty names, thirty addresses, twelve Social Security cards" and benefited from Medicaid and food stamps.[41] Fiscal conservatives condemned welfare as waste of public funds and pointed to the program as example of the excesses of Keynesianism. Social conservatives associated welfare with other permissive social policies such as abortion, feminism and the Equal Rights Amendment, and the homosexual rights movement to denounce the erosion of the family structure and the moral degradation of American society.[42]

The black conservatives of the post–civil rights era echoed the critiques of white conservatives and also appealed to their racial identity to make claims of authenticity and authority. There were two strains of critique in their analyses of welfare, one economic and one cultural. Fiscal conservatives argued that government aid to the poor was wasteful and did more harm than good. In his introductory remarks at the Fairmont Conference, economist Thomas Sowell claimed Johnson's Great Society created a web of wasteful bureaucracy that actually syphoned money away from the poor. "The cost of taking care of the poor," he argued, "is relatively small, compared to the cost of bureaucracy."[43] Fellow economist Walter Williams estimated that welfare expenditure cost the government $32,000, but welfare recipients only received a fraction of the amount.[44] Furthermore, they claimed, welfare had failed to improve the economic standing of its recipients but rather kept them trapped in poverty. Antistatists like Sowell and Williams believed that the government created more problems than it solved. While government intervention was sometimes necessary—for the abolition of slavery and Jim Crow laws, for example—when the state sought "to play a positive role," Sowell argued, "they not only failed but they've had counterproductive results."[45] The antistatist economists also assailed other government statutes, employing the same principles. Walter Williams argued that a federally mandated minimum wage "systematically discriminates against the most disadvantaged members of the labor force."[46] Employers discriminated against young and low-skilled workers, particularly black teenagers, Williams contended, because they were the least productive and thus could not produce the value of the minimum wage. Antistatist black fiscal conservatives maintained that the state should not seek to engineer reform in black communities, but rather allow the free market to more efficiently distribute benefits to those in poverty.

In the 1990s, the black conservatives' most damning critiques of welfare assailed the cultural and social implications of government assistance. They charged that government dependency threatened the autonomy of the black poor. Public intellectual and neighborhood activist Robert Woodson argued that welfare "fostered dependency on government assistance and stifled the initiative of small entrepreneurs with programmed-to-fail bureaucratic restrictions."[47] Furthermore, black conservatives also claimed that AFDC and other government assistance programs exacerbated the pathological culture of poverty that existed in black ghettos by weakening the family and undermining any sense of personal responsibility.[48] The "entitlement" programs, most notably the AFDC, they asserted, "cracked the ridge-pole of the black heritage—the black family—and set into motion the dialectic among personal and social forces that is responsible for the cycle of welfare dependency seen in cities today."[49] The AFDC created the welfare mother, who was rewarded by the government with a consistent paycheck for remaining unemployed, shunning marriage, and having children out of wedlock. "Welfare policies right now," Robert Woodson asserted in 1992, "discourage family formation. People are made dependent . . . You cannot have programs that treat people as impotent children and then expect them to act like responsible adults."[50] Conservative commentator Star Parker also criticized the relationship of dependency that characterized the relationship between blacks and the government. A former welfare recipient, Parker compared welfare to the institution of slavery, asserting, "Uncle Sam has developed a sophisticated poverty plantation operated by a federal government, overseen by bureaucrats, protected by media elite, and financed by the taxpayers." Like American slavery, welfare broke down the traditional family structure, she argued, by "removing the man's responsibility to care for his family" and "freeing women to face up to their end of the responsibility."[51] "If a woman gets pregnant out of wedlock," Parker claimed, "Uncle Sam will pick up the bill for the abortion; if she decides to keep the child, he'll buy the groceries."[52] Meanwhile, the state did seemingly nothing to encourage traditional family formation even though, Parker contended, "there is clear evidence that family breakdown contributes to low academic and employment achievement, propensity for crime, drug use, and sexual promiscuity."[53] Welfare, black conservatives like Star contended, not only made its recipients entitled and complacent, the institution compromised the values of blacks living in poverty.

Nonetheless, black conservatives did not hesitate to blame who they perceived was truly at fault for sustaining black poverty: the black poor themselves. They believed a "ghetto-specific" culture that blacks created bore much of the responsibility for the dysfunction in urban communities. In this ghetto culture, promiscuity, teenage pregnancies, and abortion were the norm; hard work and thrift were discouraged; education was not a priority; and vice and violence were glorified. Children lacked respect for their elders and for traditions, as their parents failed to discipline them and teach them the values needed to transcend their economic status.[54] While most black conservatives acknowledged that the historical and structural forces of racism and segregation played a role in creating black poverty and urban disorder, they insisted that racism was not the sole explanation. Glenn Loury argued, "Whatever fault may be placed upon racism in America, the responsibility for the behavior of black youngsters lies squarely on the shoulders of the black community itself."[55] Black conservatives believed their "tough love" was necessary for black self-improvement.

These tough love critiques of black cultural pathology came not only from conservative intellectuals in ivory towers, but also from black public figures whose admonishments had a much larger audience. These critiques were often couched in anecdotes and lessons but sometimes were more severe and accusatory. In his bestselling memoir, *My American Journey*, Colin Powell emphasized "a need for a return to traditional values" in the black community.[56] At the 2000 Republican National Convention, he was even more explicit, asserting, "We need to restore the social model of married parents bringing into the world a desired child, a child to be loved and nurtured, to be taught a sense of right and wrong ... Simple to say, difficult to achieve, yet the ideal toward which we must never stop striving."[57] Other public figures were less forgiving in their chastisements. At a May 2004 gala honoring the fiftieth anniversary of the *Brown v. Board of Education* decision, comedian Bill Cosby chastised impoverished black communities in what became known as the "Pound Cake Speech." Cosby lamented, "Ladies and gentlemen, the lower economic and lower middle economic people are not holding their end in this deal. In the neighborhood that most of us grew up in, parenting is not going on."[58] He assailed the high rate of incarceration and crime in black communities famously yelling, "People getting shot in the back of the head over a piece of pound cake! Then we all run out and are outraged, 'The cops shouldn't have shot him!' What the hell was he doing with the pound cake in his hand?"[59] Like the black conservative intellectuals, Cosby shifted the blame from racism to black people's misbehavior, arguing, "We cannot blame white people." Though Cosby's remarks garnered applause and moments of uncomfortable laughter from the audience, black liberals hurled sharp appraisals. Michael Eric Dyson argued that Cosby's views were representative of many in the conservative "Afristocracy"—the black upper-middle class and elite—who had been criticizing the behavior and values of the black poor since the era of Booker T. Washington. "Cosby's overemphasis on personal responsibility, not structural features," Dyson asserted, "wrongly locates the source of poor black suffering—and by implication its remedy—in the lives of the poor."[60] Dyson's appraisal of Cosby's conservative "Blame-the-Poor Tour" was representative of the critiques of black liberal scholars such as Manning Marable and Cornel West, who underscored the intractability of structural racism in their analyses of black poverty and their challenges to black conservatism.

Nonetheless, black conservatives claimed figures like Dyson were part of the "totalitarian and non-representative" civil rights establishment and consequently were part of the problem.[61] The civil rights establishment was comprised of leftist intellectuals and leaders of the civil rights organizations like the NAACP, the National Urban League, and the Southern Christian Leadership Conference, who, conservatives argued, policed the political discourse on racial issues and had a "monopoly over the civil rights mantle."[62] The establishment leaders supposedly condoned black lawlessness, came to the defense of gangsters and hoodlums who terrorized black communities, lionized criminals and illicit culture, and ignored the issue of "black-on-black crime" and the self-destruction of black communities.[63] Furthermore, black conservatives believed the civil rights establishment created a profitable civil rights industry that relied upon the preservation of urban poverty and the welfare state. Thomas Sowell declared, "Poverty used to be a condition but now it's an industry. Grants, careers, turf, movements and bureaucratic enterprises all depend on poverty."[64] The black conservative dissidents also argued that the establishment leaders profited from the perpetuation of white guilt. Glenn Loury held, "The growing black 'underclass' has become the constant reminder to many Americans of a historic debt owed the black community." Loury added, "[T]he suffering of the poorest blacks creates a fund of political capital which all members of the group can draw the pressing of racially-based claims."[65] The civil rights establishment, Loury claimed, then used the "victim-capital" to lobby for interventionist programs like minority set-asides and affirmative action, which benefited the black middle class more than the black poor. Shelby Steele expanded on the analysis of white guilt, arguing that the civil rights establishment used white guilt as a form of "valuable currency" to shame white liberals into funding the profitable civil rights industry. Thus, black and white liberals removed any sense of personal responsibility and motivation for self-improvement within poor black communities.[66] The black conservatives contended the civil rights establishment was out of touch with the realities of the black underclass. Political scientist Michael C. Dawson reasoned, "Black conservatives view themselves as the fiercest defenders of the poor and disadvantaged black community—warriors who attack middle-class complacency, smugness, and abandonment of the black poor."[67] Black conservatives believed that they were the true "partisans of the poor" and representatives of a silent majority of blacks who too were concerned about black America's moral crisis.[68]

Black conservatives recommended several solutions to address the problem of black poverty in the post–civil rights era. Most believed that self-help should undergird the process of reform, agreeing that state intervention in the form of welfare and other social services had only worsened the problems of the black poor. Yet, they offered different views on the most effective path to recovery and reform. Antistatists and neoconservatives insisted that the market, free from the intervention of the state, would best lift the black poor out of poverty. Robert Woodson, a sociologist by training, advocated free enterprise and market-based local initiatives. With funding from the American Enterprise Institute, he founded the grassroots National Center for Neighborhood Enterprise in 1981. Through the organization's "micro-enterprise approach," Woodson sought to empower neighborhoods by encouraging business development, improving schools and homes, and building a sense of community among black residents.[69] Woodson believed neighborhood-level enterprise would encourage residents of impoverished areas to feel a sense of ownership and investment in their neighborhoods. Through community-based ownership and self-improvement, blacks would achieve economic freedom and free themselves from the dependency of the welfare state.

Black conservatives also believed that the key to poor blacks' advancement out of the ghettos and into the American middle class was a restoration of the values that blacks had apparently lost in the post–civil rights era. Thomas Sowell argued that the development of human capital, or an ethnic group's skills, values, and other forms of "cultural equipment," was important for group socioeconomic advancement.[70] These skills and values, which for Sowell included thrift, diligence, and enterprise, needed to be reinforced in black communities in neighborhood institutions such as schools, churches, and civic and voluntary organizations, as well as in family units. These traditional institutions, Sowell maintained, "helped the black family [survive] slavery, discrimination, poverty, wars, and depressions" until the black family "began to come apart as the federal government moved in with its well-financed programs to 'help.'"[71] Glenn Loury also championed a return of traditional values, arguing, "What is important to the alleviation of black poverty and racism is not the economic structure of the United States nor the racist behavior of whites, but African Americans' behavior."[72] Loury contended, "It is time to recognize that further progress toward the attainment of equality for black Americans, correctly understood, depends most crucially at this juncture on the acknowledgement and rectification of the dysfunctional behaviors that plague black communities, and that so offend and threaten others."[73] He presented two paths—one based in the self-help politics of Booker T. Washington and another dependent on entitled demands of the state.[74] The black working class and poor needed to look inward and focus on the "inside game" of self-improvement, rather than the "outside game" of petitioning for amends for historical treatment. Only then, Loury suggested, would they earn the equality they demanded.

Linguist and cultural critic John McWhorter described the crisis of values in African American culture as a self-sabotaging "Cult of Victimology." The grip of the "Cult of Victimology," McWhorter contended, "encourages the black American from birth to fixate upon remnants of racism and resolutely downplay all signs of its demise."[75] Thus, the Cult of Victimology encouraged black people to refuse to take responsibility for their own failures and weaknesses. Nowhere was this troubling culture of self-sabotage more visible than in hip hop and rap music, McWhorter argued in 2006's *Winning the Race*. He contended that since the 1960s, black communities, particularly impoverished ones, had been plagued by what he deemed the culture of therapeutic alienation. He defined this cultural flaw as "alienation unconnected to, or vastly disproportionate to, real life stimulus, but maintained because it reinforces one's sense of psychological legitimacy, via defining oneself against an oppressor characterized as eternally depraved."[76] Blacks adopted the antiestablishment attitude of the New Left hippies of the 1960s, but their once meaningful and constructive resistance to the dominant social order became just "a fashion statement," gutted of any revolutionary potential. "The lyrics of rap music," he claimed, "are therapeutic alienation set to a catchy beat."[77] A child of the hip hop generation, McWhorter did not entirely oppose rap music, unlike many other black conservatives. He claimed to enjoy listening to some of it, though he has been critical of the violence and misogyny common in the lyrics. However, he challenged the political potential of the cultural form, as scholars of hip hop Tricia Rose and Imani Perry have suggested. "The music, we are told, is 'revolutionary,' putting the urgency of black poverty in white America's faces and pointing the way to a better future for poor blacks in America," he claimed. "This is nonsense."[78] McWhorter, like Thomas Sowell and Glenn Loury, thus insisted that values and culture matter and that transformation in black America must start from within.

Conservatives on the black Right believed that the moral destruction of the black family in particular was at the core of the decline of black communities. Abortion, many claimed, was one of the primary factors undermining the strength of the black family. One of its most vocal black conservative opponents is Christian and conservative writer Star Parker. As a former "welfare brat" who had four abortions, Parker used her personal experiences to attack abortion, which she called "subsidized murder," in her conservative activism.[79] Several other black conservatives have also been public opponents of abortion. Peter Kirsanow, a black conservative commissioner on the US Commission on Civil Rights, claimed that abortion was "the defining issue for black conservatism."[80] He argued that abortion "cheapened" black life and undermined the stability of the black family, much like the institution of slavery. He contended, "Just as slavery was justified on the basis that blacks were not human, the abortion industry largely depends on the fiction that the unborn child is somehow not quite human."[81] Kirsanow also suggested that abortion was particularly detrimental for the black community, arguing, "We err if we think that black Americans are not negatively impacted by abortion on demand."[82] He echoed many other black conservatives, including black nationalists such as the members of the Nation of Islam, who have framed abortion as "black genocide."[83] Black antiabortion activists have also adopted the rhetoric of the Black Lives Matter (BLM) movement. Star Parker declared at a prolife march in Selma, Alabama, in 2015, "If black lives matter, then black children matter, then black babies matter."[84]

Conservatives on the black Right, particularly those from the black church, also assailed same-sex marriage as detrimental to the black family. Prominent black pastors have been on the forefront of constructing an anti-LGBT black conservative rhetoric. Atlanta-based minister Eddie Long notably held a "Stop the Silence" march to advocate for an amendment banning same-sex marriage in Georgia.[85] In 2015, the Coalition of African-American Pastors (CAAP), led by Reverend William Owens, organized a protest against same-sex marriage in the wake of the impending US Supreme Court decision. The pastors declared that they would lead a massive protest of "civil disobedience" if the ruling were to come down in favor of same-sex marriage. When the Court did rule that bans on same-sex marriage were unconstitutional in June 2015 in the *Obergefell v. Hodges* decision, Reverend Owens vowed that the CAAP would continue the fight to defend traditional marriage. "We remain committed to faith, family, and justice–and we will defend the rights of all believers to follow their conscience without persecution," Owens declared, "There remain millions of people throughout this country who believe that marriage should only be recognized between a man and a woman."[86] Consequently, conservative black ministers have castigated traditional civil rights organizations such as the NAACP for supporting marriage equality and other protections of LGBT Americans. Reverend Owens criticized black leaders, such as Barack Obama, who have compared the movement of gay, lesbian, and transgender people to the African American civil rights movement. Owens accused the Obama administration of "extorting" and "usurping" the legacy of the civil rights movement. He declared, "Black Pastors will not allow the homosexual and transgender community to rob Black Americans of their battle for civil rights!"[87] In debates about religion, traditional values, and other moralistic social issues, the black conservatives found common ideological ground with the "conservative blacks" who filled the pews of evangelical churches.[88] Yet, on other issues such as affirmative action and the continuing salience of race, black conservatives and conservative blacks clashed.

Along with welfare, affirmative action became a defining issue for the black conservatives of the post–civil rights era. The term "affirmative action" first came into use with John F. Kennedy's Executive Order 10925 in 1961, an order that urged that government-funded contractors "take affirmative action" to deter discrimination in defense contract hiring. The order also established the Committee on Equal Employment Opportunity, a precursor to the Equal Employment Opportunity Commission.[89] Following the passage of the Civil Rights Act of 1964, Lyndon Johnson issued Executive Order 11246, which prohibited discrimination based on race, sex, religion, or country of origin for federal defense contractors. However, affirmative action as a policy of quotas, timetables, and preferences was formulated during Richard Nixon's administration. Nixon expanded the Equal Employment Opportunity Commission and issued the Revised Philadelphia Plan, which gave the state more power to enforce Johnson's Executive Order 11246 with proscribed goals and timetables for minority hiring. Many companies and universities created their own recruitment policies based on quotas and gender and race-based preferential hiring and admissions policies.[90] These more interventionist forms of affirmative action quickly came under fire, culminating in the Supreme Court case *Bakke v. Regents of California* (1978).[91] After the *Bakke* decision upheld the constitutionality of race-based admissions policies, conservatives intensified their attacks on the policy, with black conservatives as the most vocal critics.

The earliest challenges came from the economists—Thomas Sowell, Walter Williams, and Glenn Loury—who focused their attacks on the inefficiency of affirmative action. Sowell and Williams argued that the interventionist policy interrupted the free market as it "[imposed] unwarranted governmental restrictions on voluntary exchange."[92] The free market would provide opportunities for blacks, women, and the other underrepresented groups because, they argued, the "operating market does not recognize race or gender but works according to economic laws that minimize these factors."[93] They also claimed that the policy was inefficient because it did not help those it was intended to help. While proponents of affirmative action pointed to the growth of the black middle class as evidence of the policy's efficacy, Loury argued, "The policy advances under the cover of providing assistance to disadvantaged persons when in fact, by its very nature, its ability to assist poor blacks is severely limited."[94] "It is now beyond dispute that the principal beneficiaries of affirmative action are relatively well-off blacks," Loury asserted, arguing that affirmative action, like welfare, was ultimately a self-serving measure for the black middle class and the civil rights establishment. Robert Woodson echoed Loury, claiming, "Not all blacks are equally 'disadvantaged.'"[95] Thomas Sowell insisted that the most underprivileged members of black society were hurt the most by affirmative action. In order to fulfill the demands of state-mandated "quotas and timetables," he contended that companies would hire the most "unusually" qualified minority applicants. Minority applicants who were less qualified than typical applicants, those that affirmative action policies were intended to aid, would be disadvantaged in the application process.[96] Thus, the policy benefited African Americans who would not have needed the help in the first place. Black conservatives insisted that affirmative action was an economically inefficient "symbolic policy" that was yet another ploy of the black bourgeoisie to maintain their class position at the expense of the black poor.[97]

Black conservatives also believed that affirmative action was un-American, statist, and immoral. Anne Wortham argued affirmative action was based on the un-American premises of "collectivism" and "socio-cultural determinism," while Jay Parker claimed, "[Affirmative action] violates our very basic principles of individual freedom and our hope for continuing progress."[98] They believed that the system of quotas and preferences was essentially state-funded social engineering that undermined the freedom of the marketplace and struck at the liberty of American citizens. Black conservatives also "objected to the moral perversity embodied in preferential treatment."[99] Thomas Sowell insisted that policy created an entire new class of victims: whites, particularly white men. "Live people are being sacrificed because of what dead people did," Sowell contended.[100] In discriminating against white people, affirmative action, black conservatives alleged, violated the equal protection clause of the Fourteenth Amendment, much like Jim Crow laws. Racial preference, they suggested, undermined the goals of the civil rights movement and colorblind vision of Martin Luther King Jr.'s "I Have a Dream Speech." Ward Connerly, a businessman who helped end affirmative action in California as a regent of the University of California in 1996, claimed, "Affirmative action has become a major detour in our journey to a fair and equitable society."[101] Furthermore, Sowell, whose scholarship on race and economics was international in scope, argued that quotas did not work in other multiethnic nations, such as Brazil and India, that tried out the policy in the hope of rectifying historical economic disparities. In a few cases, notably Malaysia and Indonesia, quotas caused violent ethnic clashes.[102] While most black conservatives did not predict bloodshed in the streets, many believed that affirmative action was, in essence, reverse racism and thus contradictory to the nation's ideals of equal opportunity and nondiscrimination.

In the 1990s, black conservatives began to claim that affirmative action was also psychologically damaging to its supposed beneficiaries and to African Americans broadly. The practice, Glenn Loury argued, "introduces uncertainty into the process by which individuals make inferences about their own abilities."[103] Because employers and universities supposedly lowered their standards to accept unqualified minority candidates, African Americans would come to doubt their own abilities and their self-esteem consequently would plummet. Black conservatives claimed that affirmative action and other race-preference programs fostered a "victim mentality" among African Americans. As Robert Woodson argued, "A victim mentality has been not only demeaning but dangerous for the young people who have taken this message to heart. In effect, they have been told, 'You are a victim of society.'"[104] Shelby Steele and John McWhorter, two black conservative academics who came into prominence in the 1990s, expanded upon the supposed psychological effects of affirmative action. Steele, a former professor of English and fellow at the Hoover Institute, argued that affirmative action instilled self-doubt with African Americans. In his 1995 award-winning book, *The Content of Our Character,* Steele wrote, "I think that one of the most troubling effects of racial preferences for blacks is a kind of demoralization, or put another way, an enlargement of self-doubt." "Under affirmative action," he continued, "the quality that earns us preferential treatment is an implied inferiority."[105] Both whites and, more damagingly, blacks accepted this implied inferiority, which put "blacks at war with an expanded realm of debilitating doubt, so that the doubt itself becomes an unrecognized preoccupation that undermines their ability to perform, especially in integrated situations."[106] The self-doubt instilled by affirmative action and other race-based programs created a "cycle of internalized victimization," which blacks used as a tool for increased political capital. However, the cycle was ultimately self-sabotaging for black Americans.[107] John McWhorter echoed Steele in his examinations of black culture and politics. He claimed that affirmative action fostered the "Cult of Victimology" and treated "victimhood not as a problem to be solved but an identity to be nourished."[108] Blacks, from the ghettos to the departments of Ivy League universities, were so blinded by their hyper-race consciousness, McWhorter claimed, they were unable to stop the cycle of self-destruction. Steele and McWhorter believed that it was not racism or discrimination that was holding blacks back, but rather blacks' own obsession with being the victims of racism.

Hence, black conservatives alleged that racism was no longer the determining factor in the lives of African Americans in the post-civil rights era. They claimed it was not the primary cause of black poverty or the socioeconomic and educational disparities between blacks and whites. Though racism had been a central aspect of African Americans' experience in the United States, racism was, to use McWhorter's phrase, "receding" since the triumph of the civil rights movement. Libertarians Sowell and Williams argued that racism was irrational in the free market, and "market mechanisms alone [were] sufficient enough to erode racist behavior."[109] Other black conservatives pointed to the expanding black middle class, the shrinking percentage of blacks living in poverty, and the increasing number of black college graduates, doctors, lawyers, and business executives.[110] In the eyes of black conservatives, these figures demonstrated that racism was no longer preventing blacks from entering positions of power. Black conservatives maintained that blacks exaggerated the role racism continued to play. Led by the "race hustlers" of the civil rights establishment such as Jesse Jackson and Al Sharpton, they argued, African Americans were preoccupied by race and routinely used racism as an excuse for their failings and laziness. Race consciousness also fostered an undue hatred of white people and the American way of life, which prevented black people from entering the American mainstream. As Jesse Peterson wrote about race consciousness, "An 'us-against-them' mentality results, and one's individuality begins to recede behind a wall of racial anger and personal hostility that is poisonous to the person."[111] This black rage was another form of self-sabotaging behavior that kept African Americans from advancing and achieving the American Dream.

Black conservatives believed that in their obsession with racial identity, African Americans constructed an ideal of "authentic blackness" that necessitated ideological conformity among black Americans and separatism from the mainstream. Conservatives, committed to the ideals of liberty and individualism, found this aspect of race consciousness particularly troubling. Anne Wortham argued that the danger of race consciousness was that an individual's identity was "to be analyzed and understood not on the basis of his identity as man qua human being, but as man qua racial being."[112] Blacks then became fixed in "racial robot thinking," making decisions not based on what they actually wanted to think or do but what they perceived as something a black person should think or do.[113] The commitment to ethnocentricity with narrow boundaries, black conservatives believed, was dangerous because it encouraged blacks to adhere to a counterproductive set of values that prevented black assimilation into American society. Thus, black conservatives were critical of the ways in which they believed Afrocentrism and racial solidarity motivated African Americans to express hatred for their country. Consequently, they were also wary of multiculturalism in education and ethnic studies, which they believed isolated black Americans from the rest of American culture. Shunning the concept of racial collectivity, black conservatives esteemed the American ideals of individualism and nonconformity and argued that through them, they were able to "transcend race" entirely.[114] They depicted themselves as "dissidents," "iconoclasts," and members of a "new black vanguard," who refused to be "muzzled" by the conformist civil rights establishment.[115] Because they were able to reason as individuals, black conservatives claimed to expose truths that were not apparent to African Americans engaged in a race-conscious "group think." "Personal responsibility," Shelby Steele asserted, "is the brick and mortar of power."[116] Moreover, he continued, "Blacks must be responsible for actualizing their own lives."[117]

In their critiques of affirmative action, black conservatives also challenged the state-driven overemphasis on college admissions, arguing that education reform should instead be directed at the primary and secondary education levels. "A PhD," Steele argued, "must be developed from preschool on."[118] In the 1980s and 1990s, the state of black education was deeply troubling to both liberals and conservatives. While liberals argued Great Society reforms did not go far enough and that public education needed increased funding and regulation, conservatives held that the state of public education in the post–civil rights era demonstrated the failures of an interventionist state. Liberal solutions such as increased spending, integration, and experimental pedagogy, black conservatives argued, only worsened the problems in black schools.[119] Black conservatives suggested several solutions for the crisis of black education, all of which involved scaling back state involvement in education. Thomas Sowell and Walter Williams advocated overhauling public education entirely. They recommended privatizing the system and allowing the market to take command. They argued that this system would be more cost effective and would give families more choice in their children's education.[120] Other suggestions were less drastic and focused on providing parents with more autonomy within the public education system. The school voucher program was a popular proposal. The voucher would provide parents who could not afford to send their children to private schools with a tax break or credit to pay for private schools for their children. The proposal would provide low-income parents with the same choice that middle- and upper-class parents had on how best to educate their children. Conservatives believed vouchers would restore control of children's education to the parents, thus, as Jesse Peterson argued, "[recognizing] the preeminence of the family in the social order."[121] Unlike other black conservative proposals, school vouchers had a great deal of support within black communities. In 2000, 60 percent of African Americans polled supported vouchers.[122]

In short, black conservatives believed black children and the black community as a whole suffered in the post-civil rights era because the state had a stranglehold over their lives. Liberals had made African Americans into a problem population, a people to be experimented with, fixed, and tested. Black liberals in the civil rights establishment, they argued, were willing to accept status as victims in exchange for money and political clout. The liberal establishment was content to allow blacks to remain dependent and self-sabotaging. The black dissidents of the post-civil rights era sought to challenge the civil rights establishment and the hegemony of Democratic liberalism among black Americans. They sought to provide an alternative that was grounded in liberty and respect for the individual and the household; an assent to the colorblind free market; and the traditional values of family, integrity, and tradition that had guided African Americans through slavery, segregation, and the civil rights movement.

CONCLUSION

The black conservatives of the post-civil rights era emerged at a pivotal period in African American history. Following the expansion of African American civil and political rights during the civil rights era, the direction of African American politics was uncertain and contingent. Conservatism, an ideology deeply rooted in the African American political tradition, was one of many political strategies on the table for debate. Conservatism became particularly visible with the rise of the bombastic and provocative black conservatives of the Reagan era. Seeking to challenge the Great Society interventionist state and the racial consciousness of identity politics, black conservatives attacked the excesses of liberalism. Though many claimed to "transcend" their racial identity, black conservatives were most vocal in discussions concerning race. In their highly publicized critiques, they shaped the parameters of debate over welfare, affirmative action, education, and African American culture.

The black conservatives of the post-civil rights era drew a number of sharp critiques from black liberals and leftists. Benjamin Hooks, executive direction of the National Association for the Advancement of Colored People from 1972 to 1992, assailed the new black conservatives as "a new breed of Uncle Tom," who were "some of the biggest liars the world ever saw."[123] Poet and political activist Amiri Baraka described black conservatives as "racists" and "pods growing in the cellars of our politics."[124] Clarence Thomas, one of the most visible black conservatives of the post-civil rights era perhaps received the most cutting criticism from black liberals. Political scientist Manning Marable claimed that Thomas "ceased to be African American," while filmmaker Spike Lee claimed that Malcolm X, were he still alive, would decry Thomas as "handkerchief-head, chicken-and-biscuit-eating Uncle Tom."[125] Several on the black Left have condemned Thomas and others on the black Right as race traitors, who, in their sycophantic acquiescence to the conservative ideology of the New Right, placed themselves outside the bounds of the black community and authentic blackness. Consequently, these new black conservatives found a niche in the think tanks, political action committees, and academic departments of the New Right. They remained highly visible—serving in positions such as secretary of state (Colin Powell and Condoleezza Rice) and chairman of the Republican National Committee (Michael Steele)—yet they were seemingly token exceptions rather than representatives of a sizeable segment of the African American political landscape. By 2000, the ambitious goals and optimistic hope for a potential black conservative revolution that had undergirded the 1980 Fairmont Conference had seemingly dissipated. As illustrated by the dwindling number of blacks aligned with the conservative Republican Party and the continuing marginalization of black conservative figures, black conservatives failed to naturalize black conservatism and present conservative ideology as a viable and worthwhile political alternative to liberalism. With their rancorous critiques of black culture and celebrated black figures, their denial of the continuing significance of race, their affiliations with antagonistic white conservatives, and their failure to promote proactive solutions for the improvement of black communities, black conservatives isolated themselves from black America and limited the transformative potential of their politics. They continued to operate in the liminal space between black America and the New Right.

Nevertheless, black conservatives' effort to influence the rhetoric and ideologies of black America's politics was perhaps not a complete failure. Strains of black conservative thought often emerge from the mouths of progressives in discourses concerning race, politics, and culture. President Barack

Obama has cribbed from black conservative buzzwords when advocating for self-improvement in black communities. In initiatives such as My Brother's Keeper and in numerous addresses to black audiences, President Obama has called for personal responsibility, the restoration of traditional values, and an emphasis on the family. In his 2013 commencement address at Morehouse College, the historically black all-male college, Obama told the graduates of their "individual responsibilities" and exhorted, "Nobody cares how tough your upbringing was. Nobody cares if you suffered some discrimination."[126] Obama emphasized the importance of personal responsibility and individual choices in defying the legacies of systemic racism and poverty. Almost immediately after his address, Obama came under attack from black progressives who accused the president of "finger wagging" at poor blacks and reinforcing the archaic politics of respectability. They also charged the president with undervaluing the intractability of structural racism and wrongly blaming black families and culture.[127] Nonetheless, the president's comments on family and personal responsibility found many supporters among black conservatives such as John McWhorter, who defended the president, writing, "The black man who told us to hope disses the idea that hopelessness is higher wisdom. Do keep at it, Mr. President."[128]

Historian Michael Ondaatje has noted, "At every epoch in the nation's history in which there was a significant transformation in the status of African Americans, individual black conservative spokespersons had emerged, counseling racial caution, submission, and even retreat."[129] Booker T. Washington and the elitist black conservatives of the late nineteenth and early twentieth centuries emerged from the revolution of the Civil War and Reconstruction, urging pragmatism and accommodation in the face of racial violence and disorder. The new black conservatives of the post-civil rights era similarly arose from the upheaval of America's second reconstruction, the civil rights movement, cautioning against surrender to the all-encompassing power of the state and the abandonment of traditional values. Black America may perhaps be witnessing a new uprising of black conservatism in the age of Obama. With the rise of prominent black conservative figures such as Ben Carson, Congresswoman Mia Love, Senator Tim Scott, and a growing network of younger black conservatives connected through blogs and online forums such as Crystal Wright's Conservative Black Chick and Richard Ivory's Hip Hop Republican, black conservatives are perhaps attempting a renaissance. Nevertheless, even if conservatives remain outsiders in African American politics, strains of conservative thought persist in black political discourse and continue to inform debates about the past and future of black America.

NOTES

1. Clarence Thomas, "No Room at the Inn: The Loneliness of the Black Conservative," in *Black and Right: The Bold New Voice of Black Conservatives in America*, ed. Stan Faryna, Brad Stetson, and Joseph G. Conti (Westport, CT: Praeger, 1997).

2. Though many scholars use the term "neoconservative" in reference to the group of black conservatives who came to prominence after the civil rights movement, in this chapter I use it to refer only to former liberals or radicals who became conservative, and I use "new black conservative" to refer to the broad group of black conservatives of the post-civil rights era.

3. Angela K. Lewis, *Conservatism in the Black Community to the Right and Misunderstood* (New York: Routledge, 2013), 75.

4. Lewis, *Conservatism*, 75.

5. As quoted in Michael L. Ondaatje, *Black Conservative Intellectuals in Modern America* (Philadelphia: University of Pennsylvania Press, 2011), 20.

6. Before delineating the components of black conservative thought, Eisenstadt discusses the tricky nature of honing in on a cohesive definition of black conservatism, writing, "Any generalization about black conservatism is subject to the following two limitations, (1) It will not be true of all black conservatives, (2) it will be true of many individuals who are not black conservatives." Peter Eisenstadt, "Introduction" in *Black Conservatism: Essays in Intellectual and Political History*, ed. Peter Eisenstadt (New York and London: Routledge, 1999), x-xii.

7. Peter Eisenstadt, "Southern Black Conservatism, 1865-1945: An Introduction" in *Black Conservatism*, ed. Eisenstadt, 61.

8. Angela Dillard, *Guess Who's Coming to Dinner Now? Multicultural Conservatism in American* (New York: New York University Press, 2002), 14.

9. Ibid., 29.

10. On the development of the New Right see Kim Phillips-Fein, *Invisible Hands: The Making of the Conservative Movement from the New Deal to Reagan* (New York: W. W. Norton, 2009); Bruce J. Schulman and Julian E. Zelizer, *Rightward Bound: Making America Conservative in the 1970s* (Cambridge, MA: Harvard University Press, 2008); Lisa McGirr, *Suburban Warriors: The Origins of the New American Right* (Princeton, NJ: Princeton University Press, 2001); Dan T. Carter, *The Politics of Rage: George Wallace, the Origins of the New Conservatism, and the Transformation of American Politics* (New York: Simon and Schuster, 1995).

11. See Ira Berlin, *Many Thousands Gone: The First Two Centuries of Slavery in North America* (Cambridge, MA: The Belknap Press of Harvard University Press, 1998).

12. Rhett Jones, "Black Creole Cultures: The Eighteenth Century Origins of African American Conservatism," in *Dimensions of Black Conservatism in the United States: Made in America*, ed. Gayle T. Tate and Lewis A. Randolph (New York: Macmillan, 2002), 14.

13. Eisenstadt, "Southern Black Conservatism, 1865-1945," xiv–xv; Sondra O'Neale, *Jupiter Hammon and Biblical Beginnings of African American Literature* (Metuchen, NJ: Scarecrow, 1993), 11.

14. O'Neale, *Jupiter Hammon*, 86.

15. Julie Winch, "James Forten, Conservative Radical," in *Black Conservatism*, 8.

16. Ibid.

17. Ibid.

18. Kevin Kelly Gaines, *Uplifting the Race: Black Leadership, Politics, and Culture in the Twentieth Century* (Chapel Hill: University of North Carolina Press, 1996), 38–40.

19. Ibid., 28.

20. Dillard, *Guess Who's Coming to Dinner Now?* 36–37.

21. See Martin Summers, *Manliness and Its Discontents: The Black Middle Class and the Transformation of Masculinity, 1900–1930* (Chapel Hill: University of North Carolina Press, 2004); Evelyn Brooks Higginbotham, *Righteous Discontent: The Women's Movement in the Black Baptist Church, 1880–1920* (Cambridge, MA: Harvard University Press, 1993).

22. Walter Friedman, "The African American Gospel of Business Success," in *Black Conservatism*, 140–41.

23. Dillard, *Guess Who's Coming to Dinner Now?* 41–42.

24. Lewis, *Conservatism*, 40.

25. Oscar R. Williams Jr., "The Lonely Iconoclast: George Schuyler and the Civil Rights Movement," in *Dimensions of Black Conservatism*, 165.

26. Ibid., 173.

27. Eisenstadt, xxiii.

28. Leah Wright-Rigueur, *The Loneliness of the Black Republican: Pragmatic Politics and the Pursuit of Power* (Princeton: Princeton University Press, 2015), 9.

29. Ibid., 97–105.

30. Tomiko Brown-Nagin, *Courage to Dissent: Atlanta and the Long History of the Civil Rights Movement* (New York: Oxford University Press, 2011), 2.

31. See N. D. B. Connolly, *A World More Concrete*.

32. See N. D. B. Connolly, "Games of Chance: Jim Crow's Entrepreneurs Bet on 'Negro' Law and Order," in *What's Good for Business: Business and American Politics Since World War II*.

33. Joshua D. Farrington, "Build, Baby, Build: Conservative Black Nationalists, Free Enterprise, and the Nixon Administration," in *The Right Side of the Sixties: Reexamining Conservatism's Decade of Transformation*, ed. Laura Jane Gifford and Daniel K Williams (New York: Palgrave Macmillan, 2012), 65.

34. Christopher Alan Bracey, *Saviors or Sellouts: The Promise and Peril of Black Conservatism, from Booker T. Washington to Condoleeza Rice* (Boston: Beacon, 2008), 123.

35. Ibid., 124.

36. Dillard, *Guess Who's Coming to Dinner Now?* 10.

37. Thomas Sowell, *A Personal Odyssey* (New York: Free, 2000), 288.

38. Thomas Sowell, *Fairmont Papers*, 4–5.

39. Ondaatje, *Black Conservative*, 94.

40. Michael Katz, *The Undeserving Poor: From the War on Poverty to the War on Welfare* (New York: Oxford University Press, 1989), 163–68.

41. Ondaatje, *Black Conservative*, 101.

42. Katz, *The Undeserving Poor*, 165.

43. Thomas Sowell, "Politics and Opportunity: The Background," in *The Fairmont Papers: Black Alternatives Conference San Francisco December 1980* (San Francisco: The Institute for Contemporary Studies, 1981), 7.

44. Ibid., 7–8.

45. Ondaatje, *Black Conservative*, 103–104.

46. Walter Williams, "Legal Barriers to Black Economic Gains: Employment and Transportation," in *The Fairmont Papers*, 27–28.

47. Ondaatje, *Black Conservative*, 104–105.

48. Black conservatives were joining in an intellectual conversation about the sources of black poverty that had been particularly vocal since the publication of Daniel Moynihan's *The Negro Family: The Case for National Action* also known as the Moynihan Report, in 1965. Moynihan, then an assistant secretary of labor, argued that the historical forces, most notably slavery and segregation in housing, employment, and education, had fostered structural inequities and created a pathology culture of poverty in black communities by destabilizing the black family.

49. Joseph G. Conti and Brad Stetson, *Challenging the Civil Rights Establishment: Profiles of a New Black Vanguard* (Westport, CT: Praeger, 1993), 49.

50. As quoted in Conti and Stetson, *Challenging the Civil Rights Establishment*, 51.

51. Star Parker, *Uncle Sam's Plantation: How Big Government Enslaves Poor and What We Can Do About It* (Nasville: Thomas Nelson, 2010), 110.

52. Ibid.

53. Ibid., 5.

54. Conti and Stetson, *Challenging the Civil Rights Establishment*, 50–62.

55. Glenn Loury, "The Moral Quandary of the Black Community," in *One by One from the Inside Out: Essays and Reviews on Race and Responsibility in America* (New York: Free, 1995), 37.

56. Colin Powell and Joseph E. Persico, *My American Journey* (New York: Random House, 1995), 599.

57. As quoted in Bracey, *Saviors or Sellouts*, 165.

58. As quoted in Michael Eric Dyson, *Is Bill Cosby Right: Or Has the Black Middle Class Lost Its Mind?* (New York: Basic Civitas Books, 2005), 141–42.

59. Dyson, *Is Bill Cosby Right*, 59.

60. Ibid., 5.

61. Dillard, *Guess Who's Coming to Dinner Now?* 64.

62. Conti and Stetson, *Challenging the Civil Rights Establishment*, 5.

63. Joseph H. Brown, "The Moral Vacuum in Black America Must Be Filled," in *Black and Right: The Bold New Voice of Black Conservatives in America*, ed. Stan Faryna, Brad Stetson, and Joseph Conti (Westport, CT: Praeger, 1997), 95.

64. Joseph G. Conti and Brad Stetson, *Challenging the Civil Rights Establishment: Profiles of a New Black Vanguard* (Westport, CT: Praeger, 1993), 115.

65. Loury, *One by One*, 47.

66. Shelby Steele, *White Guilt: How Blacks and Whites Together Destroyed the Promise of the Civil Rights Era* (New York: HarperCollins, 2006), 35.

67. Michael C. Dawson, *Black Visions: The Roots of Contemporary African-American Political Ideologies* (Chicago: University of Chicago Press, 2001), 282.

68. Ondaatje, *Black Conservative*, 92; Dillard, 295–96.

69. Ondaatje, *Black Conservative*, 44.

70. Thomas Sowell, *Race and Culture: A World View* (New York: Basic Books, 1994), xii; *The Economics and Politics of Race: An International Perspective* (New York: Morrow, 1983), 234–35.

71. As quoted in Conti and Stetson, *Challenging the Civil Rights Establishment*, 105.

72. As quoted in Bracey, *Saviors or Sellouts*, 135.

73. Loury, *One by One*, 72.

74. As quoted in Conti and Stetson, *Challenging the Civil Rights Establishment*, 204.

75. Ibid., xi.

76. McWhorter, *Winning the Race*, 6.

77. Ibid., 318.

78. Ibid., 315.

79. Star Parker, *Pimps, Whores, and Welfare Brats: The Stunning Conservative Transformation of a Former Welfare Queen* (New York: Pocket Books, 1997), 37.

80. Peter Kirsanow, "A Black Conservative Looks at Abortion," in *Black and Right*, 115.

81. Ibid., 116.

82. Ibid., 119.

83. Mary Ziegler, "Roe's Race: The Supreme Court, Population Control, and Reproductive Justice," *Yale Journal of Law and Feminism* 25 (2013): 26–27.

84. Ken Blackwell, "Indeed Black Lives Matter—Especially the Unborn!" Family Research Council, http://www.frc.org/op-eds/indeed-black-lives-matter-especially-the-unborn (accessed August 26, 2016).

85. Jonathan Walton, *Watch This! The Ethics and Aesthetics of Black Televangelism* (New York: New York University Press, 2009), 126.

86. "Marriage Pledge," Coalition of African American Pastors, http://caapusa.org/marriage-pledge/sign-marriage-pledge/ (accessed August 26, 2016).

87. "CAAP Discusses Gender Identity, the President, and Theft of Civil Rights Legacy," Coalition of African American Pastors, May 18, 2016, http://caapusa.org/2016/05/caap-discusses-gender-identity-the-president-and-theft-of-civil-rights-legacy/.

88. According to polls conducted by the Pew Research Center, black support for same-sex marriage has risen gradually from its low of 19 percent in 2004 to 42 percent in 2016. African Americans in general have tended to be less supportive of same-sex marriage than whites. See "Changing Attitudes on Gay Marriage," Pew Research Center, Washington, DC, May 16, 2016, http://www.pewforum.org/2016/05/12/changing-attitudes-on-gay-marriage/.

89. Ondaatje, *Black Conservative*, 56.

90. Ibid., 56–57.

91. Ibid., 59.

92. William A. Drake and Robert D. Holsworth, *Affirmative Action and the Stalled Quest for Black Progress* (Urbana: University of Illinois Press, 1996), 18.

93. Ibid.

94. Glenn C. Loury, "Performing without a Net," in *The Affirmative Action Debate*, ed. George E. Curry and Cornel West (Reading, MA: Addison-Wesley, 1996), 51.

95. Robert L. Woodson, "Personal Responsibility," in *The Affirmative Action Debate*, 111.

96. Thomas Sowell, "Affirmative Action Harms the Disadvantaged," *The Wall Street Journal*, July 28, 1981, 28.

97. Loury, "Performing without a Net," 51.

98. Ondaatje, *Black Conservative*, 61

99. Conti and Stetson, *Challenging the Civil Rights Establishment*, 64.

100. Ondaatje, *Black Conservative*, 61.

101. Faye J. Crosby, *Affirmative Action Is Dead, Long Live Affirmative Action* (New Haven: Yale University Press, 2004), 35.

102. See Thomas Sowell, *Affirmative Action around the World: An Empirical Study* (New Haven: Yale University Press, 2005).

103. Loury, "Performing without a Net," 54.

104. Woodson, "Personal Responsibility," in *The Affirmative Action Debate*, 116.

105. Shelby Steele, *The Content of Our Character: A New Vision for Race in America* (New York: St. Martin's, 1995), 116.

106. Ibid., 117–18.

107. Frank Harold Wilson, "Neoconservatives, Black Conservatives, and the Retreat from Social Justice," in *Dimensions of Black Conservatism*, 189.

108. John McWhorter, *Losing the Race: Self-Sabotage in Black America* (New York: Simon and Schuster, 2000), xi.

109. Bracey, *Saviors or Sellouts*, 129.

110. Conti and Stetson, *Challenging the Civil Rights Establishment*, 105; McWhorter, 166–69.

111. Jesse L. Peterson, *From Rage to Responsibility: Black Conservative Jessie Lee Peterson and America Today* (St. Paul, MN: Paragon House, 2000), 22.

112. Conti and Stetson, *Challenging the Civil Rights Establishment*, 132.

113. Ibid., 132

114. Sherrie Smith, "The Individual Ethos: A Defining Characteristic of Contemporary Black Conservatism," in *Dimensions of Black Conservatism*, 12.

115. Conti and Stetson, *Challenging the Civil Rights Establishment*, 21.

116. Steele, *The Content of Our Character*, 33.

117. Ibid., 34.

118. Ibid., 122.

119. Ondaatje, *Black Conservative*, 130.

120. Ibid., 143; Dillard, 20.

121. Peterson, *From Rage to Responsibility*, 92.

122. Bracey, *Saviors or Sellouts*, xvi.

123. Patrick Allitt, *The Conservatives: Ideas and Personalities throughout American History* (New Haven: Yale University Press, 2009), 271.

124. Dillard, *Guess Who's Coming to Dinner Now?* 15.

125. Brando Simeo Starkey, *In Defense of Uncle Tom: Why Blacks Must Police Racial Loyalty* (New York: Cambridge University Press, 2015), 258.

126. Barack H. Obama, Remarks by the President at Morehouse College Commencement Ceremony, May 19, 2013, Office of the White House Press Secretary, whitehouse.gov.

127. Ta-Nehesi Coates, "How the Obama Administration Talks to Black America," *The New Yorker,* May 20, 2013; Vanessa Williams, "To Critics, Obama's Scolding Tone with Black Audiences Is Getting Old," *The Washington Post,* May 20, 2013.

128. John McWhorter, "It's About Time Obama Stuck Up for His 'Respectability Politics,'" washingtonpost.com, May 14, 2015.

129. Ondaatje, *Black Conservative,* 7.

- CHAPTER FIVE -

STEPS IN AND PLACES OUTSIDE

*The Reception of Black Feminist Intellectuals and
Black Feminist Theory in Modern America*

BENITA ROTH

In her landmark work, *When and Where I Enter: The Impact of Black Women on Race and Sex in America,* Paula Giddings recounts the history of African American women activists resisting slavery by articulating a consciousness of the oppressions they faced as blacks and as women. Giddings quotes the speeches of Maria Stewart, a free black woman who advocated for her people before abolitionist audiences in the early 1800s. Stewart's words showed a "distinct ethos," wherein struggles against race and gender oppressions were intertwined.[1] She combined concerns for black rights and women's rights a decade and a half before the convening of the Seneca Falls women's rights convention in 1848. Rejecting prevailing visions of "true womanhood" that excluded her and other black women, Stewart argued against the idea that black women were somehow responsible for their own—or their race's—plight, placing the responsibility for the ills of slavery squarely on the slave owners. Simultaneously working within the boundaries of the religious discourse of the time and pushing against the conventions of docility imposed by the cultural norm of true womanhood, Stewart advocated that black women become more public and more daring in their efforts against slavery, that they emulate "the spirit of men, bold and enterprising," and that they sue for their rights and privileges.

Maria Stewart, speaking well before the organization of the "first wave" of feminist protest, was an early example of a black, female, and activist intellectual approach to understanding the position of the black women in the United States. Black women activists' understanding of the complex and at times contradictory relationships of race and sex oppression prompted them to advocate for the full contribution of all members of the race in opposing injustices.[2] Throughout their history in the Americas, many black women activists put forward an analysis of the multiplicative nature of oppressions in black women's lives and consequently the need for a vision of social change on multiple fronts. Even a movement like 1920s Garveyism, where gender politics were to some degree characterized by ideals of "Victorian womanhood,"[3] produced leaders such as Amy Jacques Garvey, the second wife of black nationalist Marcus Garvey. She was a key player in the movement's Universal Negro Improvement Association (UNIA) in the United States and in Jamaica and a strong advocate for black women's equality; she authored numerous editorials and articles about women in the nationalist movement in her role as editor of the Garveyite journal *Negro World*.[4]

The first half of the twentieth century also witnessed the participation of black women in socialist and communist US-based parties. As historian Eric McDuffie has noted, these "Black left feminists ... constituted the most radical group of black women in the United States and globally during the mid-twentieth century."[5] Black Left feminists were engaged in practical politics to improve the conditions for blacks as workers; some black women, like Claudia Jones, rose up through the party hierarchy while advocating a "triple jeopardy" approach to understanding black women's oppression as workers, women, and blacks.[6] While McCarthyism preemptively severed the ties that 1950s groups like the Soujourners for Truth and Justice would form with later generations of activists, by the time the 1960s came, a number of black women on the left, like Frances Beal, cofounder of the Third World Women's Alliance (TWWA) wrote about the "double jeopardy" of being black and female, a reduction of one axis of oppression whose absence was short-lived, as the naming of the TWWA's newspaper, *Triple Jeopardy*, attests.[7]

Black women activists indeed played central roles in the movements that emerged in the post-World War II era of popular protest, where liberation movements proliferated, cooperated, and sometimes collided. In the black civil rights/black liberation movement, black women worked in organizations devoted to civil rights and also in those organized for peace, for workers' rights, and for women's rights. As relationships among organizations and movements were complicated, the demands on the energies of black women were great. Moving inside and among different movements, most black women activists continued to theorize a consistent politics of their position in their movements, in their communities, in America, and in the world. They self-consciously spoke from social locations that they felt gave them a unique ability to analyze the specific workings of racial and gender hierarchies. In movement terms, they occupied positions at the "interstices" of the black civil rights organizing of the 1950s and 1960s and feminist organizing that developed in mass fashion by the mid-1960s.[8] Without homogenizing theoretical diversity, or arguing that all black women activists agreed as to how to position themselves within existing movements, it is striking how much intellectual continuity postwar black women activists evinced vis à vis their predecessors. Following in the footsteps of figures like Maria Stewart, Amy J. Garvey, and Claudia Jones, many postwar black women activists challenged the widespread "Victorian Philosophy of Womanhood" within their communities by calling themselves "feminists," even while they made clear to white feminists that racism could not be ignored by their movement.[9] And black women became visible figures in more liberal feminist circles: Shirley Chisholm's run for US president in 1972 put a black woman at the forefront of a mainly white feminist movement, while the flamboyant figure of Florynce Kennedy agitated for Chisholm while she tried to get white feminists and black liberationists to see the commonalities in their struggles.[10]

Postwar black feminist activists in a variety of movements thus formulated analysis of the interconnectedness of power relations that was subsequently taken up by black feminists situated in the academy. The black feminist theoretical perspective of the "intersectionality"—of the mutually constitutive nature of oppressive forces in American society—became hegemonic within women's and gender studies in the United States and mainstreamed in gender and women's research. Despite the incorporation of black feminist theory into academic women's studies, black feminist public intellectuals are invisible in the larger public political sphere; as Patricia Hill Collins has noted, there is a gendered demarcation between the few selected black public intellectuals anointed by media and black domestic intellectual workers.[11] The most public of black female figures—Oprah Winfrey—has distanced herself for most of her career from feminist organizing and the black activist community, such that even in her success, she embodies the gendered split between the male public black intellectual "thinker" and the female everyday-oriented "doer." But the recent rise of the BLM movement—whose founders were women and whose inclusionary view of those for whom they fight reflects an intersectional logic—has put black feminist intersectional analysis before the American public in an unprecedented way. The history of postwar black feminist contributions to American critical theory should make us think differently about the relationship between intellectual production and activism, and it might even lead us to counter mainstream media efforts to anoint leaders and ignore the groundswell of activist-intellectuals pushing for change.

BLACK FEMINIST TRIPLE OPPRESSION POLITICS IN US COMMUNIST ORGANIZATIONS

Black women in the American communist Left in the early and midtwentieth century positioned themselves as the most oppressed and thus the necessary vanguard in that internationalist movement. Activists/theoreticians like Grace Campbell, Louise Thompson, Thyra Edwards, Claudia Jones and others participated in the Communist Party in the United States and grassroots organizations, developing what Thompson in 1936 called a "triple exploitation" view of black women's position as workers, women, and blacks.[12] In McDuffie's view, this formulation of black women's being at the bottom of intersecting hierarchies of class, race, and gender "prefigured" similar analyses by black feminists in the 1960s and 1970s. Black left feminists developed these politics as Marxists, but untraditional ones; while Communist Party USA (CPUSA) looked to organize black (male) workers on shopfloors, black Left feminists looked to the plight of female domestic workers, standing on street corners in New York City, waiting to be picked for a day's work by wealthier white women.

Claudia Jones's 1949 essay "An End to the Neglect of the Problems of the Negro Woman!" expressed black Left feminism's view of how communist politics could aid blacks struggling for freedom, and how black women and men could aid the party by focusing its work on the most exploited workers.[13] Jones was born in Trinidad-Tobago in 1915 and came to the United States nine years later. She became active in the NAACP and Urban League while still in high school in New York City. She was active in the fight to free the Scottsboro Boys and joined the CPUSA in 1936 at age of nineteen. She became an activist in US communist politics for decades after that, with the FBI keeping tabs on her all the while. She became the editor for "Negro Affairs" for the *Daily Worker,* and she wrote a column for the *Daily Worker*'s Sunday magazine on women's issues, entitled "Half the World."[14] In 1953, Jones was convicted for violating the Alien Registration Act of 1940 (the so-called Smith Act), largely on the basis of her continued work for the party, and she was imprisoned for almost a year; she was then deported under the McCarran Internal Security Act of 1950, as her many efforts to become an American citizen had been denied. Jones spent the few remaining years of her life in Great Britain, where she started a newspaper for the West Indian community called the *West Indian Gazette*. Ill health, exacerbated by the stay in prison, took its toll, and she died at the age of forty-nine in 1964. Jones is buried, as biographer Carole Boyce Davies has noted, just to "the left of Karl Marx" in London's Highgate Cemetery.

Jones was a prolific writer and poet, but her most famous and most prescient work was "An End to the Neglect of the Problems of the Negro Woman!" In the essay, addressed chiefly to fellow leftists, Jones reprimands the party and leftist progressives for their failure to understand the particular position of Negro women in the United States. She places the Negro woman at the center of the family, as a "mother, as Negro, and as worker [who] fights against the wiping out of the Negro family." The Left's failure to understand the position of black women as the "most oppressed stratum of the whole population" means that leftists had failed to confront their own "chauvinism," that is their own prejudices against Negro women.[15] Prefiguring arguments later made by black feminist theorist Patricia Hill Collins, about controlling images that constrain black women's lives in America, Jones wrote that "[in] the film, radio, and press, the Negro woman is not pictured in her real role as breadwinner, mother, and protector of the family, but as a traditional 'mammy' who put the care of children and families of others above her own."[16]

Jones's essay also contains an examination of black women's role in slavery—including instances where black men did not examine their own male chauvinism—and specifically cites Christianity as a force pushing black women down. At the same time, she lauds the central position of black women as the backbone of black community organizing and laments their lack of participation in trade unions and party organizations. She faults the party for failing to organize domestic laborers, and she has these words for white feminists who fail to understand their privilege: "Chauvinism on the part of progressive white women is often expressed in their failure ... to realize that this fight for equality of Negro women is in their own self-interest, inasmuch as the super-exploitation of Negro women tends to depress the standards of all women."[17] Jones goes on to cite specific instances of chauvinism in the Party and also describes the heroics of activist Negro women in the same party circles.

Jones's analysis, however bounded in Communist rhetoric, was ahead of its time in some ways, although consistent with the kinds of writings that black Left feminists were disseminating at the time. Her emphasis on black women as the most oppressed and therefore the vanguard of the communist movement presages very similar arguments made by black feminists who came out of the civil rights and liberation movements from the 1960s on, as I will discuss below. But in one way, Jones was not quite the protointersectional feminist that some might hope she was; she wrote quite clearly that "the Negro question in the United States is *prior* to, and not equal to, the woman question," seemingly placing gender oppression as product of racial (and perhaps class) oppression.[18] She nonetheless links race, gender, and class continuously in her essay, concluding that Negro women were "a powerful lever for bringing forward Negro workers—men and women—as the leading forces of the Negro people's liberation movement, [and] for cementing Negro and white unity in the struggle against Wall Street imperialism."[19]

Were Jones's ideas lost in the backlash against the Left in 1950s America, or in the early 1960s severing of the Old Left from the New Left? Certainly, it was difficult for communist black feminists to make much headway during the 1950s, when Cold War politics dominated mainstream political space, and black civil rights protest dominated the social movement sector. Nonetheless, as McDuffie notes, black Left feminists continued organizing, and in some ways the 1950s represented the height of their independent organizing. The group Sojourners for Truth and Justice, founded in New York City in 1951, was a short-lived but theoretically important example of triple jeopardy thinking melded with a transnational feminist approach to thinking about black women's place in the United States and the world.[20] The group included communist and noncommunist women, and their inclusion of communist women violated some civil rights organizations' proscriptions against working with communists. In October of 1951, their first convention in Washington, DC drew 132 women from all over the country; Claudia Jones could not attend because she was barred by the government from traveling outside of New York City. In its short life, members of Sojourners participated in US-based and international struggles; several members signed the petition to the United States "We Charge Genocide," put forward by the civil rights Congress comparing racial violence in the United States to the Holocaust.[21] Members were also active in publicizing and aiding the antiapartheid struggle in South Africa, drawing links between black women's oppression there and in the United States.

The ideas and internationalist perspectives evidenced in black Left feminist thought and organizing were recapitulated a scant decade later in the writings and activism of 1960s-1990s Black feminists who emerged from the civil rights movement. This time, the ideas about the linked nature of oppressions in black women's lives and the utility of the analysis of those linkages would become more widespread and would prove to be a major contribution to feminist theory inside and outside the academy.

Beginning in the very early 1960s, black feminist theorists emerged from space they occupied within the interstices of the black civil rights/black liberation movement and feminist movements in the 1960s and 1970s. Following the "organizing their own" ethos of 1960s and 1970s left politics, they formed a variety of organizations from the center to the far left.[22] In an era where bridging racial divides among feminists was difficult, few black feminist voices from the left were heard in mainstream media; the task of challenging the American body politic to live up to the promises of rights and opportunities was taken up by black feminist figures with closer ties to liberal white feminists. Congresswoman Shirley Chisholm, the first black woman to run for a major party's presidential nomination, and Florynce Kennedy, a provocative civil rights lawyer who toured with feminist icon Gloria Steinem to bring feminist messages to communities across the United States, were much better known than the black feminists agitating in the leftist social movement sector. Both Chisholm and, especially, Kennedy remain underappreciated as public intellectuals, despite their visibility at the time, but leftist black feminists theorized a so-far enduring vision of interacting oppressions—that is, the intersectionality of oppressions—that has become pervasive in women's and gender studies and that has of late shown signs of escaping into mainstream political vocabularies.

As the black civil rights movement fragmented in the mid-to late 1960s, transforming itself partially into a more liberationist movement, black women activists saw the "Victorian Philosophy of Womanhood" linger and sit uncomfortably next to increasing militancy about race. Writing in novelist/activist Toni Cade Bambara's landmark 1970 collection, *The Black Woman*, civil rights activist Gwen Patton highlighted the contradictions within the movement about black women's roles. As Patton saw it, black women and many black men recognized that the fully domesticated private role was a privilege of white womanhood and unattainable for black women. On the other hand, many members of the black activist community, both male and female, argued that women had to step back from public responsibilities within organizations in order to right the wrongs done to black manhood by slavery, Jim Crow, and contemporary racism. These contradictory ideas had their analogue in real-life dramas involving the position of women in the civil rights movement—the way that, as Charles Payne has put it, "the men led, but the women organized."[23] The public face of leadership in the civil rights movement was a male face, and many regarded that as essential to the cause; key activists such as Ella Baker who handled crucial responsibilities were nonetheless kept as behind-the-scenes or "interim" directors, regarded as facilitators rather than real leaders.[24] While participants in the movement recognized the essential contributions of black women and celebrated the emergence of charismatic black women leaders such as Fannie Lou Hamer, it was rare for a woman like Hamer to break through what was consistently a "great man" narrative of the movement.

Hamer's radicalism, like Ella Baker's—their insistence on grassroots, radical democratic participation—came to be underplayed over time, especially as the movement became younger and more Northern.[25] Hamer, Baker, and other black women leaders in the civil rights movement emerged between the mid-1950s and mid-1960s, when the movement was predominantly rooted in local community institutions in the South.[26] But by the midsixties, when the movement's social base shifted, becoming younger and more Northern, there was an infusion of a narrowly masculinist version of black nationalism. Black women were discouraged from keeping the positions of responsibility that they had held and were expected to take increasingly subservient roles behind the scenes. These role constrictions sat poorly with many black women, who argued that male activists were being influenced by a white middle-class conception of traditional gender roles that had critics in the black community and that contradicted the revolutionary goals of some movement activists. At the same time, white women's liberation groups were becoming a visible presence on the left. Emerging black feminists were equally critical of what they saw as white feminists' preoccupation with issues that were relevant only to white middle-class women's lives and thus attributed the limitations of both movements in large part to their failure to maintain consistent class critiques of injustice.[27]

By the mid-1960s, white feminists were organizing within liberal and leftist sectors of American society, with most scholars of postwar white feminism seeing at least two organizationally distinct feminist movements: one that emerged from professional women's networks within government and liberal foundations and unions; another that came out of radical Left political circles, chiefly situated on college campuses and large Northern cities.[28] Black women played central roles as activists for women's rights in liberal institutions such as the Ford Foundation, in liberal unions, and on President Kennedy's Presidential Commission on the Status of Women.[29] They were central figures in the formation of the liberal feminist group National Organization for Women (NOW), with labor activist/ Equal Employment Opportunity commissioner Aileen C. Hernández voted in as NOW's second president.[30]

While many black women, including Hernández, grew disillusioned with the ability of white feminists to incorporate concerns about race, these emergent liberal feminist organizations included black women from the beginning and sometimes gave them platforms from which to agitate for change. The most public black feminist of the 1970s was undoubtedly Congresswoman Shirley Chisholm, who ran for president in 1972.[31] Chisholm was the daughter of immigrants from Barbados who grew up both there and in New York City. She was a stellar student at Brooklyn College and a member of civil rights organizations who became active in the Democratic Party in Bedford-Stuyvesant. Chisholm's biographer, Barbara Winslow, captures the challenges Chisholm faced at every point of her long career in politics:

> Once on the political stage as a "first"—the first African American woman from Brooklyn elected to the New York state Legislature, the first African American woman elected to Congress, and then the first African American woman to make a run for the Democratic Party nomination for president—she found she had to fight constantly against the racial and gender prejudices of everyone around her. The media, the Congressional Black Caucus . . . and civil rights and feminist leaders often dismissed, underestimated, or patronized her. She held her ground, insisting that she was her own person—"Unbought and Unbossed" was her trademark slogan . . . Her support for social justice, feminism, radical Black nationalists, students, and prisoners fighting injustice, as well as her opposition to U.S. foreign policy, places her to the left of center and certainly outside the politics of the Democratic party today. Yet she chose not to participate in the social justice, civil rights, antiwar, or women's demonstrations, instead staying within the confines of the electoral political process.[32]

Winslow notes that Chisholm's run for president was more than a stunt; she thought herself qualified and intended to take her delegates to the convention in Miami and push the Democratic Party to the left. After her run, she stayed in Congress for ten more years, eventually leaving to teach and help found the National Political Congress of Black Women.

To the left of Chisholm—but still more than willing to work with liberal feminists—civil rights lawyer Florynce Kennedy repeatedly tried to maneuver between liberal feminist, left feminist and black liberationist circles during the 1960s and 1970s, all the while welcoming whatever media coverage came her way. In her recent biography, historian Sheryl M. Randolph traces

Kennedy's activist path, from a lawyer defending the civil rights of entertainers, including singer Billie Holiday, to a political hostess holding parties and salon-type activities for leftists in New York City, to writing a weekly column for a local black newspaper and hosting a radio program. Kennedy was firmly entrenched in a milieu that linked struggles against racism, classism, and US imperialism; she made connections throughout the 1960s and 1970s to Black Power and liberal and radical feminisms, involving herself in Black Power/black liberation projects such as the mid-1960s Black Power Conference and the Media Workshop and bringing her views about linked oppressions of race and gender to her work with NOW, arguing that the nascent organization should ally itself with Black Power. While NOW rebuffed those attempts, Kennedy continued to come to meetings of New York City's NOW chapter, and she brought white feminists Ti-Grace Atkinson and Peg Brennan to the Black Power conference, where they were decidedly unwelcome. But these rejections did not stop Kennedy from continuing to speak for what we would now call an intersectional view of liberation. While she was seldom successful in making the links among organizations that she wanted to see, she was, as Randolph notes a "bridge leader," employing sociologist Belinda Robnett's concept of a female civil rights activists who moved behind the scenes trying to link organizations seeking social change.[33]

Kennedy was a different kind of bridge leader in that she did not operate only behind the scenes. She had a high profile as a black feminist when she paired herself with Gloria Steinem on a speaking tour that took them to college campuses and local feminist groups in 1970; she was public in her support of Shirley Chisholm's historic run for president; and she was instrumental in establishing grassroots support for the insurgent Feminist Party (which actually nominated Chisholm for president a year before her attempt to gain the Democratic nomination). Kennedy also played a catalyzing role in the formation of the National Black Feminist Organization (NBFO) in 1973. As an activist, Kennedy operated as a kind of catalyst and did not usually stick with organizations for the long haul; however, as a visible black feminist who (most?) often appeared in front of white audiences and who was not afraid of making the case for liberation in provocative and sometimes profane ways, Kennedy helped to lay some groundwork for the acceptance of a black feminist politics and of a feminist black politics as well.

On the left, black feminists moved to form their own organizations that developed along a separate organizational path from white women's liberation groups. Their "separate road to feminism" was a reflection of a strand of 1960s leftist thinking that emphasized the need for self-determination by oppressed groups and was in line with older articulations by black women activists about the need to simultaneously challenge racial and gender hierarchy.[34] In forming black feminist organizations and seeking racial and gender liberation, they were the postwar daughters of Maria Stewart, rather strikingly intellectualized, as activists considered theory-making to be a form of activism in and of itself. Students at historically black colleges and universities formed the vanguard of the civil rights movement, not just with their bodies but also through their engagement with radical theory. Feminist movement activists who had mobilized in earnest by the mid-1960s sprang from networks formed in the civil rights movement and in other national liberation movements and were likely to be "middle-class" in trajectory if not in background. Feminists who organized on the left around newly emerging women's issues were, for the most part, highly educated young women who were interested in uncovering the history of gender oppression and understanding its current day manifestations, in order to end it. The idea that a proper understanding of sexism was the only way to eradicate it was analogous to the way in which New Left participants sought an end to class oppression and imperialism through a study of varieties of Marxism. In seeking large-scale social change and transformation, feminists organizing within and outside racial/ethnic movements saw the redress of their grievances as predicated on arriving at accurate, persuasive analyses of inequality and injustice.

Within the black oppositional community of the 1960s, emerging black feminists searched for proper theory as the predicate for proper activism. A widely read example of black feminist activist ideology was the position paper produced by Frances Beal and a number of other authors who were founders of the Third World Women's Alliance (TWWA), one of the most influential of the black feminist groups formed in the postwar era.[35] The TWWA was an offshoot of the Student Nonviolent Coordinating Committee (SNCC); in its initial incarnation it was a black women's committee within SNCC.

In 1969 Frances Beal and others wrote "Double Jeopardy: To Be Black and Female," which was published in 1970 in two important feminist anthologies: Toni Cade Bambara's *The Black Woman* and Robin Morgan's more well known *Sisterhood Is Powerful*.[36] In "Double Jeopardy," Beal and her coauthors laid responsibility for the cultural ideal of black "manhood" squarely at the feet of American capitalism. They argued that the construction of masculinity and femininity was driven by the need of American capitalists to sell products. Black women, who had historically worked outside the home, could not conform to the idea of a "typical" (i.e., white) middle-class woman, staying home and buying these consumer products. It therefore made no sense, argued Beal, for the black community to support a system that was not designed for them. Beal and the other members of the TWWA pointedly criticized male, black liberation activists for taking their guidelines for gender analysis "from the pages of the *Ladies Home Journal.*"[37] While TWWA members like Beal were sympathetic to black men's suffering at the hands of white society, like other black feminists, they nonetheless maintained that the black woman had been "the slave of a slave" and that black women's dignity and sexual personhood had always been as much under assault as black men's.[38] In line with the TWWA's anti-capitalist and anti-imperialist politics, Beal and the collective argued that consistent class, gender, and race analysis by the black movement was required in order to purge the movement of its inappropriate white middle-class goals. Black feminists and other organized black women, could, in the TWWA's opinion, productively steer the entire black movement's course, if others in the community would only let them.

Beal and her coauthors in the TWWA exemplified a striking consistency within postwar black feminism about the need for activism that was theoretically informed, and that simultaneously addressed the interlocking forces of race, gender, and class domination. Without ignoring differences of emphases among them, this group of black feminist activists included Pat Robinson of The Black Women's Liberation Group of Mount Vernon/New Rochelle, New York, which was among the first black feminist groups formed in the 1960s. Robinson, who had a background as a black activist and an advocate for birth control, cowrote widely circulated position papers with an explicitly militant, black feminist and anti-capitalist agenda.[39] Other lesser known black feminist figures who shared visions of intersectional black feminist politics include MaryAnne Weathers of the TWWA; Nina Harding, a thirty-one year old black studies major at the University of Washington, Seattle, a mother, employee of the Seattle Opportunities Industrialization Center, and author of the 1970 pamphlet "The Interconnections Between the Black Struggle and the Woman Question"; and Margaret Wright, a union activist and member of a Los Angeles-based women's liberation group.[40] More publicly-recognized black women activists like Pauli Murray tied together concerns for racial and gender liberation. Murray emerged from her work in postwar liberal foundations and government commissions, writing about feminist issues and becoming the nation's first black female Episcopal priest.[41]

Black women fiction writers also engaged questions of feminism in various ways. Toni Cade (later Toni Cade Bambara), a novelist and short story writer, edited the afore-mentioned collection *The Black Woman*. Novelists Toni Morrison and Alice Walker were both critical of organized white feminism and committed in their political writings to a broad intersectional perspective. Morrison saw white feminists as blind to the material reality of black women's lives but tempered her criticism with the speculation that the appearance of prominent black women within the ranks of white women's liberation might broaden the movement so that it would one day be fighting for a more broadly based set of rights which included economic survival.[42] Alice Walker's dissatisfaction with the failure of white feminists to engage all aspects of liberation led to her invention of the term "womanism" to describe the feminism of black women and other women of color.[43] Finally, in the postwar period, some black female writers became well known specifically for being black feminists, with some adding another "street" to the intersection—that of sexuality. Audre Lorde; bell hooks; Michelle Wallace; Sweet Honey in the Rock founder Bernice Johnson Reagon; Angela Davis; and Gloria Hull, Patricia Bell Scott, and, especially Barbara Smith, coeditors of the 1982 anthology *All the Women Are White, All the Men Are Black, but Some of Us Are Brave* engaged in a dialogue with organized white feminism and antifeminists in the black activist and increasingly the black academic community.[44]

By the end of the 1980s, the Combahee River Collective (CRC) had added sexuality as another axis of oppression that needed to be fought along with those of gender, race, and class. The CRC was an offshoot of the NBFO that formed in the Boston/Cambridge area. The group became well known for its position paper "A Black Feminist Statement" which appeared in feminist anthologies.[45] In the summer of 1974, CRC members decided to become independent from the NBFO; they were a small group, with most members active in lesbian and socialist feminist groups. The CRC added an explicitly prolesbian, antihomophobia stance to black feminist vanguard center politics, arguing, "If Black women were free, it would mean that everyone else would have to be free since our freedom would necessitate the destruction of all the systems of oppression."[46] Members of CRC stressed the need to take on simultaneous oppressions through discussion that would enable black women to better understand their position. In its focus on intellectual development coupled with activism as a way of life, the CRC was aided by being situated in Boston/Cambridge's extremely vibrant local activist milieu. From 1977 to 1979, the CRC met locally and also held a series of six retreats between 1977 and 1979 in order to think about their efforts as black feminists.[47] Among the work that CRC members read was Toni Cade

Bambara's collection *The Black Woman*, a work that influenced the CRC's "A Black Feminist Statement." Like other black feminist groups, the CRC placed itself in the difficult space of being critical of other black community and white feminist organizations. CRC members saw themselves as fighting at the juncture between these organizations, doing so without "racial, sexual, heterosexual or class privilege to rely upon."[48] As a black lesbian-identified group, the CRC rejected black liberationist politics that could not even admit to the existence of lesbian relationships. At the same time, CRC members rejected lesbian separatism, by the late 1970s a dominant strand in white feminist cultural politics.[49] CRC members argued that lesbian separatism left out "far too many people, particularly Black men, women, and children."[50] In practice, CRC members were active in struggles such as showing support for Kenneth Edelin, a Boston African American physician who was arrested for performing a legal abortion; they became involved in local efforts to assure the hiring of black laborers for a school being built in the black community; they championed the case of L. L. Ellison, a black woman prisoner at Framingham State Prison who had killed a guard in self-defense against sexual assault; and they worked to publicize the murders of a dozen black women in the late 1970s, charging the city and local media with neglect of the issues.[51] In 1979, in response to a series of murders of young women in the Boston area, the CRC published a pamphlet entitled "Why Did They Die?"[52] Twelve black women and one white woman had been killed in the first half of 1979, and police had failed to act swiftly after the murders; their disregard led to meetings within the affected communities and the forming of an organization called CRISIS, which further publicized the murders, organized self-defense classes, and set up neighborhood watches. The CRC pamphlet was designed to be reproduced without permission; it included self-defense tips along with an analysis of schisms between the organized black and white feminist communities. It was reprinted in *Radical America* in 1979, where the editors characterized the CRC as a minority voice within the black community which had nonetheless seen success in spreading awareness of black feminism.

The CRC was never very large, but despite its size and somewhat fractious history, it was an example of black feminist success on its own terms.[53] The members of the CRC, perhaps more explicitly than other black feminist groups, articulated an alternative to universalistic visions of sisterhood that erased differences between women, and its statements offered a way to think about the proliferation of identities around which feminist (and other) organizing was happening.

As feminist mobilization waxed and the black movement waned in the 1960s and 1970s, black feminists were able to make their theories central to feminist studies in the United States. Postwar black feminist protest produced a generation of activist/theorists who developed historically based explanations about the particular nexus of oppressions that black women faced. These theoretical and activist writings came to be seen as coalescing into a feminist theory of "intersectionality" that has become the dominant perspective animating gender studies.[54]

INTERSECTIONALITY AND ITS ROOTS IN THE VANGUARD CENTER: THEORY BUILT FROM ACTIVISM

In 1989, Kimberlé Crenshaw published an article in *The University of Chicago Legal Forum* entitled "Demarginalizing the Intersection of Race and Sex: A Black Feminist Critique of Antidiscrimination Doctrine, Feminist Theory and Antiracist Politics." Crenshaw is a critical race legal scholar at UCLA and Columbia.[55] In this article, and in subsequent work, Crenshaw argued against what she saw as a lack of attention paid in the law to the specific lived experiences of black women. She used real world examples to illustrate the ineffectiveness of law enforcement and judicial responses to the concrete circumstances of black women's lives with a view to demonstrating the law's blind spots regarding the confluence of racial and gender oppression. Crenshaw wrote of the "need to account for multiple grounds of identity when considering how the social world is constructed," arguing that black women's position in American society could not be captured by viewing their needs as solely generated by their membership in a historically dominated racial/ethnic group or as solely a result of their gender status.[56] Consequently, Crenshaw posited that communities of color were actually "coalitions" rather than homogenous groups where all members had identical interests. She maintained that identity politics, while viable, were thus oversimplified; even within oppressed racial/ethnic communities, some members were relatively privileged, and others were treated worse by dominant institutions. Crenshaw therefore concluded that legal theorists had to understand the specific history and current incarnations of that different treatment in order to create effective legal standards that would actually protect black women as blacks *and* as women.[57]

"Intersectionality" is the term that came into use after Crenshaw's work was disseminated within critical race studies, ethnic studies, and women's and gender studies. It has become the dominant perspective in American women's studies and has been influential internationally, with Crenshaw herself invited to take part in United Nations-sponsored meetings of the global antiracist and feminist community.[58] Her writings on intersectionality emerged at a time when American white feminist activists were dealing in earnest with critiques of the racial politics of the supposedly unified feminist movement. While second-generation critiques of intersectionality have noted the multiple ways in which the perspective has been employed and the subsequent lack of analytical clarity that promiscuous use of the perspective has encouraged, most critics acknowledge the concept's power for feminist theory making.[59] However, Crenshaw's persuasive formulation of intersectionality was not fashioned out of wholly new ideas but in line with the emphases of black women activists historically. As noted, intersectional thinking as a theoretical perspective was present in the writings of black women communists and socialists in the United States; in the post-World War II period, black feminist activists constructed an intersectional ideology of simultaneous liberation from racial, sexual, and class oppression as part of their politics. They placed themselves at the "vanguard center" of various movements, seeing themselves as the key group whose liberation would hasten everyone else's.[60] Theorizing their place at the intersection of oppressive structures, black feminists saw their struggle as central, in a manner analogous to the way that Marxists argued that the liberation of the proletariat would overturn capitalist class domination.

Intersectionality has subsequently had a decades-long journey through intellectual circles. A 2013 special issue of the gender studies journal *Signs* took an overview of what has come to be known as intersectionality studies, as did a special issue of the *DuBois Review*.[61] In 2016, three feminist scholars, including black feminist scholar Patricia Hill Collins, published books on intersectionality's history and promise.[62] Second-generation debates about intersectionality have centered on a number of questions, with black feminist scholars showing concern for how the concept is deployed. Jennifer Nash has succinctly summed up the debates as trying to answer the question of "*who* is intersectional?" As Nash has put it, "(i)ntersectionality's reliance on Black women as the basis for its claims to complex subjectivity renders Black women prototypical intersectional subjects whose experiences of marginality are imagined to provide a *theoretical value-added*." Nash further argues that intersectional theorists have "obscured the question of whether *all* identities are intersectional or whether only multiply marginalized subjects have an intersectional identity."[63]

Nash keeps the question of the extending intersectional analysis beyond the study of the marginalized an open one, while other feminist theorists have argued that intersectionality's popularity has led to the erasure of marginalized women from many analyses, an outcome directly counter to what Crenshaw, not to mention activist theorists, intended. Jordan-Zachery, writing about the state of research on black women's lives in political science, argues that even researchers who use intersectionality as a guideline in theory, have in practice only focused on the lives of black women elected to public office; this research emphasis obscures what might be very differently lived politics on the part of other black women. More forcefully, Floyd-Alexander has argued that many feminist researchers, particularly those in political science and sociology, have employed intersectionality in a way that obscures the focus on the black women whose lives, theorizing, and research gave birth to the concept. Floyd-Alexander argues that researchers who expand intersectionality beyond the boundaries of exploring black women's lives engage in one or both of two problematic strategies of erasure: "bait and switch," in which "Black women stand as a proxy for would-be white victims," that is, where black women's lives are explored only to really focus a lens on how white women are affected by some phenomenon; and "universalizing," where "activists or other political actors suggest that a particular issue goes beyond the experience of women of color and is relevant to a broader community of women, the effect of which is to typically highlight the plight of white women and not that of Black women."[64]

These and other critiques are to be expected, as the intersectional perspective, broadly defined, dominates American feminist studies. Today, works with an intersectional perspective occupy pride of place as part of the nearly two hundred undergraduate women's studies programs at universities and colleges in the United States, thirty-one master's-level programs, and sixteen PhD programs.[65] While feminist theorists debate the utility and underpinnings of the intersectional perspective, the perspective itself seems lodged in place, despite concerns about how it requires complex contextual grounding in doing research itself.[66] Postwar black feminist theory is current feminist theory. In contrast, black studies has not been captured by black feminist or other perspectives, despite the individual prominence of some black feminists within the field. American black studies as a field is rather more fragmented than American women's studies, with nationalists, multiculturalists, diasporeans, feminists, socialists, and others engaged in more active battles over what the dominant perspective within the field should be.[67]

THE PUBLIC WORLD: THE INVISIBILITY OF BLACK FEMINIST INTELLECTUALS AND NEW VISIBILITY IN THE BLM MOVEMENT

Intersectional perspectives have a radical history and retain their activist edges, but until very recently, black feminist intellectuals who espouse this perspective have not been visible in the American body politic. Rather, popular political discourse still paints the position of the black woman as one that involves making a painful existential choice between being black and being female, with questions of class and sexuality seldom even making it into the discussion. This logic of irreconcilable choice was underscored in the reporting on the role of black women in the 2008 presidential race. Given that the top two contenders for the Democratic Party nomination were a black man and a white woman, one might have thought that black women were in an especially good place to identify with a candidate. However, a 2007 article in the *New York Times* posited the existence of a "Clinton-Obama Quandary for Many Black Women." The reporter's stance about the position of black women was that they had to be painfully ambivalent about the question of for whom to vote, their "loyalties" tested by the "puzzling" choice that confronted them. The idea that black women couldn't really lose given the Obama-Clinton primary match-up did not occur to the reporter, despite quotes from black women that indicated that no such quandary existed for them. One black woman in South Carolina was quoted as stating, "[t]his is history here.... On both sides. Either way, it's history. So let's see what history going to bring in." Another told the reporter that "[w]hoever it is ... we just ask the Lord to bless them and take care of them."[68]

The "either/or" logic of popular politics—loyalty must be demonstrated to the "larger" black community or the "larger" feminist community—is, of course, the same logic that prompted black feminists to assert the necessity of having an intersectional perspective. But while black feminist theory has become central to feminist studies in the academy and beyond, it is hard to think of a black feminist who is a well-known public figure. Angela Davis is a recognizable name to many (older) Americans, but she is more vilified for her past radicalism and imprisonment than celebrated for her continued radicalism and continuing research. Davis is a professor emerita at the University of California, Santa Cruz, in the history of consciousness and feminist studies programs, retiring in 2008 after more than seventeen years spent teaching at the school. She was a keynote speaker at the 2009 annual meeting of the National Women's Studies Association (whose president, Beverly

Guy-Sheftal, is the founder of the Women's Research and Resource Center at Spelman College). Although in demand as a speaker before college and academic crowds, Davis has a much lower profile than black male academic figures such as Cornel West and Henry Louis Gates, both of whom receive regular—if sometimes unwanted—attention from the mainstream media.

Patricia Hill Collins—herself a lauded black feminist sociologist and a recent president of the American Sociological Association—has argued that the prominent place of a few chosen intellectual stars reflects America's deeply gendered and racialized ideas about public and private political space. Hill Collins sees public political/media space as not just neutrally about work and government but as fundamentally male, with a "private sphere of gender and sexuality to give it meaning."[69] She examines the current position of "Black intellectual celebrities" by contrasting their lives to that of W. E. B. Du Bois, who never had a "cozy academic position" from which to work.[70] Significantly, Hill Collins notes that Du Bois himself, though sympathetic to feminism, had more attenuated ties to the intellectual concerns of such important black women activists as Anna Julia Cooper and Ida B. Wells-Barnett. Citing Hazel Carby, Hill Collins argued that the gendered division of labor—whereby Wells-Barnett, for example, was deemed an "activist" and Du Bois an "intellectual"—"suggests that scholars routinely relegate women to the realm of 'domestic intellectual labor,' whose purpose is to remain invisible and support the accomplishments of male intellectuals."[71] This gendered and racial division of labor is supported by mainstream media, which, in order to maintain the fiction of a post–civil rights movement color-blind America, find a few black faces to tout; according to Hill Collins, these selected black intellectuals "function in this allegedly color-blind context that buys, sells, and rents people and their images for popular consumption."[72] Black public intellectuals—male, tenured, freed of most day-to-day teaching responsibilities—have different roles than the "Black domestic intellectuals" whom Hill Collins sees as carrying the bulk of the burden for educating black youth. In Hill Collins's view, the inclusion of a few African American luminaries in the public political sphere functions as a new "veil" which obscures the reality of the continuing exclusion of large numbers of African Americans from academic life. The new veil consists of a short list of black public intellectuals whose mass-media visibility belies their actual numbers and establishes a pecking order among them. Some become academic superstars, like Henry Louis Gates and Cornel West. Consulted less often as a black public intellectual, writer Toni Morrison rounds out the top three. Some are unabashedly self-promoting, like Michael Eric Dyson; others, like

Manning Marable, often find themselves in the limelight yet shy away from media attention. The brilliance or intellectual commitment of this list of academic superstars is less the issue here than the ways in which mass media and institutions of higher education make use of them.[73]

At any given moment, there is only room for a few black intellectual "stars" to cross over, leaving those domestic intellectuals working at the lower echelons of universities overburdened and undersupported. These domestic intellectuals are disproportionately black women who are charged with actually educating students and who are often seen by those very institutions as not producing enough "scholarly" work. Thus, the black public luminary/black domestic intellectual split is a gendered split, where received wisdom about the proper places of women and men in the private sphere is grafted onto the purportedly public space of the academy.

To be fair, there are times when the luminaries themselves are attacked.[74] But Hill Collins's larger point seems defensible, insofar as public intellectual space is gendered and racialized: black feminist intellectuals are invisible to the public at large. The most significant black female voice of our times—Oprah Winfrey—is literally one concerned with taking care of our domestic lives. Winfrey's various personae—as talk show host, mother confessor, taste maker, book promoter, political operator, actress, film producer, magazine creator, and, most recently, cable network owner/inspiration—have elevated her to the level of media-celebrated demigoddess and made her one of the richest celebrities in the world.[75] But despite her media moguldom, Winfrey's celebrity is a domesticated one, and until very recently, it is also celebrity that is attenuated in terms of its relationship to the movements that made her position possible. In her introduction to a 2009 collection of essays called *Stories of Oprah: The Oprahfication of American Culture*, coeditor Kimberly Springer wrote that while Winfrey is regularly cited as one of the most influential people in the United States, the measure of her influence is economic, and not intellectual. Winfrey sees her influence on the public as a result of her being a role model; her message is inextricably linked to her lifestyle, which is packaged and sold (mostly) to women. In packaging her message as part of her lifestyle, Springer notes that Winfrey "credits neither the civil rights nor women's movement activism with contributing to her successful rise from news anchor to media giant. Instead she credits inner strength and spirituality."[76] Winfrey has been quoted as eschewing the role of black leader, emphasizing instead her possession of unproblematic black and female identity in a postracial world: "People feel you have to lead a civil rights movement every day of your life, that you have to be a spokeswoman and represent *the race*. . . . Blackness is something I just am. I'm Black. I'm a woman. I wear a size 10 shoe. It's all the same to me."[77]

Despite the statement above, Winfrey has also been quoted as saying that she sees herself as part of a tradition of black women trying to succeed in America.[78] This individualist take on the tradition of black movement activism extends as well to Winfrey's complicated stance vis à vis feminist movement activism. Winfrey does not claim an explicitly "feminist" label. Instead, she is what Jennifer Rexroat, using Patricia Misciagno's term, calls a de facto feminist, and her place in the media broadly supports the tenets of American liberal feminism.[79] According to John Howard, Winfrey's view of black women activists in American history decontextualizes them from the communal struggles in which they participated: "[E]ach is understood as an individual, an admirable role model of personal fortitude and striving."[80] But Rexroat contends that Winfrey's decontextualized feminism is still feminism: her "everywoman" persona embodies the contradictions of contemporary de facto feminism, which is based on the possession of a "feminist consciousness, at the expense of feminist praxis."[81] By refusing to identify with the feminist movement, Winfrey is able to "deliver feminist messages" without "risking the alienation of her audience, advertisers, and the mass public."[82]

Winfrey's relationship to the history, if not the present, of the black civil rights movement has shifted in recent years, evidenced by her involvement with two films about the experience of black Americans fighting segregation: *Lee Daniels' The Butler* (2013) and *Selma* (2014).[83] Winfrey had been an executive producer on director Daniels's acclaimed film *Precious*; he wrote a part for her in *The Butler* and convinced the busy Winfrey, who had not acted since her role in the 1998 film adaptation of the Toni Morrison novel *Beloved*, to take it. Winfrey played Gloria, the wife of Cecil Gaines, the White House butler of the title. Gaines is used as a lens to understand the position of blacks under segregation, the changes wrought in black lives by the black civil rights movement, and the way in which the movement splintered as the 1960s wore on. While working on *The Butler*, Winfrey met the young British-Nigerian actor David Oyelowo, who played the Gaines's son, Louis. In the movie, Louis rejects what he sees as his father's capitulation to white racism; in one of the film's most powerful scenes, Gloria slaps Louis for disrespecting his father.

Oyelowo and Winfrey became good friends, and Winfrey went on to become a producer on *Selma*, a film that dramatized the events surrounding the 1965 marches from Selma to Montgomery, Alabama. *Selma* was directed by a black female director, Ava DuVernay, and starred Oyelowo as the Reverend

Martin Luther King Jr.; Winfrey had a small part as the activist Annie Lee Cooper, who famously confronted the local police by trying to register to vote. *Selma* was well received by most critics, and the film received Academy Award nominations for best picture and best original song, winning the latter. Oyelowo and DuVernay were snubbed in the nomination process. Winfrey participated in press junkets, was present at a White House screening of the film, and walked with others across Selma's Edmund Pettis Bridge to commemorate the fiftieth anniversary of the original event.[84] In her public statements about her roles in making these films, Winfrey paid homage both to the extraordinary efforts of select individuals such as King and Cooper and to the necessity of the civil rights struggle as a collective effort.

In stark contrast to her embrace of a legacy of collective black struggle, there are no equivalent gestures on Winfrey's part of rapprochement with the feminist movement as a movement per se. And given her position in the public sphere, some readers might wonder if Winfrey should be considered an intellectual as such, let alone a black feminist one. But Winfrey embodies the way that post World War II black feminist activism has split into two directions: one in the confined realm of women's studies within the academy, and thus largely hidden from mainstream view; the other, hypervisible in everyday media, but almost completely disassociated from the movements and movement-related ideas that spawned it. In the American public realm, Winfrey's fame is predicated on being black but more because she most often speaks of herself as an individual who has achieved because of her inner strength and spiritual steadfastness. In contrast, within gender studies, black feminists' theories have seen success on the basis of being about black women's day-to-day lives, and the universality of black feminist insights are seen as predicated on the ability to speak the truth about the intersection of *social* statuses.

The bifurcation of black feminism may be easing a touch, as social movement activists have renewed the imperative of intersectional thinking about oppressions in black lives. If we look beyond the emergence of discrete black public intellectual figures, we can see where black feminist intersectional thought is having its biggest impact: on the ground. It is difficult to know exactly when an academic concept escapes the academy and becomes part of popular discourse, but in the past several years, "intersectionality" and "intersectional" have done just that. The word gained attention when Dr. William Barber II, one of the leaders of the Moral Mondays movement of clergy and lay people seeking social justice, explained how participants understood current progressive struggles as linked to each other.[85] *New York*

Times columnist Charles Blow used it when writing about the troubles of a black, gay cousin.[86] Debates about 2016 presidential candidate Hillary Clinton's brand of feminism include queries about how intersectional that feminism is, especially since she doesn't use the word "intersectional," which at least one political writer thinks still bears the taint of the academy.[87] But yet another article describes the activism of a young New York City Muslim activist in the BLM movement as "loud, strident and inflected with both street smarts and the tropes of 'intersectionality,' as the trending term has it," showing that at least for the *Times* readership, the term does not need to be explained.[88]

Black feminist intersectional theory has directly influenced the BLM movement, one of the most visible (and in some circles, vilified) social movements of the past decade. Although this movement has sometimes been seen as "hashtag activism—referring to the viral popularity of its "#Blacklivesmatter" Twitter hashtag campaign—BLM has been able to draw many participants to marches and demonstrations that occur in real life. It had founders who created a website, a Facebook page, and a political presence that has continuously brought protestors out in cities where police have killed black civilians under what the group sees as unjust and unjustifiable circumstances. BLM was founded in 2013 by Patrisse Cullors, Opal Tometi, and Alicia Garza, as a means of fighting the continuing violence perpetrated by law enforcement against ordinary black women and men.[89] The three founders of BLM have been and continue to be involved in other social justice groups. Cullors works for the Ella Baker Center for Human Rights in Oakland, California, a predominantly black community; Tometi, the daughter of Nigerian immigrants, works at the Black Alliance for Just Immigration; and Garza is the special projects director of the National Domestic Workers Alliance.

Garza describes BLM's "herstory" as having been formed by black queer women, whose existence was subject to erasure. Garza and her cofounders insist on the specificities of the black experience in the United States as an underpinning for progressive social change.[90] She characterizes what she sees as the mission of BLM:

> Black Lives Matter is a unique contribution that goes beyond extrajudicial killings of Black people by police and vigilantes. It goes beyond the narrow nationalism that can be prevalent within some Black communities, which merely call on Black people to love Black, live Black and buy Black, keeping straight cis Black men in the front of the movement while our sisters, queer and trans and disabled folk take up roles in the

background or not at all.[91] Black Lives Matter affirms the lives of Black queer and trans folks, disabled folks, Black-undocumented folks, folks with records, women and all Black lives along the gender spectrum. It centers those that have been marginalized within Black liberation movements. It is a tactic to (re)build the Black liberation movement.[92]

BLM's simultaneous insistence on inclusivity in forming a community for liberation, and specificity in naming what black people in America have faced, has garnered a great deal of attention from social and other media and huge amounts of criticism for going against standard American discourses of democratic access being best obtained through political pluralism. Regardless of critiques, BLM has been sought out by candidates for US president for endorsements, although they announced that they would not endorse anyone.[93] The group has begun to get support from more mainstream feminists; the New York Women's Foundation awarded Garza, Tometi, and Cullors its "walking stick award" for political trailblazers, an award previously given as well to Hillary Clinton.[94] Even *Cosmopolitan*, a magazine better known for its tips on sex than politics, interviewed Garza, Tometi, and Cullors recently for a short but remarkably direct piece where the three women conveyed their perspective on racial/ethnic, gender, and economic justice, with Tometi stating, "We live intersectional lives.[95]

What is notable in looking at BLM is how Tometi's use of the term "intersectional" to describe black women's lives is how it serves as an example of how intersectionality has escaped from the academy to make a full circle journey back to activist roots. BLM clearly is conceptualized by its architects and by many participants as a coalition built on sets of differences: the differences between what black people and white people experience facing the police; the differences among participants in black movements as they encounter power, especially but not only the marginalization of queer voices within the black community; the way that common interests in stopping the militarization of the police, and in addressing the mass incarceration crisis that the United States can be found in differently positioned communities. BLM is really only intelligible through an intersectional lens that highlights its coalitional nature, not only because its founders use the word, but because they operate according to intersectional logic. BLM's intersectionality—its black feminism—was incorporated into its roots, and many if not most media accounts note the active presence of black women at BLM events. Nonetheless, there are those who argue that in the national debate over police violence against black communities, the visibility of violence committed against black women by police has been submerged. Kimberlé Crenshaw and others at the Center for Intersectionality and Social Policy Studies have started a campaign, in association with the African-American Policy Forum, to increase that visibility, called "Say Her Name." As Crenshaw put it,

> Although Black women are routinely killed, raped, and beaten by the police, their experiences are rarely foregrounded in popular understandings of police brutality . . . Yet, inclusion of Black women's experiences in social movements, media narratives, and policy demands around policing and police brutality is critical to effectively combatting racialized state violence for Black communities and other communities of color.[96]

Crenshaw's activist "Say Her Name" project speaks both to the newly visible presence of the BLM movement and the ensuing obscurities that happened even as the movement was becoming part of a national political agenda. From this, we can see how the project of intersectional analysis of social injustice is a never-ending one.

CONCLUSION

In conclusion, it will certainly not solve the problem of the invisibility of black feminist intellectual production to visually prop up a few black feminists and make them prominent as personalities. That might be warranted, gratifying, and interesting, but larger points remain as to the uneven impact that black feminist intellectuals have had postwar. To summarize: black radical feminists in US communist politics developed views of the interconnected nature of domination in black women's lives, advocating for a "triple oppression" view of the situation of black women. In the 1960s and 1970s, black feminists in left-wing and mainstream liberal feminist circles advocated in what would come to be called an intersectional manner. As a result of that agitation, black feminists in the academy articulated intersectional theories about the position of women and people of color in the United States and in the world at large. The neglect of the intersectional view of academics has been mitigated somewhat by the articulation of an intersectional point of view within coalitional grassroots efforts such as BLM.

The historical record, ever in need of updating, should show black feminist *consistency* of advocacy of the need to mutually and simultaneously address racial and gender oppression over time. These black feminist intersectional perspectives, rooted in activism, have had a paradigm-changing effect on current academic feminism. One can only imagine the kind of "dead end" of irrelevancy that American feminism—no longer a mass movement, but institutionalized in many places and beleaguered all at the same time—may have run into without the incorporation of the intersectional perspective into its center. Currents of black feminist theory, past and present, challenge scholars to think in complex fashion about social structures and life within them. Whatever the public presence of black feminists in the American intellectual landscape, their work continues to inform the expansion of knowledge about living under domination in America and in other parts of the world.

NOTES

1. Paula Giddings, *When and Where I Enter: The Impact of Black Women on Race and Sex in America* (New York: Bantam Books, 1984), 50.

2. Ibid.; Deborah Gray White, *Too Heavy a Load: Black Women in Defense of Themselves 1894-1994* (New York and London: W. W. Norton, 1999); Duchess Harris, *Black Feminist Politics from Kennedy to Clinton* (New York: Palgrave Macmillan, 2009); Julia S. Jordan-Zachery, "Am I a Black Woman or a Woman Who Is Black? A Few Thoughts on the Meaning of Intersectionality," *Politics and Gender* 3, no. 2 (2007): 254-63; Gerda Lerner, ed., *Black Women in White America: A Documentary History* (New York: Vintage Books, 1972); Benita Roth, *Separate Roads to Feminism: Black, Chicana, and White Feminist Movements in America's Second Wave* (New York: Cambridge University Press, 2004); Kimberly Springer, *Still Lifting, Still Climbing: Contemporary African American Women's Activism* (New York: New York University Press, 1999); Kimberly Springer, *Living for the Revolution: Black Feminist Organizations, 1968-1980* (Durham, NC: Duke University Press, 2005).

3. Karen S. Adler, "'Always Leading Our Men in Service and Sacrifice': Amy Jacques Garvey, Feminist Black Nationalist," *Gender and Society* 6 (September 1992): 346-75; Gray White 1999, 121; E. Frances White, "Listening to the Voices of Black Feminism," *Radical America* 18, nos. 2-3 (1984): 7-25.

4. Adler, "'Always Leading Our Men in Service and Sacrifice.'"

5. Eric McDuffie, *Sojourning for Freedom: Black Women, American Communism, and the Making of Black Left Feminism* (Durham and London: Duke University Press, 2011), 3.

6. Carole Boyce Davies, *Left of Karl Marx: The Political Life of Black Communist Claudia Jones* (Durham and London: Duke University Press, 2007); Angela Davis, *Women, Race and Class* (New York: Vintage Books, 1983); McDuffie, *Sojourning for Freedom*.

7. Frances Beal, "Double Jeopardy: To Be Black and Female," in *The Black Woman: An Anthology*, ed. Toni Cade (Bambara) (New York: New American Library, 1970), 90-100.

8. Kimberly Springer, "The Interstitial Politics of Black Feminist Organizations," *Meridians: Feminism, Race, Transnationalism* 1, no. 2 (2001): 155–91.

9. Gwen Patton, "Black People and the Victorian Ethos," in *The Black Woman: An Anthology*, ed. Toni Cade (Bambara) (York and Scarborough, Ontario: Mentor Books, 1970), 143–48.

10. On Chisholm see Barbara Winslow, *Shirley Chisholm: Catalyst for Change* (Boulder, CO: Westview, 2013) and Chisholm's autobiography *Unbought and Unbossed* (Washington, DC: Take Root Media, 2010); on Kennedy see Sherie M. Randolph Florynce *"Flo" Kennedy: The Life of a Black Feminist Radical* (Chapel Hill: University of North Carolina Press, 2015).

11. Patricia Hill Collins, "Black Public Intellectuals: From Du Bois to the Present" *Contexts* 4, no. 4(2005): 22–27. Reprinted in *The Contexts Reader*, ed. Jeff Goodwin and James M. Jasper (New York and London: W. W. Norton).

12. McDuffie, *Sojourning for Freedom*, 112.

13. Claudia Jones, "An End to the Neglect of the Problems of the Negro Woman!" *Political Affairs* (June 1949). Reprinted as a pamphlet by the National Women's Commission of the Communist Party, USA. The version I cite from can be found at https://palmm.digital.flvc.org/islandora/object/ucf%3A4865.

14. Boyce Davies, *Left of Karl Marx*, 77–84.

15. Jones, "An End to the Neglect," 1949, 4.

16. Ibid., 7. Patricia Hill Collins noted the pernicious effects of such "controlling images" as the "mammy" in her work *Black Feminist Thought: Knowledge, Consciousness and the Politics of Empowerment* (New York: Routledge, 2008).

17. Jones, "An End to the Neglect," 12.

18. Ibid., 15, emphasis in the original.

19. Jones, "An End to the Neglect," 17.

20. McDuffie, *Sojourning for Freedom*, 173–92.

21. Ibid., 176.

22. Roth, *Separate Roads to Feminism*.

23. Charles Payne, "Men Led, but Women Organized: Movement Participation of Women in the Mississippi Delta," in *Women in the Civil Rights Movement: Trailblazers and Torchbearers 1941–1965*, ed. Vicki L. Crawford, Jacqueline Anne Rouse, and Barbara Woods (Bloomington and Indianapolis: Indiana University Press, 1990), 1–12.

24. Barbara Ransby, *Ella Baker and the Black Freedom Movement: A Radical Democratic Vision*(Chapel Hill: University of North Carolina Press, 2005); Belinda Robnett, *How Long? How Long? African-American Women in the Struggle for Civil Rights* (New York: Oxford University Press, 1997).

25. Doug McAdam, *Political Process and the Development of Black Insurgency 1930–1970* (Chicago: University of Chicago Press, 1982); Nigel Young, *An Infantile Disorder? The Crisis and Decline of the New Left* (London and Henley: Routledge and Kegan Paul 1977).

26. Vicki L. Crawford, Jacqueline Ann Rouse and Barbara Woods, eds, *Women in the Civil Rights Movement: Trailblazers and Torchbearers 1941–1965* (Bloomington and Indianapolis: Indiana University Press, 1993); Bernice McNair Barnett, "Invisible Southern Black Women Leaders in the Civil Rights Movement: The Triple Constraints of Gender,

Race and Class," *Gender and Society* 7, no. 2 (1993): 162-82; Charles Payne, "Ella Baker and Models of Social Change," *Signs* (Summer 1989): 885-99; Payne 1990; Robnett, *How Long?*

27. Springer, "The Interstitial Politics of Black Feminist Organizations"; Roth, *Separate Roads to Feminism*.

28. Jo Freeman, *The Politics of Women's Liberation* (New York and London: Longman, 1975); Myra Marx Ferree and Beth B. Hess *Controversy and Coalition: The New Feminist Movement across Four Decades of Change*, 3rd ed. (New York and London: Routledge, 2000).

29. Harris 2009; Susan M. Hartmann, *The Other Feminists: Activists in the Liberal Establishment* (New Haven and London: Yale University Press, 1999).

30. Roth, *Separate Roads to Feminism*.

31. Chisholm, *Unbought*; Winslow, *Shirley Chisholm*.

32. Winslow, *Shirley Chisholm*, 2.

33. Robnett, *How Long?*

34. Roth, *Separate Roads to Feminism*.

35. Kristen Anderson-Bricker, "'Triple Jeopardy': Black Women and the Growth of Feminist Consciousness in SNCC, 1964-1975," in *Still Lifting, Still Climbing*, ed. Kimberly Springer, 49-69; Benita Roth, "The Vanguard Center: Intra-movement Experience and the Emergence of African-American Feminism," in *Still Lifting, Still Climbing: Contemporary African American Women's Activism*, ed. Kimberly Springer, 70-90; Benita Roth, "Race, Class, and the Emergence of Black Feminism in the 1960s and 1970s" *Womanist Theory and Research* 2, no. 1 (Fall 1999); Roth, *Separate Roads to Feminism*; Springer, "The Interstitial Politics of Black Feminist Organizations," in *Living for the Revolution*.

36. According to Beal, the concept of the intersection of race, class, and gender in the essay was a collective effort, although Beal was the principal writer and was therefore assigned authorship (2000 interview with the author).

37. Beal, "Double Jeopardy," 92.

38. Ibid., 92.

39. Patricia Robinson and the Mount Vernon/New Rochelle Group. "Poor Black Women's Study Papers by Poor Black Women of Mount Vernon, New York," in *The Black Woman: An Anthology*, ed. Toni Cade (Bambara) (York and Scarborough, Ontario: Mentor Books, 1970a), 189-97; "Statement on Birth Control," in *Sisterhood Is Powerful*, ed. Robin Morgan (New York: Vintage Books, 1970b): 360-61.

40. Nina Harding, "The Interconnections between the Black Struggle and the Woman Question" (rpt., Seattle: Radical Women, 1970); Women's Liberation Ephemera Files, Special Collections, Northwestern University; Maryanne Weathers, "An Argument for Black Women's Liberation as a Revolutionary Force," position paper issued by Third World Women's Alliance, Cambridge, MA, October 1968a; Social Action Files, State Historical Society, Madison, Wisconsin; Weathers, "Black Women and Abortion," position paper issued by Third World Women's Alliance, Cambridge, MA, October 1968b; Margaret White, "I Want the Right to Be Black and Me," in *Black Women in White America: A Documentary History*, ed. Gerda Lerner (New York: Vintage Books, 1972), 607-8.

41. See the seven articles in the roundtable in *The Journal of Women's History*, 2002; "Pauli Murray's Notable Connections" 14, no. 2 (Summer); Harris, *Black Feminist Politics*.

42. Toni Morrison. "What the Black Woman Thinks about Women's Lib," *The New York Times Magazine,* August 22, 1971.

43. Alice Walker, *In Search of Our Mother's Gardens: Womanist Prose*(San Diego, New York, and London: Harcourt Brace Jovanovitch, 1983).

44. Angela Y. Davis, *Women, Race and Class* (New York: Vintage Books, 1983); bell hooks, *Ain't I a Woman: Black Women and Feminism* (Boston: South End, 1981); hooks, *Feminist Theory: From Margin to Center* (Boston: South End, 1984); Bernice Johnson Reagon, "Coalition Politics: Turning the Century," in *Home Girls: A Black Feminist Anthology,* ed. Barbara Smith (New York: Kitchen Table/ Women of Color Press, 1983), 343–56; Audre Lorde, *Zami: A New Spelling of My Name* (Freedom, CA: Crossing, 1982); Lorde, *Sister Outsider: Essays and Speeches*(Freedom, CA: Crossing, 1984); Michelle Wallace, "A Black Feminist's Search for Sisterhood," in *All the Women Are White, All the Men Are Black, but Some of Us Are Brave: Black Women's Studies,* ed. Gloria T. Hull, Patricia Bell Scott, and Barbara Smith (New York: Feminist, 1982): 5–17; Wallace, *Black Macho and the Myth of the Superwoman* (London and New York: Verso, 1996); Hull, Gloria T., Patricia Bell Scott and Barbara Smith, eds. *All the Women are White, All the Men are Black, But Some of Us are Brave: Black Women's Studies* (New York: Feminist, 1982).

45. The statement appeared in Cherrie Moraga and Gloria Anzaldúa's collection *This Bridge Called My Back* (New York: Kitchen Table/Women of Color Press, 1981) and former CRC member Barbara Smith's collection *Home Girls* (New York: Kitchen Table/Women of Color Press, 1983).

46. The Combahee River Collective, "Combahee River Collective Statement, 1981," in *Home Girls,* ed. Barbara Smith (New York: Kitchen Table, 1983), 215.

47. Harris, *Black Feminist Politics.*

48. Combahee River Collective, "Combahee River Collective, 1981," 214.

49. Alice Echols, *Daring to Be Bad: Radical Feminism in America, 1967-1975* (St. Paul: University of Minnesota Press, 1989).

50. Combahee River Collective, "Combahee River Collective, 1981," 214.

51. Combahee River Collective, "Combahee River Collective, 1979."

52. Harris, *Black Feminist Politics.*

53. Ibid.; Roth, *Separate Roads to Feminism*; Springer, "The Interstitial Politics of Black Feminist Organizations." White, "Listening to the Voices of Black Feminism."

54. Kimberlé Crenshaw, "Demarginalizing the Intersection of Race and Sex: A Black Feminist Critique of Antidiscrimination Doctrine, Feminist Theory and Antiracist Politics," *The University of Chicago Legal Forum* (1989): 139–67; Kimberlé Crenshaw, "Mapping the Margins: Intersectionality, Identity Politics and Violence against Women of Color," in *Critical Race Theory: The Key Writings That Formed the Movement,* ed. Kimberlé Crenshaw, Neil Gotanda, Gary Peller, and Kendall Thomas (New York: New, 1995). "Mapping the Margins" was first printed in the *Stanford Law Review* 43, no. 6 (1991): 1241–99.

55. A twentieth-anniversary conference on the concept of "intersectionality" centered around Crenshaw's work and was held at UCLA in March 2010. In 2013, the women's studies journal *Signs* devoted a special issue to a reconsideration of intersectionality. See *Signs* 38, no. 4 or http://signsjournal.org/.

56. Crenshaw, "Mapping the Margins," 358.

57. Ibid. During the 1980s, feminist scholars in a number of disciplines moved toward intersectional theory without naming it as such. In anthropology, see Karen Sacks "Toward a Unified Theory of Class, Race and Gender" *American Ethnologist* 16, no. 3 (1989); in philosophy, see Elizabeth V. Spelman, "Theories of Race and Gender/The Erasure of Black Women," *Quest: A Feminist Quarterly* 5, no. 4 (1982): 36–62; in sociology, see Deborah H. King, "Multiple Jeopardy, Multiple Consciousness: The Context of a Black Feminist Ideology" *Signs* 14, no. 1 (Autumn 1988): 42–72; and Bonnie Thorton Dill, "Race, Class and Gender: Prospects for an All-Inclusive Sisterhood," *Feminist Studies* 9, no. 1 (Spring 1983). Thorton Dill has also contributed recently to *Ms.* Magazine on the subject of intersectionality; see Bonnie Thorton Dill, "Intersections," *Ms.* 19, no. 2 (Spring 2009): 65.

58. Nira Yuval-Davis, "Intersectionality and Feminist Politics," *European Journal of Women's Studies* 13, no. 3 (2006): 193–209.

59. Avtar Brah and Ann Phoenix, "'Ain't I a Woman? Revisiting Intersectionality," *Journal of International Women's Studies* 5, no. 3 (2004): 75–86; Hae Yeon Choo and Myra Marx Ferree, "Practicing Intersectionality in Sociological Research: A Critical Analysis of Inclusions, Interactions, and Institutions in the Study of Inequalities," *Sociological Theory* 28, no. 2 (2010): 129–49; Myra Marx Ferree, "Inequality, Intersectionality and the Politics of Discourse: Framing Feminist Alliances," in *The Discursive Politics of Gender Equality: Stretching, Bending and Policy-Making*, ed. Emanuela Lombardo, Petra Meier, and Mieke Verloo (New York: Routledge, 2009), 86–104; Leslie McCall, "The Complexity of Intersectionality," *Signs: Journal of Women in Culture and Society* 30, no. 3 (2005): 1771–1800; Gill Valentine, "Theorizing and Researching Intersectionality: A Challenge for Feminist Geography," *The Professional Geographer* 59, no. 1 (2007): 10–21; "Intersectionality and Feminist Politics."

60. Roth, "The Vanguard Center: Intra-movement Experience and the Emergence of African-American Feminism," 70–90; Roth, "Race, Class, and the Emergence of Black Feminism in the 1960s and 1970s"; Roth, *Separate Roads to Feminism*.

61. See *Signs: Journal of Women in Culture and Society* 38, no. 4 (Summer 2013); *The DuBois Review: Social Science Research on Race* 10, no. 2 (Fall 2013).

62. The books are *Intersectionality*, by Patricia Hill Collins and Sirma Bilge (Wiley 2016); *Intersectionality: An Intellectual History*, by Ange-Marie Hancock (Oxford 2016); and *Intersectionality: Origins, Contestations, Horizons*, by Anna Carastathis (Nebraska 2016).

63. Jennifer Nash, "Re-Thinking Intersectionalisty," *Feminist Review* 89 (2008): 8–9.

64. Nikol G. Alexander-Floyd, "Disappearing Acts: Reclaiming Intersectionality in the Social Sciences in a Post-Black Feminist Era," *Feminist Formations* 24, no. 1 (Spring 2012): 8–9. The recent controversies over "expanding" the activist hashtag #Blacklivesmatter to #alllivesmatter might be fruitfully read against Floyd-Alexander's critique of universalism. See the discussion about BLM below.

65. See *Ms.* 2009.

66. Jordan-Zachery, "Am I a Black Woman or a Woman Who Is Black?"

67. Patricia Hill Collins, *Fighting Words: Black Women and the Search for Justice* (Minneapolis: University of Minnesota Press, 1998); Barbara Ransby, "Afrocentrism, Cultural Nationalism, and the Problem with Essentialist Definitions of Race, Gender, and Sexuality," in *Dispatches from the Ebony Tower: Intellectuals Confront the African American*

Experience, ed. Manning Marable (New York: Columbia University Press, 2000), 216–23; Fabio Rojas, *From Black Power to Black Studies: How a Radical Social Movement Became an Academic Discipline* (Baltimore: Johns Hopkins Univrsity Press, 2007).

68. Katherine Q. Seelye, "Clinton-Obama Quandary for Many Black Women," *New York Times*, October 14 2007. Accessed online at http://www.nytimes.com/2007/10/14/us/politics/14carolina.html?_r=1andscp=1andsq=clinton%20ºbama%20quandary%20Blackandst=cse.

69. Hill Collins, "Black Public Intellectuals: From Du Bois to the Present," 136.

70. Ibid., 137.

71. Ibid.

72. Ibid., 140.

73. Ibid., 141. Hill Collins wrote before Melissa Harris-Perry started becoming a well-known figure on cable news shows. Harris-Perry is now the Maya Angelou Presidential Chair at Wake Forest University, where she is also the executive director of the Pro Humanitate Institute and a founding director of the Anna Julia Cooper Center. Harris-Perry had her own two-hour current events show on weekend mornings on MSNBC from 2012 through 2016. In contrast, MSNBC aired the Reverend Al Sharpton's show nightly in prime time.

74. Henry Louis Gates's arrest in July 2009 and the subsequent White House "beer summit" placed him at the center of a US media firestorm for several weeks (Seelye 2009); Cornel West's 2002 troubles with Harvard president Lawrence Summers received less attention but still was covered by several media outlets, including *The Boston Globe* and *The New York Times*.

75. Web portals to Winfrey's various media ventures can be found online at http://www.oprah.com.

76. Kimberly Springer, "Delineating the Contours of the Oprah Culture Industry," in *Stories of Oprah: The Oprahfication of American Culture*, ed. Trystan T. Cotton and Kimberly Springer (Oxford: University Press of Mississippi, 2010), ix.

77. John Howard, "Beginnings with O," in *Stories of Oprah: The Oprahfication of American Culture*, ed. Trystan T. Cotton and Kimberly Springer (Oxford: University Press of Mississippi, 2010),10, emphasis in the original.

78. Jennifer Rexroat, "'I'm Everywoman': Oprah Winfrey and Feminist Identification," in *Stories of Oprah: The Oprahfication of American Culture*, edited by Trystan T. Cotton and Kimberly Springer (Oxford: University Press of Mississippi, 2010), 19–32.

79. Rexroat, "'I'm Everywoman,'" 19. Winfrey, for example, has links to *Ms.* magazine, having accepted their Woman of the Year Award in 1989 and having been interviewed in the pages of *Ms.* several times. As Rexroat states, "Whether or not Oprah considers herself to be a feminist role model, it is clear that *Ms.* Magazine does" (2009, 31, note 1).

80. Howard, "Beginnings with O," 11.

81. Rexroat, "'I'm Everywoman,'" 20.

82. Ibid., 28.

83. There are numerous articles in the popular press about the two films and Winfrey's roles in them. See http://www.nytimes.com/2013/08/11/movies/oprah-winfrey-and-forest

-whitaker-on-the-butler.html?_r=0; http://www.gq.com/blogs/the-feed/2013/08/the-gqa-the-butlers-david-oyelowo-on-getting-slapped-around-by-oprah.html; http://www.nytimes.com/aponline/2015/01/16/us/politics/ap-us-obama-selma-movie.html; http://www.theguardian.com/us-news/2015/jan/19/oprah-david-oyelowo-selma-martin-luther-king.

84. http://variety.com/2015/film/news/oprah-winfrey-ava-duvernay-attend-white-house-screening-of-selma-1201407670/;http://www.huffingtonpost.com/2015/01/18/selma-mlk-march_n_6498088.html.

85. http://bittman.blogs.nytimes.com/2014/12/13/rev-dr-william-barber-ii-on-todays-protest-movements/.

86. http://www.nytimes.com/2015/06/29/opinion/charles-blow-my-murdered-cousin-had-a-name.html.

87. http://www.nytimes.com/roomfordebate/2015/07/08/is-hillary-clintons-feminism-out-of-style/feminism-is-not-a-conflict-of-generations.

88. http://www.nytimes.com/2015/08/09/nyregion/linda-sarsour-is-a-brooklyn-homegirl-in-a-hijab.html.

89. The group's website is www.Blacklivesmatter.com; it also has a Facebook page (https://www.facebook.com/BlackLivesMatter/?fref=ts) with nearly 100,000 "likes."

90. http://www.thefeministwire.com/2014/10/Blacklivesmatter-2/.

91. "Cis" or "cisgender" denotes an individual who identifies with the gender to which they were assigned at birth and is contrasted to "trans" or "transgender," which describes an individual who does not identify with the gender to which they were assigned at birth.

92. http://www.essence.com/2015/09/22/Black-lives-matter-activists-will-not-endorse-2016-presidential-candidate.

93. Ibid.

94. http://www.nywf.org/2015/05/nywfs-2015-celebrating-women-breakfast-event-recap/.

95. http://www.cosmopolitan.com/entertainment/a47842/the-women-behind-Blacklivesmatter/.

96. For the African-American Policy Forum, see www.aapf.org; for the full "Say Her Name" report, go to http://static1.squarespace.com/static/53f20d90e4b0b80451158d8c/t/55a810d7e4b058f342f55873/1437077719984/AAPF_SMN_Brief_full_singles.compressed.pdf.

- CHAPTER SIX -

INTELLECTUAL PREDICAMENTS

Black Nationalism in the Civil Rights and Post-Civil Rights Eras

SIMON WENDT

In 1964, after leaving the black nationalist Nation of Islam (NOI), militant activist Malcolm X founded the Organization of Afro-American Unity (OAAU) to further the cause of black nationalism in the United States. The OAAU's program insisted that African Americans ought to begin their liberation by freeing themselves from white America's racist mindset. According to Malcolm X, black Americans needed to "change the thinking of the Afro-American by liberating" their "minds through the study of philosophies and psychologies, culture and languages that did not come from" their "racist oppressors."[1] A closer look at black nationalism in the United States during the civil rights and post-civil rights eras demonstrates, however, how difficult it was to put such strategies into action. Viewed from a postcolonial studies perspective, Malcolm X and other black activist intellectuals were faced with the same dilemma that native intellectuals confronted in their attempts to throw off the yoke of colonialism and imperialism. As postcolonial theorist Leela Gandhi reminds us, "anti-colonial nationalism remains trapped within the structures of thought from which it seeks to differentiate itself." What anticolonial activists and postcolonial critics have grappled with, Gandhi maintains, is the question of whether they ought to "concede the mimetic nature of anti-colonial nationalisms, or submit to the paradox that the very imagining of anti-colonial freedom is couched in the language of colonial conquest."[2] Attempting to find new forms of antiracist expression while struggling with the fact that these seemingly novel ideas were based on Anglo-European intellectual traditions, black nationalist thinkers of the civil rights and post-civil rights eras struggled with a very similar predicament.

Analyzing black nationalist thought from the 1950s through the 1990s, this chapter explores this particular quandary. It focuses on the thought of what political scientist Dean Robinson has called "paraintellectuals," a group of black thinkers that constituted "an essentially new and increasingly important stratum of intellectuals who spoke and wrote about black politics, but who did not necessarily originate from the black middle class." Unlike black nationalist academics, these paraintellecutals reached larger audiences and largely "determined what would count as black nationalism."[3] They tended to be activists rather than scholars, and their ideas emanated directly from their experiences as organizers in black communities. What Malcolm X, Stokely Carmichael, Huey Newton, and other paraintellectuals shared was the fact that the basis for their nationalist thinking was a "lived" rather than "learned" analysis of the problems that confronted black America. Focusing on these thinkers promises to yield particular insights into black intellectuals' legacy that moves us closer to the lives of ordinary African Americans. Adopting a postcolonial studies perspective helps us better understand the predicaments that black intellectuals confronted when rejecting white racism and white culture while inadvertently relying on concepts and theories that were a product of that culture.[4]

Several scholars have argued that the United States ought to be seen as a postcolonial state as well as a neocolonial nation that continues to oppress subaltern groups. Amritjit Singh and Peter Schmidt explain: "Anti-colonial resistance at its founding worked to secure an economy that thrived by appropriating the labor of racially-defined 'aliens' not allowed the 'inalienable' rights of full citizenship. While the US defined itself as the world's first independent and anti-colonial nation-state it simultaneously incorporated many of the defining features of European colonial networks—including the color line—into its economic and cultural life."[5] Within this context, postcolonial critic Gayatri Spivak has pointed out that African Americans are comparable to colonized people whose "liberation" did not necessarily mean the end of racial oppression. "In the struggle against internal colonization, it is the African-American who is postcolonial in the United States," Spivak writes.

> In its own context, postcoloniality is the achievement of an independence that removes the legal subject-status of a people as the result of struggle, armed or otherwise. In terms of internal colonization, the Emancipation, Reconstruction, and civil rights were just such an achievement. Furthermore, postcoloniality is no guarantee of prosper-

ity for all but rather a signal for the consolidation of recolonization. In that respect as well, the condition of the African-American fits the general picture of postcoloniality much more accurately than the unearned claims of the Eurocentric well-placed migrant.[6]

Conceptualizing black nationalist paraintellectuals as colonial and postcolonial thinkers who grappled with the reality of internal colonization and its legacy opens up fresh perspectives on the history of black intellectual thought in general and black nationalism in particular. Consequently, it seems worthwhile to reconsider the theoretical insights of Martiniquan psychiatrist Frantz Fanon, whose *Black Skins, White Masks* (1952) and *The Wretched of the Earth* (1961) influenced generations of African American activists. In these seminal works, Fanon explored the interrelationship between race, sexuality, and colonialism, as well as the significance of anticolonial activism for oppressed peoples. Most importantly, Fanon examined the role of native intellectuals in colonial and postcolonial societies, highlighting the ambiguities in their attempts to produce anticolonial nationalist thought while partaking in cultural practices that were introduced by the white oppressor.[7]

Studying post-civil rights black nationalists from this perspective promises to enhance our understanding of the peculiarities and ambiguities of their thought. First, it sheds light on the predicament that these thinkers faced in their attempts to forge a black nationalist ideology that was inextricably linked to Anglo-European traditions. Second, it sharpens our understanding of the colonial analogy that many African American paraintellectuals used to describe and explain the racist oppression that confronted people of color in the United States. And finally, such a perspective highlights the gendered nature of black nationalism, which appropriated, adapted, and reinterpreted Anglo-European and "African" notions of femininity and masculinity.

Nationalism can be defined as an ideological movement that propagates the existence of a unique and sovereign nation. It argues that the interests of this nation take precedence over the interests of all other social groups. But what exactly is a nation? Political scientist Anthony Smith defines a nation as a named population that shares a historic territory and that has common myths and memories, a mass public culture, a single economy, and common rights and duties for all members.[8] This definition is problematical because there are nations that neither share a territory, nor have a single economy, nor have common myths and memories. Definitions of this kind frequently conflate nation with state. Being a legal and political concept, a state is a body of autonomous public institutions that wields control and coercion within a recognized territory. States are not communities. The concept of the nation-state assumes complete correspondence between the nation and the territory that is under state control. That, too, however, is not always the case. As Walker Connor has pointed out, the essence of what constitutes a nation frequently remains intangible. "This essence," Connor writes, "is a psychological bond that joins a people and differentiates it, in the subconscious conviction of its members, from all other people in a most vital way." But the "nature of that bond and its well-spring," Connor says, "remains shadowy and elusive."[9]

Scholars' uneasiness with definitive definitions of what constitutes a nation stems from a shift in perspective in studies on nationalism in the last two decades. Prior to the 1990s, theorists of nationalism debated primarily the origins of nations. So-called modernists argued that nations were a product of modernity. Only in the wake of modernity, they argued, was it actually possible to really think the nation. Their opponents, who were labeled ethnicists, did not deny the modernity of nations but emphasized their premodern origins, arguing that certain notions of ethnicity provided the basis for modern national identities. This debate is closely related to the emergence of two ideal types that scholars continue to use to describe nationalisms: civic nationalism and ethnic nationalism. In the case of civic nationalism, people become members of a nation because they pledge allegiance to that nation's political institutions and values. In the case of ethnic nationalism, membership qualifications are tied to a specific ancestry and culture, which are believed to be shared by all members of the nation. Most nations lean toward one or the other form of nationalism, but in most nations, both forms exist side by side.[10]

While current scholarship does not ignore these earlier discussions, it puts more emphasis on the artificial nature of nations and asks different questions. Rather than thinking of the nation as something real or even natural, scholars now focus on its constructedness, indeterminacy, and contingency. Nations are understood as cultural constructs that are far more heterogeneous than nationalist movements and earlier generations of scholars of nationalism wanted to make their audiences believe. Concepts such as Eric Hobsbawm's "invented traditions" and Benedict Anderson's "imagined communities" were precursors to this shift in perspective.[11] Following in their footsteps emerged a generation of scholars who were heavily influenced by cultural studies, postcolonial studies, and poststructuralist theory. They rejected grand narratives, stressed difference rather than universalism, and turned to such topics as race, multiculturalism, and gender. What these scholars are interested in is how the nation is constituted in various times and places and what active role people played in making sense of national identity. Nationalism is no longer viewed as something that people have no control over. Rather, it is seen as something that people create together. Finally, scholars now examine nationalism and power relations within societies, since nations are seen as complex sites of control and domination.[12]

In light of the difficulties of finding a general definition of nationalism, it is not suprising that historians have similarly struggled to define black nationalism. As early as 1970, John Bracey, August Meier, and Elliot Rudwick alluded to the relative vagueness of the term, pointing out that it "has been used in American history to describe a body of social thought, attitudes, and actions ranging from the simplest expressions of ethnocentrism and racial solidarity to the comprehensive and sophisticated ideologies of Pan-Negroism or Pan-Africanism."[13] Writing eight years later, Raymond L. Hall echoed his colleagues' comments. According to Hall, black nationalism was characterized by "complex and diverse political, cultural, territorial, and economic themes; it includes an almost bewildering variety of ideas about almost every aspect of social organization and belief."[14] Only Wilson Jeremiah Moses, who studied what he called the period of "classical black nationalism" (1850–1925), proposed a narrower definition, insisting that the "essential feature of" classical black nationalism was "its goal of creating a black nation-state or empire with absolute control over a specific geographical territory, and sufficient economic and military power to defend it."[15] With regard to black nationalist thought in the second half of the twentieth century, scholars remain hesitant to use such narrow definitions. Wahneema Lubiano, for instance, writes: "Black nationalism in its broadest sense is a sign, an analytic, describing a range of historically manifested ideas about black American possibilities that include any or all of the following: racial solidarity, cultural specificity, religious, economic, and political separatism."[16] And E. Frances White has proposed to regard it simply "as an oppositional strategy that both counters racism and constructs conservative utopian images of African-American life."[17]

As Dean Robinson has rightly pointed out, it is important to recognize the historical specificity of various forms of black nationalism between the eighteenth and twenty-first centuries, lest it become an ahistorical, unchanging body of intellectual thought. Robinson clearly states: "There is no 'essential' black nationalist tradition, despite similarities; the positions of nationalists of different eras have diverged because their nationalisms have been products of partly similar but largely unique eras of politics, thought, and culture."[18] Despite these considerable differences between various forms of black nationalism, however, it is important to define it, if only for analytical purposes. For that reason, I propose to define black nationalism as a body of intellectual thought that calls for racial solidarity and black self-determination, which is legitimated through claims that African Americans have common origins, a common history, a common culture, and a common destiny. Territorial autonomy or sovereignty may or may not be part of that quest for solidarity and self-determination.

CLASSICAL BLACK NATIONALISM

Before we turn to black nationalism during the civil rights and post-civil rights eras, it seems imperative to have a brief look at black nationalist thought prior to the 1960s and 1970s. Nationalism as an intellectual tradition emerged only in the late eighteenth century, which makes it difficult to speak of black nationalism before that period. Yet a nascent group consciousness did develop among African Americans during that time, fueling institutionalized forms of racial solidarity, racial unity, race pride, and identification with the African continent. As early as 1787, Prince Hall, the leader of an African lodge in Boston, petitioned the General Court of Massachusetts to allow a group of people of color to emigrate to Africa. In the following decades, the Haitian Revolution and its black leader, Toussaint L'Ouverture, inspired black nationalist thinkers in the United States. During the first half of the nineteenth century, an increasing number of blacks reacted to racist discrimination and the consolidation of racial slavery with calls for separate black institutions and economic self-help. Individuals like militant author David Walker, as well as a growing national black convention movement, advocated race pride and more militant resistance to slavery. Identification with Africa resolved a growing number of black intellectuals to emigrate to Africa or the Caribbean to establish separate black communities. Among the earliest advocates of emigration to Africa were black ship owner Paul Cuffee and black sail manufacturer James Forten. Combining nationalist thinking with economic interest and religious zeal to Christianize Africa, Cuffee was able to resettle a small group of African Americans in Sierra Leone in 1815. However, due to the activities of the American Colonization Society, a white slaveholders' organization that sought to remove free African Americans from America while keeping slavery intact, more and more black intellectuals abandoned colonization. Although black nationalism was less popular between 1830 and 1850, thinkers such as Edward Wilmot Blyden, Alexander Crummel, Henry Highland Garnet, and Martin R. Delany moved closer to this particular intellectual perspective in the decade leading up to the Civil War.[19]

While black nationalism and emigrationist sentiment was all but muted during the Civil War and Reconstruction—a consequence of the end of slavery and constitutional amendments that seemed to promise racial equality—the emergence of racial segregation and disfranchisement in the 1880s and 1890s revived the black nationalist tradition. Race pride, racial solidarity, and self-help became central pillars of the various strains of radical thinking that emerged during that period. In addition, an increasing number of thinkers advocated separate institutions and, in some cases, a separate nation-state as a long-term goal. Emigration to Africa continued to be advocated by some, but it was not as popular as it had been during the pre-Civil War era. One of the most ardent advocates of emigration during this period was Henry McNeal Turner, bishop of the African Methodist Episcopal Church, who called for mass migration to Africa. Even though such radical solutions were no longer widely advocated, more and more black nationalists moved toward some form of Pan-Africanism, the idea that black people around the world had common interests and ought to build international alliances to throw off the yoke of racial oppression.[20]

In the first two decades of the twentieth century, the Jamaican activist Marcus Garvey became the most influential black nationalist thinker in America, managing to build one of the largest black mass movements in US history. In 1914, he founded the Universal Negro Improvement Association (UNIA), which advocated black unity, race pride, and black self-help. Two years later, Garvey traveled to the United States, where he established a UNIA branch in New York City and subsequently managed to organize numerous other branches in the United States, the West Indies, Latin America, and Africa. By 1919, Garvey had established himself as a well-known radical in Harlem and managed to recruit hundreds of thousands of followers. The appeal of Garvey's organization stemmed primarily from its emphasis on race pride and economic self-improvement. Intending to make being black "a virtue," Garvey taught his followers about the glorious past of nonwhite civilizations and declared Jesus to be black. In UNIA auxiliaries such as the African Legion, the Black Cross Nurses, or the black Boy Scouts, African Americans proudly wore uniforms and bore titles, which white citizens traditionally denied them. On the pages of the organization's newspaper

Negro World, Garvey praised blacks' accomplishments and challenged racist stereotypes.[21]

As part of his plan to achieve complete black self-reliance, Garvey also founded various business enterprises, an idea that he had adopted from African American leader Booker T. Washington. The UNIA operated numerous businesses, including a publishing house, several cooperative grocery stores, a restaurant, and a steam laundry. In 1919, Garvey also established the Black Star Line, an all-black operated steamship company that he hoped would enable his organization to establish trade relations with black people around the world. One year later, the UNIA's first international convention took place in New York City, where delegates from dozens of countries passed a declaration that demanded an end to discrimination and disfranchisement in the United States and denounced white colonialism in Africa. During the convention delegates discussed Garvey's "Back to Africa Movement," which sought to establish a UNIA base in Liberia to achieve the organization's long-term goal to free Africa from colonial rule and to establish an independent black nation. Despite his popularity among ordinary African Americans, Garvey's militancy earned him numerous enemies, who made concerted efforts to destroy his movement. In 1923, these efforts led to his conviction for mail fraud and ultimate deportation to Jamaica in 1927. His attempts to save the flagging movement in the following years ultimately proved unsuccessful.[22]

Garvey's departure marked the temporary end of black nationalism in the United States. From the late 1920s to the late 1950s, black nationalist thought played virtually no role in African American activists' discussions about possible strategies to attain racial equality. There continued to exist a few small groups that called for a black nation-state or advocated emigration, including the Ethiopian Peace Movement, which was founded in 1932, and the National Movement for the Establishment of a Forty-Ninth State, which was established two years later. Around the same time, W. D. Fard founded the Detroit-based Nation of Islam (NOI), a small and obscure sect that combined black nationalism with Islamic and Christian elements.[23] But during the 1930s and 1940s, the influence of these organizations was negligible. The temporary demise of this black intellectual tradition was a consequence of the Great Depression and the New Deal as well as the activism of trade unionists and communists who suggested that only interracial brotherhood would help African Americans win racial equality. In addition, newly established liberal civil rights organizations such as the National Association for the Advancement of Colored People (NAACP), which was founded in 1909, increasingly dominated discussions about the question of which course the black freedom struggle should take, and that course was thought to be one of interracial cooperation rather than black nationalism.[24]

Despite this temporary hiatus in black nationalist thought, Garvey and his UNIA in particular are historically significant because the Jamaican activist's thinking reflected a number of aspects that characterized classical black nationalism. Like Garvey, many black militants believed that their quest for nationhood was guided by divine providence. In addition to the religious dimension of their thinking, black nationalists of the classical period sought to foster a new black cultural tradition, even though their sense of aesthetics was modeled on white European ideas. In a similar fashion, many black nationalists shared white thinkers' prejudices toward Africa. They frequently praised the accomplishments of black people in Egypt and Ethiopia because they regarded themselves as direct descendants of the powerful civilizations that had emerged there. West Africa, by contrast, received no such lavish praise. Despite the fact that most African Americans' ancestors hailed from that region, black nationalists frequently considered it the epitome of barbarism and believed it to be in dire need of Western enlightenment. Consequently, Garvey and his predecessors preached a racial nationalism that viewed blackness and the history of racial discrimination as the central basis for national identity and, ultimately, a black nation-state. As part of this racial thinking, Pan-Africanism became a central pillar of black nationalism prior to the 1930s.[25]

POSTCOLONIAL PERSPECTIVES ON BLACK NATIONALIST THOUGHT DURING THE CIVIL RIGHTS AND POST-CIVIL RIGHTS ERAS

Black nationalism during the civil rights and post-civil rights eras shared a number of commonalities with classical black nationalism, most notably an essentialized concept of race, Pan-Africanism, the insistence on self-determination and black control of African American institutions, and the idea of black economic self-help. But there were also differences, among them modern black nationalists' rejection of Western culture, as well as a less rigid emphasis on religion. Scholars of black nationalism have utilized a number of typologies to describe its modern manifestations, distinguishing, for instance, between cultural, revolutionary, territorial, and economic nationalism. In light of the considerable overlap between these various ideologies, however, it might be more fruitful to analyze certain common themes within modern black nationalists' thinking to better understand ideological similarities and differences. As activist Roy Innis, head of the Congress of Racial Equality (CORE), pointed out in 1969, the "stages of liberation" such as culture, politics, and economy were "virtually inseparable."[26]

Examining these common themes with an eye on the postcolonial dilemma that African American thinkers confronted in the civil rights and post-civil rights eras enhances our understanding of the complexities of this important intellectual tradition. Several aspects of black nationalists' vision of nation-building testify to their efforts to distinguish themselves from white nationalists and to reject "white" ideas while simultaneously relying on Anglo-European intellectual traditions. One of these aspects is the quest for territorial separatism and a black nation-state, an idea that was particularly influential during the era of classical black nationalism but continued to be widely discussed during and after the civil rights era. One organization that consistently called for a black homeland was the NOI. After taking over the organization from its founder, W. D. Fard, Elijah Muhammad continued to merge elements of Islam, Christianity, and black nationalism, condemning whites as "devils" and preaching black pride, moral uplift, and economic self-reliance. Beginning in the 1950s, Muhammad called for and sought to establish a separate black state on US territory or elsewhere, arguing that the US government was obligated to provide such land as compensation for hundreds of years of slavery and discrimination.[27]

In the early 1960s, Malcolm X, a hustler-turned-Muslim-minister became the NOI's most visible spokesperson, preaching Muhammad's gospel, condemning civil rights leader Martin Luther King's nonviolent philosophy, and reminding his audiences that true revolutions were fought over territory. In his famous "Message to the Grass Roots," he insisted that the American Revolution "was based on land, the basis of independence."[28] Even after breaking with the NOI over a comment on the assassination of President John F. Kennedy, Malcolm X demanded that the African American population "should be separated completely from America and should be permitted to go back to our African homeland."[29]

Malcolm X can be regarded as the quintessential paraintellectual, which helps explain his tremendous influence on the black freedom struggle in the 1960s and 1970s. Born in 1925, Malcolm X, whose real name was Malcolm Little, was the son of an itinerant Baptist preacher and black nationalist organizer named Earl Little. After the death of his father and a nervous breakdown of his mother Louise Norton, Malcolm lived in various foster homes in Lansing, Michigan, before leaving school and becoming involved in the underworlds of Boston and New York City. In 1946, he was arrested and convicted of burglary and subsequently sentenced to ten years in prison. While in prison Malcolm converted to the religious teachings of Elijah Muhammad and adopted the black Muslims' strict rules of moral conduct. He also began to read ravenously, devouring philosophy, history, and many other subjects. Having become a fervent and highly articulate follower of Elijah, he was paroled and released from prison in 1952. After his release, Malcolm moved to Detroit, Michigan, where he became a member of the local NOI's Temple No. 1. Shortly thereafter, Malcolm received his X, which stood for the lost name of black Muslims' African ancestors. In the following ten years, Malcolm X became the NOI's most successful organizer, establishing numerous new Muslim temples across the country. Malcolm X also plunged into a marathon of press, radio, and television interviews, talking to *Playboy* journalists as well as to academic audiences at Harvard and Yale. By 1961, chiefly because of Malcolm X's tireless recruiting efforts, the NOI's membership had soared from a few hundred to tens of thousands. More than fifty temples—or mosques as they came to be called after 1961—had been established across the country. It is this combination of insights into racial oppression derived from personal experience, a nonacademic education, and charisma as a speaker that made Malcolm X one of the most popular spokespersons for black nationalism among ordinary African Americans.[30]

Malcolm's insistence on the acquisition of land, which was modeled on European nationalist concepts of the nation-state, had a considerable influence on post-civil rights black nationalists, regardless of whether they considered themselves cultural, territorial, or revolutionary nationalists. Leroi Jones, for instance, a poet, playwright, and activist who in 1965 founded the militant US Organization and later changed his name to Amiri Baraka, had clearly been influenced by Malcolm's militant rhetoric.[31] Writing about the Muslim minister's legacy after his assassination in 1965, Jones argued: "[A]ny talk of Nationalism also must take this concept of land and its primary importance into consideration because, finally, any Nationalism which is not intent on restoring or securing autonomous space for a people, i.e., a nation, is at the very least shortsighted."[32] Five years later, when talking to the Congress of African Peoples, Amiri Baraka continued to quote Malcolm's message. "Like Malcolm said," Baraka told his audience, "you want some land, look down at your feet."[33] Stokely Carmichael, a former member of the Student Nonviolent Coordinating Committee (SNCC) who helped popularize the term "Black Power" in 1966, also took Malcolm's message to heart. Talking to black students at Morehouse College in 1970, he said: "Revolution must be about land. It is from the land that we get everything we need for survival."³⁴ In the post-civil rights era, the Republic of New Africa (RNA) epitomized this quest for a black nation-state. At its founding meeting in March 1968, the RNA called for a separate and independent black nation, whose territory would consist of five states in the Deep South and some black enclaves in northern cities. The RNA's leader, black lawyer Milton Henry, or Gaidia Obadele as he began to call himself, warned that if the federal government refused to yield to the new nation's demands, it would initiate a "people's war" against the white enemy. In a list of demands that the RNA submitted to the US Congress in 1972, the organization unequivocally claimed that "sovereignty" was "inseparable from independent land."³⁵ Even though groups like the RNA were also influenced by anticolonial Marxism, Anglo-European traditions of nationalist thinking became the basis of black intellectuals' quest for a black nation-state.

Despite the fact that demands for a black nation-state became more muted by the 1980s, the influence of Malcolm's vision of territorial separatism remained powerful. One umbrella organization that continued to believe in the need for a black nation-state was the New African Independence Movement (NAIM), which saw itself as heir to the Republic of New Africa. The groups that belonged to NAIM frequently evoked Malcolm's "Message to the Grass Roots" speech, in which he insisted that land was the basis of any people's independence. Consequently, the battle cry of NAIM was: "Free the Land." The organization's "New Afrikan Creed" made Malcolm X the most important ideological figure for its black nationalist ideology. The Creed read: "I believe in the Malcolm X Doctrine: that We must organize upon this land, and hold a plebiscite, to tell the world by a vote that We are free and our land independent, and that, after the vote, We must stand ready to defend ourselves, establishing a nation beyond contradiction." In 1995, several NAIM groups founded the New Afrikan Liberation Front (NALF) to prepare the planned plebiscite, an idea that had originally been introduced by the RNA. Unlike their predecessors, however, NAIM organizations remained small and yielded little influence among African Americans.³⁶

Civil rights and post-civil rights black nationalists' racialized thinking similarly reflected their postcolonial predicament. To most black nationalists, race became the primary analytic category, trumping issues such as class or gender. Echoing the thinking of white supremacists, black nationalists believed that race was a biological reality that correlated with certain cultural characteristics, which they thought were inherent to each racial group.

Some groups such as the African Nationalist Pioneer Movement (ANPM), a splinter group of Marcus Garvey's UNIA, and the NOI made arguments that echoed those of racist whites. In 1959, for instance, the ANPM stated that it believed "in the purity of the Black Race, and the purity of all other races." For that reason, "miscegenation" was regarded as "race suicide," and racial separation was seen as essential to black liberation.[37] NOI leader Elijah Muhammad likewise rejected "race mixing" and implored his followers to keep the black race "pure."[38] Both groups formulated ideas that became influential in the post–civil rights era, namely the idea that the black community's racial and cultural character needed to be preserved. For that reason, integration that meant assimilation into white American society was seen as detrimental to the goal of black liberation. In the 1960s, black nationalists of various persuasions made similar racial arguments. In 1965, Leroi Jones insisted that "racial" was "biological" and that African Americans' "focus of change" would be "racial."[39] As a result, a racialized blackness became black nationalists' answer to white racism. Racial solidarity among blacks in the United States and around the world would become the basis for the quest for full equality. As Stokely Carmichael pointed out in a speech in 1968: "We must understand the concept that for us the question of community is not geography, it is a question of us black people, wherever we are. We have consciously become a part of the 900 million black people that are separated over this world. We are separated by them. We are blood of the same blood and flesh of the same flesh."[40] While such race-centered thinking was an understandable reaction to the racism of white nationalism ultimately sought to communicate an antiracist message, it mimicked and ultimately perpetuated the dichotomous thinking of white supremacists.

Despite this focus on race, however, some black nationalists gradually came to see the necessity for interracial alliances to fight what they conceived of as a common oppressor. Some even reconsidered their focus on essentialized notions of blackness. Ironically, it was Malcolm X, the most important influence on black nationalists' thinking on race, who was among the first to modify his views. In April 1964, during a pilgrimage to Mecca, Saudi Arabia, Malcolm began to reconsider some of his convictions. In letters that he sent to friends and fellow black leaders in the United States, he announced his conversion to orthodox Islam and explained his changed perception of whites. Abandoning Elijah Muhammad's "white devil" theory, he began to define whiteness primarily as attitudes and actions, a shift that opened new avenues for cooperation between African Americans and those whites who were willing to support the black freedom struggle. A subsequent journey across Africa prompted Malcolm X to further rethink his original philosophy. When meeting with the Algerian ambassador, for instance, he was puzzled by the fact that the ambassador appeared to be white even though he was considered a true revolutionary on the African continent. After that experience, he voiced doubts about black nationalism's traditional focus on race.[41]

In the case of the Black Panther Party (BPP), a revolutionary nationalist organization that was founded in Oakland, California, in 1966, it was Marxist class analysis rather than religion or international travel that convinced members of the necessity of cooperation between blacks and whites in a global struggle against the common oppressor. This idea was the result of the Panthers' changing ideology, which evolved over several stages, beginning with a black nationalist analysis that was based on racial solidarity but incorporated elements of Marxist class analysis. From 1968 to 1970, the organization advocated a fusion of Marxist socialism and revolutionary nationalism that called for class alliances. After 1970, the BPP sought to establish global socialism through revolutionary intercommunalism, which would overthrow US imperialism and capitalism through alliances among revolutionaries around the world.[42]

Yet a majority of post-civil rights black nationalist thinkers continued to voice essentialized concepts of race, and culture became inextricably linked to such racial concepts. For many, it was once more the intellectual legacy of Malcolm X that became the blueprint for their thinking. In 1964, Malcolm X explained in an interview that "the social philosophy of black nationalism involves the emphasis upon the culture of the black man, which will be designed to connect us with our cultural roots, to restore the racial dignity necessary for us to love our own kind and be in unity and harmony with our own kind and strike at the evils and vices that strike at the moral fiber of our community and our own society."[43] Like Malcolm X, most African American nationalist intellectuals insisted on the unique character of black culture, which they believed to constitute a central pillar of black nationhood. This entailed both a rejection of Western culture in general and white American culture in particular. As early as 1965, Leroi Jones stated unequivocally: "In order for the Black Man in the West to absolutely know himself, it is necessary for him to see himself first as culturally separate from the white man."[44]

The Black Power movement sought to accomplish what Malcolm X, Leroi Jones, and others had called for. As Stokely Carmichael said in *Black Power: The Politics of Liberation* (1967), "we must first redefine ourselves. Our basic need is to reclaim our history and our identity from what must be called cultural terrorism, from the depredation of self-justifying guilt."[45]

Ron Karenga's US Organization, which he founded in 1965, was one of the most ardent advocates of a strategy that sought to counter this effect of white supremacy. Karenga argued that a reaffirmation of the uniqueness and beauty of black culture had to predate any revolutionary action.[46] To those black nationalists who insisted on the importance of culture in black nation-building, the role that black intellectuals played in that endeavor was crucial. Askia Muhammad Touré (Rolland Sellings) echoed the ideas of many when he claimed in 1968 that African American intellectuals had the power to organize blacks politically, culturally, spiritually, and economically. According to Touré, black intellectuals constituted "the *living mind* of the Black Nation/Race."[47] The Black Arts Movement in particular sought to put into action the ideas of Touré, Karenga, Leroi Jones, and others.[48]

Notwithstanding the demise of the Black Power movement in the mid-1970s, the underlying insistence on the necessity and possibility to separate oneself from American white culture did not die with the end of the movement. In 1985, for instance, Louis Farrakhan, the new leader of the NOI, which he had reorganized in the 1970s, echoed Jones, Touré, and others: "We must come out of the mind, the spirit, the way, the values, the norms, the folkways, the mores, the culture of our former slavemasters and their children."[49] By focusing on the uniqueness of black culture and by insisting that there was no interrelationship between white and black culture, black paraintellectuals attempted to foster group solidarity and black pride. Just as in the case of race, however, this line of thinking adopted the dichotomous worldview of white nationalists and inadvertently confirmed them in their belief in seemingly separate and racialized cultures.

In post-civil rights black nationalists' discussions about land, race, and culture as building blocks of the black nation, Africa assumed crucial importance, since studying it was not only believed to foster a strong black identity but also appeared to provide conceptual frameworks that did not come from the white oppressor. In fact, however, Africa probably best exemplifies the dilemma of postcolonial intellectuals in formulating ideological positions that rejected ideas of the oppressor while simultaneously utilizing or confirming them.

As in the case of classical black nationalism, Pan-Africanism allowed civil rights and post-civil rights black nationalists to envision a global struggle for black liberation, but it further consolidated essentialized notions of race. Many black paraintellectuals stressed the bonds of race and the history of racial oppression that they said connected black Americans and Africans. After his break with the NOI, Malcolm X insisted that black Americans' and

Africans' origin and destiny were "the same" and that the problems they confronted were inextricably linked.[50] In the post-civil rights era, it was especially Stokely Carmichael who became an ardent advocate for Pan-Africanism. "We came from Africa, our race is African," he insisted in 1969, stating that "we are all an African people, the concept that we are all working toward building a strong, united African nation, wherever we may be, the concept that we must work toward the unification of Africa—in other words, the concept of Pan-Africanism."[51] According to Carmichael, African Americans needed to support African liberation movements and make Africa a priority of the black struggle in America, a position that he never abandoned.[52]

Unlike their predecessors, however, post-civil rights thinkers did not believe Africans to be a backward people that were in need of the civilizing influence of African Americans. Instead, they praised African culture and regarded it as a behavioral model that African Americans ought to follow. In many ways, this look toward African culture became a crucial aspect of black nation-building, since it contributed to a sense of peoplehood that white supremacists had denied them for centuries. Once more, the ideas of Malcolm X became guidelines for subsequent generations of black radicals who joined the Black Power movement. "We must recapture our heritage and our identity if we are ever to liberate ourselves from the bonds of white supremacy," he said in 1964. "We must launch a cultural revolution to unbrainwash an entire people."[53] Like Afrocentrist nationalists, Malcolm suggested that there was one monolithic and unchanging African heritage. In his eyes, looking toward Africa to uncover this heritage was an essential first step to begin the process of debunking white supremacist myths about black people. Shortly before his death, he claimed: "You can't hate the land, your motherland, the place that you came from, and we can't hate Africa without ending up hating ourselves."[54] His Organization of Afro-American Unity sought "to rediscover" black Americans' "true African culture, which was crushed and hidden for over four hundred years in order to enslave us and keep us enslaved up to today."[55] Among Malcolm's heirs, however, there was much debate as to what constituted "true" African culture, and many of them were forced to rely on "invented traditions" that were labeled "African" even though they had little basis in historical reality.

Afrocentrist nationalists in particular invented such new traditions, using what they thought to be an authentic African culture to strengthen black identity and self-esteem. In general, most Afrocentrists hold that Africa and especially ancient Egypt should be regarded as part of African Americans' cultural heritage. Black culture is seen as distinctly positive when compared to

European and white American culture, which is characterized as being devoid of any positive attributes. Ron Karenga's Kwanzaa, an alternative Christmas celebration ritual for African Americans, became one of those "invented traditions." It became an important aspect of black nation-building in the 1960s and 1970s, but it was emptied of its political meaning in the 1980s and 1990s. In fact, even though there was a resurgence of black nationalism during the latter period, Afrocentrist thought essentially became a conservative cultural movement that focused on the importance of proper values to solve the problems that confronted black America. Afrocentrist thinkers argued that teaching African Americans an "authentic" African culture would boost their low self-esteem and would ultimately help transform a seemingly defunct "culture of poverty" into a seedbed for a new black middle class. Even more so than Pan-Africanism, however, Afrocentrism relied on the same binaries that white nationalism had created, confirmed both essentialized notions of race and racist arguments about a seemingly defective black culture, and masked the dialogical relationship between white and black culture (for a more detailed discussion of Afrocentrism, see Tunde Adeleke's essay in this volume).[56]

BLACK NATIONALISTS AND THE COLONIAL ANALOGY

The argument of many post-civil rights nationalists that African Americans constituted an internal colony within the United States might be the one aspect of paraintellectuals' thinking that was least influenced by Anglo-European traditions, since it constituted a reaction to the victories of anticolonial freedom movements on the African continent. Regardless of their ideological background, many black nationalists of the 1960s and 1970s viewed black America as a colonized nation within a nation. Following the thinking of anticolonial theorists, most notably Frantz Fanon, many black intellectuals used this analogy as an analytic tool to explain patterns of racial inequalities in the United States and to legitimize militant activism that aimed to attack these inequalities. As early as 1964, the Revolutionary Action Movement (RAM), a small group of revolutionary black nationalists that was founded a year earlier, stated among its goals that it sought to "free black people from colonial and imperialist bondage everywhere and to take whatever steps necessary to achieve that goal."[57] In the case of RAM, this included violent means that were deemed necessary to bring about revolutionary change.[58]

The earliest and most elaborate discussion of internal colonization within the United States came from SNCC activist Stokely Carmichael. In *Black*

Power, Carmichael and his coauthor, Charles Hamilton, stated plainly: "black people in this country form a colony, and it is not in the interest of the colonial power to liberate them." To Carmichael and Hamilton, institutional racism and colonialism were inextricably linked, since African Americans stood "as colonial subjects in reaction to white society."[59] While they admitted that the analogy did not work perfectly, they identified three arenas in which the colonial status of African Americans became apparent. In politics, they argued, white supremacists ruled the black community like colonial masters through the strategy of "indirect rule," using black intermediaries who were responsive to white leaders and ignored the plight of the black community. In the economic realm, Carmichael and Hamilton saw similar colonial dynamics at work, claiming that the black ghettos of America—like the colonies in Africa and elsewhere—were exploited by white Americans to enrich themselves while the black community remained dependent on the larger society. In the social realm, the two thinkers identified "the most vicious result of colonialism," namely white colonizers' deliberate attempts to relegate black people "to a subordinated inferior status in the society." This form of oppression was made worse, they said, through what they interpreted as the hollow promise of assimilation, which forced blacks to dissociate themselves "from the black race, its culture, community and heritage."[60]

In the following years, Carmichael and other black thinkers elaborated on this colonial analogy in numerous speeches and publications. In a 1968 speech before the Organization of Arab Students Convention in Ann Arbor, Michigan, for instance, Carmichael explained that only black people could be regarded as colonized, while poor white people were merely exploited. The latter group, said Carmichael, was oppressed economically. Colonized people, by contrast, were not only exploited but stripped of their culture, their values, and their language. Ultimately, they were "forced to identify with the oppressor." This was a direct reference to Frantz Fanon.[61] Fanon's *The Wretched of the Earth,* first published in 1961, became a major influence on Carmichael and other black nationalists. Fanon's work could arguably be seen as one of the few intellectual models that was not primarily a product of Anglo-European traditions, even though his work applied European concepts of psychoanalysis to the Algerian anti-colonial freedom struggle.

Regardless of what their primary strategy for nation-building was, post-civil rights black nationalist thinkers frequently used the colonial analogy to legitimate their visions of black nationhood. Floyd McKissick and Roy Innis, for instance, both of whom emphasized the importance of economics for black liberation, clearly echoed Fanon. McKissick, who, after leaving the Congress of Racial Equality (CORE) in 1968, sought to create business opportunities for African Americans, viewed black communities as internal colonies that were "plagued by an imbalance of trade" and were thus dependent on white money. In his eyes, changing this condition would help solve the economic problems that African Americans faced.[62] Roy Innis, who had succeeded McKissick as CORE's chairman, similarly argued in the following years that black urban communities should cease to be "sub-colonial appendages of the cities." To Innis, there were "striking" similarities "between the so-called underdeveloped countries and our underdeveloped black communities. Both have always been oppressed; almost always there is an unfavorable balance of trade with the oppressors or exploiters; both suffer from high unemployment, low income, scarce capital." Sovereignty and autonomy, however, would enable black communities to affect these conditions.[63]

Black nationalists who put more emphasis on the acquisition of land also used the black colony analogy, as did many of those African American radicals who favored a violent revolution to bring about black liberation. The RNA, in a document submitted to the US Congress in 1972, stated unequivocally that "the black nation is a colony," whose members were entitled to reparations for slavery and racist oppression from the United States.[64] Three years earlier, RNA leader Milton Henry had explained that his organization constituted "the government for the non-self-governing blacks held captive within the United States."[65] RAM leader Max Stanford also continued to argue that African Americans had to acknowledge their status as "colonized" captives who were "held in colonial bondage inside the U.S."[66] Clearly, then, black nationalists' argument for the need to establish a black nation heavily relied on the use of analogy, and in the eyes of a large number of paraintellectuals, Africa appeared to provide the most apt comparison.

In the case of the BPP, its Marxist class analysis ultimately convinced the organization's leaders to abandon the colonial analogy. In their early years, the Panthers spoke of African Americans as a "dispersed colony" that would be able to bring about black liberation by allying themselves with other colonies. But their reading of Marx convinced its cofounder Huey Newton that the world had dissolved into a dispersed collection of communities. Given the metamorphosis of the United States into what he regarded as an empire, colonies would no longer be able to decolonize and return to some form of nationhood. As Newton pointed out in an interview in 1973, "the struggle in the world today" was "between the small circle that administers and profits from the empire of the United States, and the peoples of the world who want to determine their own destinies."[67] Newton's idea of intercommunalism represented a turning away from both the colonial analogy and the idea of black nationalism, which makes him unique when compared with similar post-civil rights thinkers.

Even though the colonial analogy was abandoned by the Panthers and others during the 1970s, which in part was a consequence of the fact that blacks were finally able to challenge at least some of the inequalities they were confronted with in the United States, a few black nationalist organizations in the 1980s and 1990s continued to argue that blacks constituted a colony within the United States. Several organizations that became part of NAIM generally argued that African Americans had become a colonized nation after they were forcibly brought to North America from Africa. Consequently, NAIM, like the RNA, still believed that this "New Afrikan Nation" would have to fight for its independence.[68]

BLACK NATIONALISM AND GENDER

While black paraintellectuals' affinity for Africa reflects certain ambiguities with regard to their postcolonial predicament, a look at the gender dimensions of black nationalism is perhaps most revealing with regard to the dilemma that black intellectuals faced when attempting to conceptualize the new black nation. Gender can be defined as the dichotomized social and cultural production and reproduction of male and female identities and behaviors. Most scholars agree that gender is a primary aspect of social organization. Culturally constructed male and female identities create and consolidate hierarchical structures within society; these structures, in turn, have an impact on the relations between the sexes.[69] The focus on the relational character of gender and on its impact on relations of power has also led to new perspectives on men and the constructed character of masculinity. The most influential concept has been sociologist R. W. Connell's idea of "hegemonic masculinity." Hegemonic masculinity, as defined by Connell, is "the configuration of gender practice which embodies the currently accepted answer to the problem of the legitimacy of patriarchy, which guarantees (or is taken for granted) the dominant position of men and the subordination of women." This dominant notion of manhood is not only grounded in patriarchal privilege but also subordinates alternative forms of masculinity, most notably homosexuality.[70]

Scholarship on the interrelationship between nationalism and gender began to proliferate in the late 1980s and initially focused on the question of how discourses on gender and nation intersected and constructed each other. Early studies focused primarily on the tensions between male nationalists' use of women as symbolic bearers of the nation and women's political marginalization. What these and subsequent works demonstrated is that women became crucial to the nationalist projects of the nineteenth and twentieth centuries, reproducing the nation symbolically, culturally, and biologically.[71]

The iconography of nationalist movements testifies to the crucial role that women played as symbols of national collectivities. In this iconography and the accompanying narratives, the nation is almost always feminized and characterized as being in need of protection. In addition, gendered narratives of nation stress the purity, modesty, and chastity of the nation and its female citizens, thus indicating how the invention of the nation was supported by the modern construction of the two sexes. This construction facilitated male dominance. For example, men attempted to control the sexuality of women, demanding that women be chaste and modest. By using this idea as a symbol of the nation, women were under even more pressure to conform to traditional gender roles, since their failure to do so would reflect negatively not only on them as individuals but on the entire nation. In a similar fashion, nationalists' tendency to depict the nation as a family perpetuated the idea that the subordination of women was a natural fact and that the nation was in effect an extension of the family.[72] But women also produce the nation culturally by becoming active transmitters and producers of its culture. Mothers in particular were regarded as crucial to nation-building, since they were expected to teach their children the national language and norms and values. Mothers were thus seen as preservers of national culture. Within this context, nationalists often depicted women as the bearers of national traditions and memory and as embodiments of conservative principles of continuity. Men, by contrast, were depicted as embodiments of the nation's progressivism and modernity.[73]

Finally, women produce the nation biologically. The ideological use of the biology of human reproduction remains the most visible example of nationalist ideologies' tendency to perpetuate gender hierarchies. Fertility of women has frequently been praised as a sign of national prosperity and virility. A consequence of this discourse is that women are often urged to have children to fulfill their gendered responsibilities as members of national collectivities. This has led to a number of attempts to regulate sexual relations between men and women as well as reproduction. Using the state as a means of coercion, nationalists have tried to prevent "improper" forms of sexuality, among them prostitution and miscegenation, and intervened in the lives of families and couples by instituting policies that regulated contraception, abortion, or childcare. Particularly since the emergence of the modern state in the late eighteenth century, women were the prime targets of these policies, which on the surface appear to be unrelated to the nation-building project, but were actually central to it. Nationalism thus becomes a major means of men's control over women's bodies.[74]

More recent scholarship has also explored the role that constructions of masculinity played in nationalist movements, nation-building, and nation-states' attempts to maintain national unity, as well as gender hierarchies. Even though women have frequently become important symbols of nationhood, nations can also be coded masculine, as can be seen in cultures that refer to a nation as the "fatherland." In addition, patriotism tends to be communicated in masculine terms. Courage and honor, for instance, are two traits that are seen as both inherently patriotic and manly, particularly during wartime. While most studies that address these issues focus on Western societies, an increasing number of scholars have studied the impact of colonialism and imperialism on the relationship between nation and manhood. With regard to British colonialism, for instance, recent studies have explored the attempts of British colonialists in the nineteenth and twentieth centuries to legitimate their rule over South Asian countries by feminizing their male inhabitants and emphasizing the "civilized" masculinity of Englishmen. In the case of the United States, Gail Bederman has called attention to the impact of American imperialism on white middle-class masculinity, which was conceived of as superior to the manhood of "uncivilized" men who were subject to US rule. Others have looked at the influence of Western notions of masculinity and nation on non-Western societies—with a particular emphasis on anticolonial nationalists—before and after achieving independence.[75]

Black nationalists' use of gender in their conceptualization of the black nation suggests that there are discernible parallels between the thinking of anticolonial nationalist activists and black militant thinkers in the United States. As in the case of former colonies, many black nationalists sought to reaffirm African American men's manhood, which had been denied to them by white supremacists for centuries. This reaffirmation of masculinity, however, mimicked European and Anglo-American heterosexist nationalisms and even tended to go beyond it by denying that women could have any role other than passive supporters in the struggle for liberation. Colonialism, then, not only denied colonized men their manhood by feminizing them, but it also exacerbated gender inequalities in postcolonial nations. In India, for instance, the powerlessness that Indian men experienced during colonialism led them to develop a more profound consciousness of their nation and their manhood. To their mind, responding to the challenge that British colonialism presented to their masculinity required both affirming their manhood through such activities as bodybuilding and controlling the body and the sexuality of women.[76]

In the case of African Americans, this denial of manhood was aggravated by sexualized violence. In the 1880s and 1890s, lynching emerged as white supremacists' dominant method to enforce the country's racial hierarchies, particularly in the American South. White southerners of all classes participated in these public rituals of murder, which turned increasingly barbaric in the ensuing decades. Frequently, hundreds of spectators witnessed the cruel spectacle, watching white men torture and mutilate their black victims. After this sadistic prelude, most African Americans were hanged; others were burned alive or died in a hail of bullets. Many whites justified these crimes by citing the need to protect their wives and daughters against black "beast rapists." Yet few of the victims, most of whom were young men, were actually accused of interracial rape. More often, this charge served as a pretext for punishing those African Americans who had violated the region's racial etiquette. For African American men, the threat of lynching became doubly humiliating, since they risked death for even looking at white women, but white men, by contrast, could sexually abuse black women with impunity.[77]

In many ways, black nationalist thinking directly addressed this legacy of racialized and sexualized violence. As early as the 1950s, the African Nationalist Pioneer Movement stated: "We are against the white race or any race taking advantage of Black Women."[78] Throughout the 1950s and early 1960s, Elijah Muhammad echoed these sentiments, arguing in 1962 "that our women should be respected and protected as the women of other nationalities are respected and protected."[79] In his "Message to the Blackman," Muhammad made explicit reference to the legacy of lynching. "Stop allowing the white men to shake hands or speak to your women anytime and anywhere," he exhorted his followers. "This practice has ruined us. They wink their eye at your daughter after coming into your home—but you cannot go on the North side and do the same with his women."[80] Women thus became symbols of masculine articulations of the black nation, which African American men needed to protect.

During the Black Power era, violence became a major rhetorical and symbolic means that black nationalists used to offset the perceived imbalance between white Americans' insistence on their manhood and black men's perceived lack of it. To many black militants, the ideas of Malcolm X became yet again an important inspiration. From Malcolm's perspective, black armed resistance represented a crucial affirmation of black masculinity. Malcolm argued that black men ought to abandon Martin Luther King's emasculating nonviolent philosophy; instead they needed to assert themselves as protectors of "their" women and their families.[81] The militant Muslim activist repeatedly suggested that "passive" resistance stood for powerlessness and effeminacy, while armed protection symbolized true black manliness. "Anybody can sit," he once dismissed nonviolent sit-in demonstrations. Women and cowards could sit, he continued, but it took "a man to stand."[82] Malcolm X was convinced that his OAAU would regain blacks' "self-respect" and "manhood" as well as their "dignity and freedom," and active armed resistance would be the first step toward achieving this goal.[83]

Another inspiration that led many Black Power activists to reevaluate their interpretation of the relationship between gender and violence came from the writings of Frantz Fanon. In his analysis of the Algerian freedom struggle against French colonial rule, Fanon argued that violence could serve as a "cleansing force," through which a colonized people would be able to free themselves from their inferiority complex and restore their self-respect.[84] As Anne McClintock has pointed out, Fanon's work provides significant insights into the inner workings of colonialism, since it questions the family analogy that colonialists used to justify colonial violence and occupation. He also acknowledged the colonial use of women as symbolic mediators and the ways in which this symbolism functioned to domesticate the colony and to undermine the patriarchal power of indigenous men. At the same time, as McClintock critically notes, Fanon deemed indigenous women's agency "a passive offspring of male agency" that could exist only in subordinated position to the actions of men.[85] This male-centered perspective probably confirmed many of the gender stereotypes that African American male nationalists harbored and convinced them that only men could be at the forefront of black liberation and black nation-building.

Both Malcolm X and Fanon fundamentally changed black militants' thinking on the role of violence in the black freedom struggle. These changing interpretations were inextricably intertwined with masculinity. For example, the BPP leaders Huey P. Newton and Bobby Seale were fascinated with the Muslim minister. Like Malcolm, they regarded nonviolence as being degrading to black masculinity and offered an alternative construction of manhood that was grounded primarily in the use of gun violence to defend the black community.[86] Defining their identities in direct opposition to what they perceived as feminine characteristics—weakness, passiveness, and powerlessness—the Black Panthers believed that they embodied the real traits of black manliness. "The black woman found it difficult to respect the black man because he didn't even define himself as a man!" Newton explained in an interview. By contrast, the Black Panthers, "along with all revolutionary black groups" had "regained" African Americans' mind and manhood.[87] In the BPP chapters that emerged across the country in the late 1960s, black militants seem to have viewed their activism from similarly gendered perspectives. In Philadelphia, for instance, as historian Matthew Countryman concluded in his study of the city's freedom struggle, the "party's hypermasculine image of the gun-toting Panther came to represent not only the right to self-defense but all the rights of manhood, including the ability to support and protect a wife and children."[88]

Some members of the original Panthers, especially black writer Eldridge Cleaver, evinced an obsession with this struggle over gender identities. Repeatedly imprisoned on drug and rape charges between 1954 and 1966, Cleaver had become a follower of the NOI in prison but broke with Elijah Muhammad after the assassination of Malcolm X in 1965. Shortly after his release in late 1966, he joined the BPP. Cleaver's *Soul on Ice,* a collection of letters and essays that he had written in prison, reflects his preoccupation with black masculinity. Alluding to the idea that women become symbolic bearers of the black nation, he explained his assaults on white women as an insurrectionary act against white men. Cleaver's scathing criticism of black homosexuality further illustrates his fear of being considered effeminate and unmanly. To him, as he explained in an essay on gay black novelist James Baldwin, homosexuality was "a sickness" that would prompt black men to adopt white principles and white behavior.[89] Philip Brian Harper has pointed out that this alleged lack of racial identification among black homosexuals became a symbol of failed manhood in the eyes of many black nationalists. For example, black poet LeRoi Jones (Amiri Baraka) used homosexuality's connotations of effeminacy to criticize the moderate wing of the civil rights movement, insulting NAACP leader Roy Wilkins in a poem as "an eternal faggot."[90] Such acrimony toward homosexuals, as historian Winifred Breines has noted, "was frequently expressed as a way to condemn black men who worked with white men. Those thought not to be strong black men were called white-identified effeminate Uncle Toms."[91] Black nationalists thus tended to adopt white nationalism's homophobia, using the same racial and gendered dichotomies that characterized Anglo-European ideological nation-building.

Unlike other black nationalist organizations, however, the BPP was self-reflective enough to reconsider the group's initial focus on masculinity, a development that was a result of their Marxist class analysis as well as the outspokenness of female BPP members. In a 1969 group interview, for example, one female member said: "[I]t's important that within the context of that struggle that black men understand that their manhood is not dependent on keeping their black women subordinate to them because this is what bourgeois ideology has been trying to put into the black man and that's part of the special oppression of black women."[92] A year later, Huey Newton publicly called for alliances with feminists and gay activists, reconsidering some of his earlier statements. Newton explicitly said that male activists needed to "be willing to discuss the insecurities that many people have about homosexuality." To Newton, this was also a pragmatic decision, since feminist and gay activists were "potential allies" that the BPP strongly needed.[93]

Despite the fact that Newton reconsidered the sexist nature of black nationalist thought, however, its machismo remained strong and was severely criticized by black feminists in the mid-1970s.[94] Yet, what recent feminist scholarship tends to neglect when analyzing the problematic nature of the gendered dimensions of black nationalism is the role of hegemonic masculinity in black thinkers' attempts to reconceptualize both "true" black manhood and the black nation. The Panthers and other nationalists countered white stereotypes and regained self-respect, but they simultaneously appropriated and reproduced hegemonic masculinity and notions of nation that this gendered thinking entailed. On the one hand, given the marginalized character of black manhood in American society, the armed defiance of the Black Panthers and other groups represented a counter-hegemonic discourse, since militant activists sought to reclaim the attributes of manhood that white men had denied African Americans for centuries. On the other hand, black nationalists reaffirmed hegemonic masculinity by perpetuating traditions of misogyny and homophobia, two aspects that were central elements of white nationalist ideology.

The continuities in paraintellectuals' masculinity-centered thinking over the course of the second half of the twentieth century are striking when one analyzes the gendered dimensions of post-civil rights black nationalism. Despite the black feminist critique of the Black Power movement's machismo, sexism and homophobia continued to permeate the thinking of black nationalists in the post-civil rights era. Ron Karenga's Afrocentric holiday Kwanzaa is a case in point. Writing in 1988, Karenga stressed the importance of the family for African Americans and insisted on the "complementarity of male and female as distinct from and opposed to the concept of conflict of genders." Just as white nationalists had done in the past, Karenga explained that the family was "the smallest example of how the nation (or national community) works." A weakened family leads to a weakened nation.[95] Karenga presented what he considered "authentic" precolonial African gender relations as models for African Americans to follow, but in effect he used the same heteronormative tenets that white nationalists had employed throughout the twentieth century to perpetuate nationalized gender hierarchies. Even though Karenga somewhat softened his views on gender in the late twentieth and early twenty-first centuries, neither Karenga nor other Afrocentrist nationalists have embraced full gender equality or revised their views on homosexuality.[96]

Louis Farrakhan likewise continues to stress the essential nature of heteronormativity for black nationalism. Farrakhan's focus on the "endangered black male" echoes the calls of many Black Power activists that black liberation had to begin with the liberation of black men from the feminization by white supremacists. Farrakhan argued not only that any attempt to improve the situation of African Americans should start with black men but that black homosexuals threatened the future of the black community by undermining both traditional gender identities and racial unity, and thus the black nation. The Million Man March, which was organized by Farrakhan's Nation of Islam in 1995, reiterated such heteronormative ideas. Designated as "Day of Atonement," the demonstration drew several hundred thousand black men to Washington, DC and exhorted them to rededicate themselves to traditional family values and the time-honored ideal of the patriarchal provider and protector. Only this rededication, Farrakhan asserted, would help the black community win the struggle against drug abuse, violence, and teenage pregnancy. In the NOI's vision of the black nation, neither women nor homosexuals or transgender persons played any role. Only if they conformed to traditional gender identities that did not challenge hegemonic masculinity would they be able to help African Americans and thus the black nation. By arguing that only black self-help and rededication to these traditional values could help the "defective" culture of poor blacks, Farrakhan echoed the tenets of conservative white nationalists who insisted that racial discrimination played a negligible role in the plight of impoverished black communities in the urban United States.[97] Post-civil rights black nationalists thus adopted the same gendered language that their Anglo-European counterparts had long utilized to create national unity while simultaneously perpetuating traditional gender hierarchies.

CONCLUSION

African American post-civil rights intellectuals confronted an ideological predicament that anticolonial thinkers had known all too well. Just as it took Europe to "invent the language of decolonization" in former colonies in Africa and Asia, it took America to invent the language of black nationalism in the United States. A number of scholars have pointed to the ambiguous consequences of this ideological mixture. Critiquing the particular language that Black Power produced in the 1960s, for instance, Eddie Glaude concludes that it "suppressed the very real tensions within the sixties revolution in that the language of nation and the idea of blackness it often presupposed collapsed the differences among African Americans into ambivalent similarity."[98] Dean E. Robinson ventures even further in his assessment. "By accepting the notion that black people constitute an organic unit, and by focusing on the goal of nation building or separate political and economic development," he writes, "black nationalism inadvertently helps to reproduce some of the thinking and practices that created black disadvantage in the first place."[99] African American radical thinkers' conceptualization of Africa and gender in particular reveals how what was conceived of as antiracism could contribute to the perpetuation of American traditions of inequality. A postcolonial studies perspective contributes to a better understanding of these complexities because it helps us conceptualize the predicaments that black intellectuals faced in their attempts to conceive of a black nation that emancipates itself from Anglo-European ideas and traditions.

Despite the ambiguities and negative consequences of black nationalism, however, it is important to stress the positive legacies of black intellectuals who espoused nationalist ideas. Stressing the cultural dimensions of the Black Power movement, William Van Deburg has argued that black nationalist thinkers and the literary and artistic achievements they produced "raised both individual and group expectations, made black folk feel good about themselves, and steered them away from 'cultural homicide.'"[100] More recently, Peniel Joseph and others have stressed the important political legacies of Black Power and related black nationalist ideologies, which Joseph says complemented changes in culture, identity, and politics. "Ultimately," he writes, "the Black Power Movement left a legacy that altered black political discourses, culture, and consciousness. More specifically, the BPM was institutionalized through the creation of Black Studies departments and programs at American universities and through the rise of black elected officials."[101] After decades of neglect and disparagement, the legacy of black nationalist thought is currently being reconsidered and reinterpreted. It remains to be seen whether this intellectual legacy will ultimately be regarded as a central element of American intellectual history.

NOTES

1. "Basic Unity Program: Organization of Afro-American Unity," in Malcolm X, *February 1965: The Final Speeches* (New York: Pathfinder, 1992), 259.

2. Leela Gandhi, *Postcolonial Theory: A Critical Introduction* (New York: Columbia University Press, 1998), 115, 118.

3. Dean E. Robinson, *Black Nationalism in American Politics and Thought* (New York: Cambridge University Press, 2001), 70.

4. Martin Kilson was the first to use the term "paraintellectuals." Harold Cruse likewise emphasized the significance of this group of black thinkers as early as the 1960s. See Martin Kilson, "The New Black Intellectuals," *Dissent* 16, no. 4 (July-August 1969): 304–10; Harold Cruse, *The Crisis of the Negro Intellectual* (New York: William Morrow, 1967).

5. Amritjit Singh and Peter Schmidt, "On the Borders between US Studies and Postcolonial Theory," in *Postcolonial Theory and the United States: Race, Ethnicity, and Literature*, ed. Amritjit Singh and Peter Schmidt (Jackson: University Press of Mississippi, 2000), 5. See also C. Richard King, ed., *Postcolonial America* (Urbana: University of Illinois Press, 2000).

6. Gayatri Chakravorty Spivak, "Teaching for the Times," in *Dangerous Liaisons: Gender, Nation, and Postcolonial Perspectives*, ed. Anne McClintock, Aamir Mufti, and Ella Shohat (Minneapolis: University of Minnesota Press, 1997), 478.

7. Fanon's works were translated into English in the 1960s. See Frantz Fanon, *Black Skin, White Masks* (New York: Grove, 1967) and Frantz Fanon, *The Wretched of the Earth* (New York: Grove Weidenfeld, 1963).

8. "The Nation: Real or Imagined? The Warwick Debates on Nationalism," *Nations and Nationalism* 2, no. 3 (1996): 359.

9. Walker Connor, *Ethnonationalism: The Quest for Understanding* (Princeton, NJ: Princeton University Press, 1994), 92.

10. The best-known representatives of these two schools are modernist Ernest Gellner and ethnicist Anthony D. Smith. On the theoretical discussions about modernists and ethnicists, see "The Nation: Real or Imagined? The Warwick Debates on Nationalism," *Nations and Nationalism* 2, no. 3 (1996): 357–70; Walter Schnee, "Nationalism: A Review of the Literature," *Journal of Political and Military Sociology* 29, no. 1 (Summer 2001): 1–18. On discussions about civic and ethnic nationalism, see David Brown, "The Ethnic Majority: Benign or Malign?" *Nations and Nationalism* 14, no. 4 (2008): 768–88; David Brown, "Are There Good and Bad Nationalisms?" Nations and Nationalism 5, no. 2 (1999): 281–302; Tim Nieguth, "Beyond Dichotomy: Concepts of the Nation and the Distribution of Membership," *Nations and Nationalism* 5, no. 2 (1999): 155–73.

11. See Eric Hobsbawm and Terence Ranger, eds., *The Invention of Tradition* (Cambridge: Cambridge University Press, 1983); Benedict Anderson, *Imagined Communities: Reflections on the Origin and Spread of Nationalism*, rev. ed. (New York: Verso, 1991).

12. The most influential works on these various aspects of nationalism have been Nira Yuval Davis and Floya Anthias, *Woman-Nation-State* (London: Macmillan, 1989); Michael Billig, *Banal Nationalism* (London: Sage, 1995); Nira Yuval-Davis, *Gender and Nation* (London: Sage, 1997); Anne McClintock, "'No Longer in a Future Heaven': Gender, Race, and Nationalism," in *Dangerous Liaisons: Gender, Nation, and Postcolonial Perspectives*, ed. Anne McClintock, Aamir Mufti, and Ella Shohat (Minneapolis: University of Minnesota Press, 1997), 89–112; Partha Chatterjee, *The Nation and Its Fragments: Colonial and Postcolonial Histories* (Princeton: Princeton University Press, 1993); Craig Calhoun, *Nations Matter: Culture, History, and the Cosmopolitan Dream* (New York: Routledge, 2007).

13. John H. Bracey Jr., August Meier, Elliott Rudwick, "Introduction," in *Black Nationalism in America*, ed. John H. Bracey Jr., August Meier, and Elliott Rudwick (Indianapolis: Bobbs-Merrill, 1970), xxvi.

14. Raymond L. Hall, *Black Separatism in the United States* (Hanover, NH: University Press of New England, 1978), 1.

15. Wilson Jeremiah Moses, "Introduction," in *Classical Black Nationalism: From the American Revolution to Marcus Garvey*, ed. Wilson Jeremiah Moses (New York: New York University Press, 1996), 2.

16. Wahneema Lubiano, "Standing In for the State: Black Nationalism and 'Writing' the Black Subject," in *Is It Nation Time? Contemporary Essays on Black Power and Black Nationalism*, ed. Eddie S. Glaude Jr. (Chicago: University of Chicago Press, 2002), 157.

17. E. Frances White, "Africa on My Mind: Gender, Counter Discourse and African American Nationalism," *Journal of Women's History* 2, no. 1 (Spring 1990): 73.

18. Robinson, *Black Nationalism in American Politics and Thought*, 3, 6.

19. On these developments, see Wilson Jeremiah Moses, *The Golden Age of Black Nationalism, 1850–1925* (New York: Oxford University Press, 1978); Sterling Stuckey, *Slave Culture: Nationalist Theory and the Foundations of Black America* (New York: Oxford University Press, 1988); John Thornton, *Africa and Africans in the Making of the Atlantic World, 1400–1800*, 2nd ed. (Cambridge: Cambridge University Press, 1998); James Sidbury, *Becoming African in America: Race and Nation in the Early Black Atlantic* (New York: Oxford University Press, 2009).

20. See Alphonso Pinkney, *Red, Black, and Green: Black Nationalism in the United States* (London: Cambridge University Press, 1976); Moses, *The Golden Age of Black Nationalism*; Stephen Ward Angell, *Bishop Henry McNeal Turner and African-American Religion in the South* (Knoxville: University of Tennessee Press, 1992); Kate Dossett, *Bridging Race Divides: Black Nationalism, Feminism, and Integration in the United States, 1896–1935* (Gainesville: University Press of Florida, 2008).

21. On Garvey's life and his organizing efforts in the United States, see Edmund David Cronon, *Black Moses: The Story of Marcus Garvey and the Universal Negro Improvement Association* (Madison: University Press of Wisconsin, 1955); Tony Martin, *Race First: The Ideological and Organizational Struggles of Marcus Garvey and the Universal Negro*

Improvement Association (Westport, CT: Greenwood, 1976); Judith Stein, *The World of Marcus Garvey: Race and Class in Modern Society* (Baton Rouge: Louisiana State University Press, 1986); Lawrence Levine, "Marcus Garvey and the Politics of Revitalization," in *Black Leaders in the Twentieth Century*, ed. John Hope Franklin and August Meier (Urbana: University of Illinois Press, 1986), 104–38; Mary G. Rolinson, *Grassroots Garveyism: The Universal Negro Improvement Association in the Rural South, 1920–1927* (Chapel Hill: University of North Carolina Press, 2007).

22. Theodore G. Vincent, *Black Power and the Garvey Movement* (Berkeley, CA: Ramparts, 1971); John Henrik Clarke, *Marcus Garvey and the Vision of Africa* (New York: Random House, 1974); Colin Grant, *Negro with a Hat: The Rise and Fall of Marcus Garvey* (New York: Oxford University Press, 2008).

23. C. Eric Lincoln, *Black Muslims in America* (Boston, MA: Beacon, 1961); Clifton E. Marsh, *From Black Muslims to Muslims: The Resurrection, Transformation, and Change of the Lost-Found Nation of Islam in America, 1930–1995*, 2nd ed. (Metuchen, NJ: Scarecrow, 1996); Edward E. Curtis IV, *Islam in Black America: Identity, Liberation, and Difference in African-American Islamic Thought* (Albany: State University of New York Press, 2002).

24. See Mark Naison, *Communists in Harlem during the Depression* (Urbana: University of Illinois Press, 1983); Robin D. G. Kelley, *Hammer and Hoe: Alabama Communists during the Depression* (Chapel Hill: University of North Carolina Press, 1990); Mark Solomon, *The Cry Was Unity: Communists and African Americans, 1917–1936* (Jackson: University Press of Mississippi, 1998); Manfred Berg, *"The Ticket to Freedom": The NAACP and the Struggle for Black Political Integration* (Gainesville: University Press of Florida, 2005); Glenda Elizabeth Gilmore, *Defying Dixie: The Radical Roots of Civil Rights, 1919–1950* (New York: W. W. Norton, 2008).

25. Moses, "Introduction," 2–3.

26. Roy Innis, "From Separatist Economics: A New Social Contract," in *Modern Black Nationalism: From Marcus Garvey to Louis Farrakhan*, ed. William L. Van Deburg (New York: New York University Press, 1997), 178.

27. Elijah Muhammad, "What Do the Muslims Want?" in *Black Nationalism in America*, 404. On Elijah Muhammad and the Nation of Islam, see Claude A. Clegg III, *An Original Man: The Life and Times of Elijah Muhammad* (New York: St. Martin's, 1997); Edward E. Curtis, *Black Muslim Religion in the Nation of Islam, 1960–1975* (Chapel Hill: University of North Carolina Press, 2006).

28. Malcolm X, "Message to the Grass Roots," in *A History of Our Time: Readings on Postwar America*, ed. William H. Chafe and Harvard Sitkoff, 4th ed. (New York: Oxford University Press, 1995), 199.

29. "An Interview by A. B. Spellman," in Malcolm X, *By Any Means Necessary*, 2nd ed. (New York: Pathfinder, 1992), 5.

30. On the life of Malcolm X, see Peter Louis Goldman, *The Death and Life of Malcolm X*, 2nd ed. (Urbana: University of Illinois Press, 1979); Eugene Wolfenstein, *The Victims of Democracy: Malcolm X and the Black Revolution* (Berkeley: University of California Press, 1981); James Cone, *Martin and Malcolm and America: A Dream or a Nightmare* (Maryknoll, NY: Orbis Books, 1991); Bruce Perry, *Malcolm: The Life of a Man Who Changed*

Black America (New York: Station Hill, 1991); William W. Sales Jr., *From Civil Rights to Black Liberation: Malcolm X and the Organization of Afro-American Unity* (Boston: South End, 1994); Michael Eric Dyson, *Making Malcolm: The Myth and Meaning of Malcolm X* (New York: Oxford University Press, 1995); Manning Marable, *Malcolm X: A Life of Reinvention* (New York: Viking, 2011).

31. On Baraka's black nationalist activism, see Komozi Woodard, *A Nation within a Nation: Amiri Baraka (LeRoi Jones) and Black Power Politics* (Chapel Hill: University of North Carolina Press, 1999).

32. Leroi Jones, "The Legacy of Malcolm X, and the Coming of the Black Nation," in Amiri Baraka, *The Leroi Jones/Amiri Baraka Reader*, ed. William J. Harris (New York: Basic Books, 2009), 163.

33. Amiri Baraka, "Speech to the Congress of African Peoples," in Van Deburg, *Modern Black Nationalism*, 154.

34. "Pan-Africanism," in Stokely Carmichael (Kwame Ture), *Stokely Speaks: From Black Power to Pan-Africanism* (Chicago: Chicago Review Press, 2007), 197, 202–03.

35. William L. Van Deburg, *New Day in Babylon: The Black Power Movement and American Culture, 1965–1975* (Chicago: University of Chicago Press, 1992), 147; "From the Anti-Depression Program of the Republic of New Africa," in Van Deburg, *Modern Black Nationalism*, 199. On the history of the RNA, see Donald Cunnigen, "The Republic of New Africa in Mississippi," in *Black Power in the Belly of the Beast*, ed. Judson L. Jeffries (Urbana: University of Illinois Press, 2006), 93–115.

36. Albert Scharenberg, *Schwarzer Nationalismus in den USA: Das Malcolm X Revival* (Münster: Westfälisches Dampfboot, 1998), 392.

37. African Nationalist Pioneer Movement, "We Advocate Complete Economic Control by the Blacks of All African Communities in America," in *Black Nationalism in America*, 487.

38. Muhammad, "What Do the Muslims Want?" 405.

39. Leroi Jones, "The Legacy of Malcolm X and the Coming of the Black Nation," 166.

40. "Free Huey," in Carmichael, *Stokely Speaks*, 129.

41. "The Young Socialist Interview," in Malcolm X, *By Any Means Necessary*, 159.

42. See Floyd W. Hayes III and Francis A. Kiene III, "'All Power to the People': The Political Thought of Huey P. Newton and the Black Panther Party," in *The Black Panther Party Reconsidered*, ed. Charles Jones (Baltimore: Black Classic, 1998), 157–76. On the history of the Black Panther Party, see Jones, *The Black Panther Party Reconsidered*; Yohuru Williams, *Black Politics/White Power: Civil Rights, Black Power, and the Black Panthers in New Haven* (New York: Brandywine, 2000); Kathleen Cleaver and George Katsiaficas, eds., *Liberation, Imagination, and the Black Panther Party: A New Look at the Panthers and Their Legacy* (New York: Routledge, 2001); Jeffrey O. G. Ogbar, *Black Power: Radical Politics and African American Identity* (Baltimore, MD: Johns Hopkins University Press, 2004); Jama Lazerow and Yohuru Williams, eds., *In Search of the Black Panther Party: New Perspectives on a Revolutionary Movement* (Durham: Duke University Press, 2006); Curtis J. Austin, *Up against the Wall: Violence in the Making and Unmaking of the Black Panther Party* (Fayetteville: University of Arkansas Press, 2006); Paul Alkebulan, *Survival Pending*

Revolution: The History of the Black Panther Party (Tuscaloosa: University of Alabama Press, 2007); Jane Rhodes, *Framing the Black Panthers: The Spectacular Rise of a Black Power Icon* (New York: New Press, 2007); Judson L. Jeffries, ed., *Comrades: A Local History of the Black Panther Party* (Bloomington: Indiana University Press, 2007); Yohuru Williams and Jama Lazerow, eds., *Liberated Territory: Untold Local Perspectives on the Black Panther Party* (Durham: Duke University Press, 2009); and Robyn C. Spencer, *The Revolution Has Come: Black Power, Gender, and the Black Panther Party in Oakland* (Durham: Duke University Press, 2016).

43. "His Best Credentials," in *Malcolm X: As They Knew Him*, ed. David Gallen (New York: Carroll and Graf, 1992), 162.

44. Leroi Jones, "The Legacy of Malcolm X," 167.

45. Kwame Ture (Stokely Carmichael) and Charles V. Hamilton, *Black Power: The Politics of Liberation* (New York: Vintage Books, 1992; repr. 1967), 34.

46. Scot Brown, *Fighting for US: Maulena Karenga, the US Organization, and Black Cultural Nationalism* (New York: New York University Press, 2003), 29, 38–39.

47. Askia Muhammad Touré (Rolland Sellings), "We Must Create a National Black Intelligentsia in Order to Survive," in *Black Nationalism in America*, 453, 457.

48. On the Black Arts Movement, see James Edward Smethurst, *The Black Arts Movement: Literary Nationalism in the 1960s and 1970s* (Chapel Hill: University of North Carolina Press, 2005); Lisa Gail Collins and Natalie Crawford, eds., *New Thoughts on the Black Arts Movement* (New Brunswick, NJ: Rutgers University Press, 2006); Amy Abugo Ongiri, *Spectacular Blackness: The Cultural Politics of the Black Arts Movement and the Search for a Black Aesthetic* (Charlottesville, VA: University of Virginia Press, 2009).

49. Louis Farrakhan, "From P.O.W.E.R. at Last and Forever," in Van Deburg, *Modern Black Nationalism*, 319. On Louis Farrakhan, see Matthias Gardell, *In the Name of Elijah Muhammad: Louis Farrakhan and the Nation of Islam* (Durham: Duke University Press, 1996); Robert Singh, *The Farrakhan Phenomenon: Race, Reaction, and the Paranoid Style in American Politics* (Washington, DC: Georgetown University Press, 1997).

50. "The Homecoming Rally of the OAAU," in Malcolm X, *By Any Means Necessary*, 146.

51. "Message from Guinea," in Carmichael, *Stokely Speaks*, 177.

52. "Pan-Africanism," in Carmichael, *Stokely Speaks*, 205; Kwame Ture, "Afterword, 1992," in Ture, *Black Power*, 196, 198, 199.

53. "The Founding Rally of the OAAU," in Malcolm X, *By Any Means Necessary*, 54–55.

54. "The Oppressed Masses of the World Cry Out for Action against the Common Oppressor," in Malcolm X, *February 1965: The Final Speeches*, 53, 55.

55. "Basic Unity Program: Organization of Afro-American Unity," in Malcolm X, *February 1965: The Final Speeches*, 258, 259.

56. Algernon Austin, *Race, Black Nationalism, and Afrocentrism in the Twentieth Century* (New York: New York University Press 2006), 110–18; White, "Africa on my Mind," 83–85.

57. Max Stanford, "Revolutionary Nationalism, Black Nationalism, or Just Plain Blackism," in *Black Nationalism in America*, 508.

58. On the history of RAM, see Akbar Muhammad Ahmad, "RAM: The Revolutionary Action Movement," in *Black Power in the Belly of the Beast*, 252–80.

59. Ture and Hamilton, *Black Power*, 5.

60. Ibid., 23.

61. "The Black American and Palestinian Revolutions," in Carmichael, *Stokely Speaks*, 132.

62. Floyd B. McKissick, "Black Business Development with Social Commitment to Black Communities," in *Black Nationalism in America*, 497. On McKissick and Soul City, see Christopher Strain, "Soul City, North Carolina: Black Power, Utopia, and the African American Dream," *Journal of African American History* 89, no. 1 (Winter 2004): 57–74; Timothy J. Minchin, "'A Brand New Shining City': Floyd B. McKisick Sr. and the Struggle to Build Soul City, North Carolina," *North Carolina Historical Review* 82, no. 2 (April 2005): 125–55; Devin Fergus, *Liberalism, Black Power, and the Making of American Politics, 1965–1980* (Athens: University of Georgia Press, 2009).

63. Roy Innis, "From Separatist Economics: A New Social Contract," in Van Deburg, *Modern Black Nationalism*, 177, 179.

64. "From the Anti-Depression Program of the Republic of New Africa," in Van Deburg, *Modern Black Nationalism*, 198.

65. The Republic of New Africa, "We are the Government for the Non-Self-Governing Blacks Held Captive within the United States," in *Black Nationalism in America*, 518.

66. Max Stanford, "A Message from Jail," in *Black Nationalism in America*, 514.

67. Kai T. Erikson, ed., *In Search of Common Ground: Conversations with Erik H. Erikson and Huey P. Newton* (New York: Norton, 1973), 30–31.

68. Scharenberg, *Schwarzer Nationalismus in den USA*, 390.

69. See Joan W. Scott, "Gender: A Useful Category of Historical Analysis," *American Historical Review* 91, no. 5 (December 1986): 1053–75; Joan W. Scott, "Unanswered Questions," *American Historical Review* 113, no. 5 (December 2008): 1422–29; Joanne Meyerowitz, "A History of 'Gender,'" *American Historical Review* 113, no. 5 (December 2008): 1346–56.

70. Tim Carrigan, Bob Connell, and John Lee, "Toward a New Sociology of Masculinity," *Theory and Society* 14, no. 5 (September 1985): 592–94; R. W. Connell, "The Big Picture: Masculinities in Recent World History," *Theory and Society* 22, no. 5 (October 1993): 597–623; R. W. Connell, *Masculinities* (Cambridge, UK: Polity, 1995), 37–38, 77; R. W. Connell and James W. Messerschmidt, "Hegemonic Masculinity: Rethinking the Concept," *Gender and Society* 19, no. 6 (December 2005): 829–59.

71. See Nira Yuval-Davis and Floya Anthias, *Woman-Nation-State* (New York: Palgrave Macmillan, 1989); Nira Yuval-Davis, *Gender and Nation* (New York: Sage, 1997); Andrew Parker, Mary Russo, Doris Sommer, and Patricia Yaeger, eds., *Nationalisms and Sexuality* (New York: Routledge, 1992); Ida Blom, Karen Hagemann, and Catherine Hall, eds., *Gendered Nations: Nationalism and Gender Order in the Long Nineteenth Century* (New York: Berg, 2000); Tamar Mayer, ed., *Gender Ironies of Nationalism: Sexing the Nation* (New York: Routledge, 2000); Yasmeen Abu-Laban, ed., *Gendering the Nation-State: Canadian and Comparative Perspectives* (Vancouver: UBC, 2008).

72. Tamar Mayer, "Gender Ironies of Nationalism: Setting the Stage," in *Gender Ironies of Nationalism*, 5–12.

73. See Tricia Cusack, "Janus and Gender: Women and the Nation's Backward Look," *Nations and Nationalism* 6, no. 4 (2000): 541–61.

74. Yuval-Davis, *Gender and Nation*, 22.

75. See Joane Nagel, "Masculinity and Nationalism: Gender and Sexuality in the Making of Nations," *Ethnic and Racial Studies* 21, no. 2 (March 1998): 242–69; Dorinne Kondo, "Fabricating Masculinity: Gender, Race, and Nation in a Transnational Frame," in *Between Woman and Nation: Nationalisms, Transnational Feminisms, and the State*, eds. Norma Alarcón and Minoo Moallem (Durham: Duke University Press, 1999), 296–319; Mrinalini Sinha, *Colonial Masculinity: The "Manly Englishman" and the "Effeminate Bengali" in the Late Nineteenth Century* (Manchester: Manchester University Press, 1995); Gail Bederman, *Manliness and Civilization: A Cultural History of Gender and Race in the United States, 1880–1917* (Chicago: University of Chicago Press, 1995), 170–215; Kristin L. Hoganson, *Fighting for American Manhood: How Gender Politics Provoked the Spanish-American and Philippine-American Wars* (New Haven: Yale University Press, 1998); Sikata Banerjee, *Make Me a Man! Masculinity, Hinduism, and Nationalism in India* (Albany: State University of New York, 2005).

76. See Steve Derné, "Men's Sexuality and Women's Subordination in Indian Nationalisms," in *Gender Ironies of Nationalism*, 237–58.

77. On the gendered complexities of lynching, see Jacquelyn Dowd Hall, *Revolt against Chivalry: Jessie Daniel Ames and the Women's Campaign against Lynching* (New York: Columbia University Press, 1979); Jacquelyn Dowd Hall, "'The Mind That Burns in Each Body': Women, Rape, and Racial Violence," in *Powers of Desire: The Politics of Sexuality*, ed. Ann Snitow, Christine Stansell, and Sharon Thompson (New York: Monthly Review, 1983), 328–49; Crystal N. Feimster, *Southern Horrors: Women and the Politics of Rape and Lynching* (Cambridge: Harvard University Press, 2009).

78. African Nationalist Pioneer Movement, "We Advocate Complete Economic Control by the Blacks of All African Communities in America," in *Black Nationalism in America*, 487.

79. Muhammad, "What Do the Muslims Want?" 407.

80. Elijah Muhammad, "From a Program of Self-Development," in Van Deburg, *Modern Black Nationalism*, 104–105.

81. Quoted in M. S. Handler, "Malcolm X Terms Dr. King's Tactics Futile," *New York Times*, May 11, 1963, 9.

82. Quoted in Perry, *Malcolm*, 282.

83. "The Founding Rally of the OAAU," in Malcolm X, *By Any Means Necessary*, 53.

84. Fanon, *The Wretched of the Earth*, 73.

85. See McClintock, "'No Longer in a Future Heaven': Gender, Race, and Nationalism," 93–97, 98.

86. Wallace Turner, "A Gun Is Power, Black Panther Says," *New York Times*, May 21, 1967, 66; "From 'In Defense of Self-Defense' II: July 3, 1967," in Huey P. Newton, *To Die for the People: The Writings of Huey P. Newton* (New York: Random House, 1972), 90.

87. "Interview with Huey Newton," in *Black Protest Thought in the Twentieth Century*, ed. August Meier, Elliot Rudwick, and Francis L. Brodwick, 2nd ed. (Indianapolis: Bobbs-Merill, 1971), 508.

88. Matthew J. Countryman, *Up South: Civil Rights and Black Power in Philadelphia* (Philadelphia: University of Pennsylvania Press, 2006), 287–88. On the gender dynamics within the Black Panther Party, see also Angely D. LeBlanc-Ernest, "'The Most Qualified Person to Handle the Job': Black Panther Party Women, 1966–1982," in *The Black Panther*

Party Reconsidered, 305-34; Tracye Matthews, "'No One Ever Asks What a Man's Place in the Revolution Is': The Politics of Gender in the Black Panther Party, 1966-1971," in *The Black Panther Party Reconsidered*, 267-304; Steve Estes, *"I am a Man!": Race, Manhood, and the Civil Rights Movement* (Chapel Hill: University of North Carolina Press, 2005); Simon Wendt, *The Spirit and the Shotgun: Armed Resistance and the Struggle for Civil Rights* (Gainesville: University Press of Florida, 2007); Linda Lumsden, "Good Mothers with Guns: Framing Black Womanhood in the *Black Panther*, 1968-1980," *Journalism Mass Communication Quarterly* 86, no. 4 (Winter 2009): 900-23; Amy Abugo Ongiri, "Prisoner of Love: Affiliation, Sexuality, and the Black Panther Party," *Journal of African American History* 94, no. 1 (Winter 2009): 69-86; Spencer, *The Revolution Has Come*.

89. Eldridge Cleaver, *Soul on Ice* (1968; repr. New York: Dell, 1992), 26, 101-6.

90. Philip Brian Harper, *Are We Not Men? Masculine Anxiety and the Problem of African-American Identity* (New York: Oxford University Press, 1996), 50.

91. Winifred Breines, *The Trouble between Us: An Uneasy History of White and Black Women in the Feminist Movement* (New York: Oxford University Press, 2006), 56.

92. "Panther Sisters on Women's Liberation," in Van Deburg, *Modern Black Nationalism*, 262.

93. "White Women's Liberation and Gay Liberation Movements: August 15, 1970," in *The Huey P. Newton Reader*, ed. David Hilliard and Donald Weise (New York: Seven Stories, 2002), 159.

94. Kimberly Springer, *Living for the Revolution: Black Feminist Organizations, 1968-1980* (Durham: Duke University Press, 2005); Breines, *The Trouble between Us*; Kimberly Springer, "Black Feminists Respond to Black Power Masculinism," in *The Black Power Movement: Rethinking the Civil Rights-Black Power Era*, ed. Peniel E. Joseph (New York: Routledge, 2006), 105-18; Anne M. Valk, *Radical Sisters: Second-Wave Feminism and Black Liberation in Washington, DC* (Urbana: University of Illinois Press, 2008).

95. Maulana Karenga, "From the Nguzo Saba (The Seven Principles): Their Meaning and Message," in Van Deburg, *Modern Black Nationalism*, 277, 278.

96. White, "Africa on my Mind," 75, 76-77, 86.

97. Irene Monroe, "Louis Farrakhan's Ministry of Misogyny and Homophobia," in *The Farrakhan Factor: African-American Writers on Leadership, Nationhood, and Minister Louis Farrakhan*, ed. Amy Alexander (New York: Grove, 1998), 276, 279; Nikol G. Alexander-Floyd, *Gender, Race, and Nationalism in Contemporary Black Politics* (New York: Palgrave Macmillan, 2007), 29-33, 61-67.

98. Glaude, "Introduction: Black Power Revisited," in *Is It Nation Time?* 10.

99. Robinson, *Black Nationalism in American Politics and Thought*, 1-2.

100. Van Deburg, *New Day in Babylon*, 304.

101. Peniel E. Joseph, "Introduction: Toward a Historiography of the Black Power Movement," in *The Black Power Movement*, 11. See also Peniel E. Joseph, "The Black Power Movement: A State of the Field," *Journal of American History* 96, no. 3 (December 2009): 751-76; Peniel E. Joseph, "The Black Power Movement, Democracy, and America in the King Years," *American Historical Review* 114, no. 4 (October 2009): 1001-16; Peniel E. Joseph, "Rethinking the Black Power Era," *Journal of Southern History*, 75, no. 3 (August 2009): 707-16.

- CHAPTER SEVEN -

AFROCENTRIC INTELLECTUALS AND THE BURDEN OF HISTORY

TUNDE ADELEKE

The black experience in America, and indeed the black experience worldwide, has borne the burden of history: the history of negation. "The Dark Continent," "Heathens," and "Barbarians," are some of the racist epithets that "enlightened" Europeans mobilized to launch the imperial phase of "The White Man's Burden." This worldview denied peoples of African ancestry a credible space among civilized beings. It nullified African history and culture and mandated Europeans to lead Africans and diaspora blacks toward civilization, historical and cultural rebirth.[1] The resultant Eurocentric ideology sought to nurture a compliant, subordinate, docile, and malleable personality. Ironically, it also induced in blacks, as well, a self-deterministic resolve to resist utilizing the very discipline (history) that Europeans had invoked to legitimize black subordination. As several scholars have demonstrated from the late Earl Thorpe, through John Ernest, to the more recent work by Stephen Hall, the negation of African history and culture induced in blacks a determination to resist with the weapon of history.[2] This interest in history birthed the nucleus of a black intelligentsia in the nineteenth century. These "Pioneers in Protest" (James W. C. Pennington, William Wells Brown, Benjamin Brawley, William Cooper Nell, William Still, and George Washington Williams, etc.) embarked on the study and research of history in order to combat the racism that permeated the intellectual culture of their times.[3]

The historical calling of the black intellectual, therefore, is rooted in the challenges and tribulations of the black experience. Long before the appearance of a professional class of black intellectuals, the challenges of historical racism compelled some blacks to seek historical knowledge. G. N. Grisham, a professor and principal of a high school in Kansas City, Missouri, described as "one of the ablest educators and most practical philosophers in the country," delivered a speech in December 1897 in which he stressed the importance of historical scholarship and urged the black scholar to "do something for his race," by helping to develop a revolutionary historical consciousness and forging "the connection between his race and civilization."[4] Grisham wanted black intellectuals to reclaim that link between Africa and civilization that leading European intellectuals had denied.[5] Grisham's motivation and vision were consistent with those of the "Pioneers." It would be left to future generations to theorize about black intellectual responsibility. As William E. B. Du Bois implied, the intellectual leadership he characterized as the "Talented Tenth" would have to engage historical studies in order to negate centuries of what Carter G. Woodson later characterized as Eurocentric miseducation.[6] The preoccupation of black intellectuals with rewriting, revising, and publicizing black history and culture became a critical repertoire of resistance. In every generation since the nineteenth century, therefore, black intellectuals engaged this struggle for historical affirmation.[7] Due to the historical circumstances, the writings of the "Pioneers" were driven more by advocacy and rehabilitation than respect for canons of historical scholarship. Most were activists drawn to history by the challenge of debunking entrenched historical fallacies.[8] By the late nineteenth and early twentieth centuries, however, Du Bois and Woodson inaugurated a school of professional historians who combined advocacy with attention to a cardinal rule of historical scholarship—research derived from credible and verifiable historical sources.[9] To be taken seriously, therefore, black intellectuals must not be driven solely by ideology and advocacy. They had to take their scholarly responsibilities seriously and be validated by established canons of historical scholarship. Du Bois, Woodson, and the New Negro History Movement (NNHM) utilized their research and scholarship to gain legitimacy for black history.[10] Black history became the foundation on which black studies would thrive from the late 1960s on.

No one understood the importance of intellectual credibility better than the late John Hope Franklin. His scholarship remains a lasting monument of intellectual excellence. As he once observed, "The dilemmas and problem of the Negro scholar are numerous and complex. He has been forced, first of all, to establish his claim to being a scholar and he had somehow to seek recognition in the general world of scholarship . . . [T]his has not been an easy and simple task."[11] Furthermore, Franklin continued, "Since American scholarship in general" denied that "Negroes were capable of being scholars," the black intellectual had to first "struggle against forces and personalities in American life that insisted that he could never rise in the intellectual sphere."[12] Earlier generations had struggled against these "forces and personalities" and won recognition for black history and ultimately black studies. However, the attainment of intellectual recognition for black studies had the unintended consequence of the ghettoization of the black intellectual. Black intellectuals became, in Franklin's words, "the victim[s] of segregation in the field of scholarship."[13] The struggle to validate the African historical tradition had resulted in the depiction of the black intellectual as someone uniquely qualified and best suited to study and research black history and experiences. Blacks were deemed to possess "peculiar talents that fitted them to study themselves and their problems."[14] Denouncing this mindset, Franklin urged the black scholar to reject this "unfortunate development" (ghettoization) by focusing on the truths and insisting that his writings be "sanctioned by universal standards developed and maintained by those who frequently do not even recognize him."[15] In other words, Franklin cautioned against combating Eurocentrism with its black equivalence; an intellectual ideology that replicated negative, anti-intellectual and racist ethos. He acknowledged that "the task of remaining calm and objective is indeed a formidable one," and the black intellectual is always tempted to "pollute his scholarship with polemics, diatribes, arguments."[16] Though Franklin understood the challenges of objectivity in the context of such overwhelming intellectual bigotry, he warned the black intellectual nonetheless against succumbing to the "attractive temptation" to fight intellectual racism with intellectual racism.[17] By succumbing to "the attractive temptation," the black intellectual would, Franklin believed, "by one act destroy his effectiveness and disqualify himself as a true and worthy scholar."[18] Franklin valued intellectual credibility. He urged black intellectuals to recognize the "difference between scholarship and advocacy" and use scholarship, "to correct the findings of pseudo scholars in other disciplines who used their writings to justify oppression of blacks."[19] The black scholar, in Franklin's words, "Must rewrite the history of this country and correct the misrepresentations and falsifications in connection with the Negro's role in our country."[20] Though he acknowledged "a place for advocacy" in scholarship, Franklin theorized the need for a clear understanding of the distinction between advocacy and scholarship.[21]

Franklin's call for a distinction between advocacy and scholarship has not received universal acclaim. A growing number of Afrocentric scholars advance a counternarrative. Building upon the historical tradition of black alienation and marginalization, Afrocentric scholars advocate prioritizing ideology and advocacy. While Franklin called for "recognizing the importance of the use of objective data in the passionate advocacy of the rectification of injustice," Afrocentric scholars challenged the need for objectivity in historical scholarship. Building on the nineteenth-century "Afrocentric" ideas and themes in the writings of Martin Delany, Henry Garnet, and Henry McNeal Turner, among others, Afrocentric scholars such as Molefi Asante, Maulana Karenga, Na'im Akbar, Dona Marimba Richards (aka Marimba Ani), the late John Henrik Clarke, and Chancellor Williams developed Afrocentrism into a full-fledged and combative ideology of intellectual resistance.

This chapter examines and discusses the many dimensions of Afrocentric constructions of the African/diaspora black historical experiences, highlighting the consequences of the failure to clearly distinguish between advocacy and scholarship. It analyzes how Afrocentric emphasis on advocacy and essentialism compromises understanding of the globalizing and complex dimensions of the African/diaspora black history and culture. Fundamentally, Afrocentrism is an ahistoristic response to issues and challenges of profound historical essence and consequences. The chapter therefore illuminates fundamental flaws in Afrocentric historiography in relation to engaging the conflict over heritage, culture, and history. It also complicates the advocacy-derived "history" Afrocentric scholars write and defend.

HISTORICAL ROOTS AND ANTECEDENTS

The rehabilitation of African and diaspora black historical experiences and cultural heritage is a daunting task black intellectuals have engaged from time immemorial. The racist worldview that birthed "the Dark Continent" invalidated African history, caricatured African culture, identified civilization with Europe and Africa with primitivism, and predictably legitimized slavery and colonialism. The historical experiences of continental Africans and diaspora blacks have been defined by racism, negation, objectification, and mystification.[22] The challenge for black intellectuals, therefore, entailed engaging and contesting this genre. The need to establish historical heritage in antiquity became an existential imperative.

Black activists and intellectuals from Frederick Douglass and the "Pioneers," down to Du Bois and Woodson vigorously contested Eurocentric historiography. They challenged Europe's claim to historical preeminence and demonstrated, as well as affirmed, the antiquity and historicity of civilization in Africa. Since Afrocentric historicism developed as a medium of black protest, it is imperative to contextualize it within the historical tradition of black resistance. Several nineteenth-century black intellectuals published to rescue African history from obscurity and establish the antiquity of civilization in Africa. This group included Martin Delany, and the "Pioneers." Collectively, they used evidence of African history, and African cultural wealth to affirm both their humanity and citizenship, and gain recognition for Africa/diaspora blacks as contributors to world history and civilization.[23] Their writings bore the seeds of a future Afrocentric genre. For example, Delany was unequivocal on the African origins of ancient Egyptian civilization. As he quizzed rhetorically, "Who were the builders of the everlasting pyramids, catacombs, and sculptors of the sphinxes? Were they Europeans or Caucasians, Asiatic or Mongolians ... Among what race of men, and what country of the globe, do we find traces of these singular productions, but the African and Africa?"[24] His answer was emphatic, "None whatever. It is in Africa the pyramids, sphinxes, and catacombs are found; here the hieroglyphics still remain. Among the living Africans traces of their beautiful philosophy and symbolic mythology still exists."[25] Underlining the antiquity of civilization in Africa, Delany declared, "And is it not known to history that Egypt was the 'cradle of the earliest civilization,' propagating the arts and sciences, when the Grecians were an uncivilized people, covering their persons with skins and clothing, anterior to the existence of the she-wolf."[26]

Du Bois's theory of the "Talented Tenth" underscored the critical role of the intellectual. As he explained it, "The Negro race, like all races, is going to be saved by its exceptional men. The problem of education, then, among Negroes must first of all deal with the Talented Tenth; it is the problem of developing the Best of this race that they may guide the Mass away from the contamination and death of the Worst, in their own and other races."[27] It should be acknowledged that Du Bois was not the first to highlight the importance of intellectual leadership. Grisham, identified earlier, aggressively challenged the prevailing Eurocentric historiography. However, it should be recalled also that long before both Du Bois and Grisham, the pioneers, had popularized this protest historiography. By the closing years of the nineteenth century leading black intellectuals had come to associate black empowerment with rehabilitating and solidifying a historical heritage. G. N. Grisham implored black scholars to develop a revolutionary historical epistemology and vigorously defend blacks "against unjust criticism and wrong."[28] Grisham further called on the black intellectual "in his exalted personality" to "furnish a standard for building aspiration, and his superior intelligence and keen foresight should offer guidance over the thousands of moral, social and political difficulties that throng the dark and devious pathway of the people."²⁹ Though cognizant of the critical need for black intellectual leadership, Grisham was equally mindful of a challenge John Hope Franklin would later underscore: the need for the black scholar to appeal beyond race. According to Grisham, "The Negro scholar must not confine himself to Negro questions. He must, in action, manifest the breadth of Terence ... mankind, humanity."³⁰ Grisham placed immense responsibility on the black intellectual. He called for an instrumentalist history that is as well cognizant of the limitations of racialist advocacy scholarship.

The movement to use African history as a counterhegemonic discipline gained momentum in the early twentieth century. Two individuals helped advance this development—Du Bois and Carter G. Woodson. They strengthened a foundation upon which future generations, including Afrocentric scholars, built. Harvard-trained historians, Du Bois and Woodson researched and published extensively to establish African history as a serious field of intellectual endeavor. They publicized the wealth of African culture and civilization and the contributions of Africans and diaspora blacks to civilization. They affirmed the historical agency of both Africans and diaspora blacks and established black history as a serious intellectual discipline.³¹ Future generations such as John Hope Franklin, Benjamin Quarles, and Earl Thorpe expanded this tradition and prepared grounds for the civil rights generation. Franklin's own landmark study, *From Slavery to Freedom*, mirrored the progressive and integrationist essence of this historiography; one defined by faith in the perfectibility of America.³² This progressive genre, which was dominant in the 1940s and 50s, soon came under scrutiny as disillusionment with the slow pace of change led to demands for a more combative historiography. Critics sought an instrumental and adversarial historiography that challenged America for failing to adhere to its democratic ideals. Advocates such as Vincent Harding and Sterling Sturkey favored jettisoning the progressive and integrationist tradition, for a combative antiestablishment black history. Harding faulted the "fathers" of Negro history for being overly optimistic about America and thereby diminished the excesses and tragedies of the history.³³ In his own critique, Stuckey accused historians of the NNHM of failure to "condemn America for her crimes against black people" and for being so blinded by optimism that they ignored the tragedies of black America.³⁴ Both proposed a radical and ideologically driven black history, developed specifically for advancing the black struggle. This was the precursor to Afrocentric historiography.

By the 1960s civil rights movement the historicity and antiquity of civilization in Africa had been affirmed. Black history had won recognition. But the struggle was far from over. The next phase was the struggle for the institutionalization of black studies and securing a critical space in American higher education for the teaching and dissemination of information about the African and diaspora black historical and cultural experiences. The establishment of black studies, however, soon illuminated a sublayer of the intellectual contest: the contest for cultural and civilizational preeminence. Black studies became, for some, not just a field for disseminating knowledge about the African and diaspora black experiences, but also for reenacting old battles over history, culture, and civilization, the most fundamental of which was the battle to resolve the question of historical preeminence: Africa or Europe, which came first? Afrocentric scholars took on this struggle with a crusading zeal. By the late 1970s, Afrocentrism had emerged as a forceful ideological and philosophical black studies/struggle paradigm.

AFROCENTRISM

The Afrocentric perspective is premised on centering Africa as the foundation of black diaspora epistemology, and it developed largely in reaction to what was perceived as a critical need for a forceful ideological response to Eurocentric historiography. Asante identifies Eurocentrism as a major threat to blacks in America. According to him, this threat has existed since the dawn of history and remains intractable despite the efforts and accomplishments of earlier generations.[35] In his view, Eurocentrism has destroyed African culture. It has de-Africanized the consciousness of blacks; arrested their economic and cultural developments; and remains a potent threat to their cultural, social, economic, and political existence. To combat this, Asante and his ideological cohorts propose Afrocentrism, which he defines as "a frame of reference wherein phenomena are viewed from the perspective of the African person . . . [and which] seeks in every situation the appropriate centrality of the African person."[36] An Afrocentric solution entails strengthening black American knowledge and awareness of African historical and cultural heritage and making Africa the foundation of knowledge. This knowledge became the defensive weapon against a pervasive and domineering Eurocentric worldview.[37]

Against the negativism and objectifications of Eurocentric historiography, Afrocentric scholars counterpoise Africans as historical actors and Africa as the basis of self-definition and identity for diaspora blacks.[38] Premised on a

Manichean conception of reality, Afrocentrism offers re-Africanization as the only viable means of resistance, survival, and eventual triumph for diaspora blacks. As Asante explains it, "We are seriously in battle for the future of our culture; Afrocentric vigilance is demanded to preserve our culture."[39] To "Africans who have lived amidst Europeans on the land of the ancestors of the Native Americans" and have in consequence been exploited materially and psychologically, and whose historical heritage has been misrepresented and maligned, Asante offers strong grounding or centering in African history as the strategy for liberation.[40] Re-establishing connections with Africa became an essential step toward empowerment.[41] Affirming the universality of the African worldview is a critical component of this paradigm. Na'im Akbar, a black psychologist, projects African cosmology as the foundation for developing social science pedagogy for human liberation. Such attributes of African cosmology as emotionalism, esoterism, irrationality, and the unity of body and spirit would, according to him, infuse education with a humane and moral imperative. When made the foundation of scholarship, the African worldview would obliterate, he believed, the negative attributes (competition, materialism, greed, violence, aggression, etc.) of Western cosmology, attributes that sustained slavery and now racism.[42]

Africa offers blacks a rich antiquity of history, culture, and civilizations, the very basis of identity, and a rallying point for group/corporate initiatives against Eurocentric threats.[43] Since the negation of African civilization and culture justified the subordination of blacks, Afrocentric scholars vigorously challenge those negative portraits and images in order to affirm, albeit philosophically and psychologically, a counterhegemonic African identity and homeland. Reversing centuries-old misrepresentations of African/diaspora black history and culture became critical to enhancing self-esteem. Convinced that blacks would never be fully integrated in America, Afrocentric "historians" represent "black" and "American" as contradictory and antagonistic. They portray America as an arena of conflict between two irreconcilable worldviews, locked in a contest for superiority. Afrocentric historiography, therefore, focuses on challenging Europe's claim to preeminence in history, civilization, morality, and culture. Afrocentric scholars seek to resolve this battle over history and civilization with a declaration of Africa's superiority.[44] They advance what Yaacov Shavit characterizes as an Afrocentric universal history that catapults Africa to the apex of global historical development.[45] They then couple this history with a monolithic construction of identity for all blacks, thus dehistoricizing almost four centuries of New World acculturation.[46]

Asante believes that to undo the psychological damage of Eurocentric miseducation, black education must be grounded in a philosophy that affirms blacks as "active historical agents." This requires vigorously contesting European superiority and offering blacks an ennobling, albeit exaggerated and mythologized, version of history.[47] Like their nineteenth-century predecessors, modern Afrocentric scholars reject the nullification of African history and civilization. They address two key challenges. First, reconstructing and establishing a credible homeland and history, and second, affirming a countervailing monolithic African identity for all blacks. This identity, as the late black psychologist Amos Wilson acknowledged, is essentially and functionally a protest identity. To be "Afrikan," he suggested, is inherently antihegemonic.[48]

The writings of the late Senegalese scholar Cheikh Anta Diop constitute the ideological bedrock of the Afrocentric genre. Perhaps his most notable contribution is rejection of the Hamitic interpretation of ancient Egyptian origins and affirmation instead of its Negroid origins and character. However, Diop went beyond reclaiming ancient Egypt for Africa to declaring its influence on classical Greece. In his view, Africans and diaspora blacks needed ancient Egypt to serve the same purpose that the classical Greco-Roman civilization served Europeans. According to him, "For us the return to Egypt in all fields is a necessary condition to reconcile African civilization with history, to be able to build a body of human sciences and to renew African culture . . . [A] look toward ancient Egypt is the best way of conceiving and building our cultural future."[49] Agreeing with Diop, Asante writes, "Afrocentrism reestablishes the centrality of the ancient Kemetic (Egyptian) civilization and the Nile Valley cultural complex as points of reference for an African perspective in much the same way as Greece and Rome serve as reference points for the Western world."[50] Asante portrays ancient Egyptian civilization as both the foundation of Africa's classical civilization and the progenitor of European civilization. By focusing on ancient Egypt, blacks, Amos Wilson argued, "are trying to take back what European historiography has stolen, completely falsified, to erase the new false identities it placed on the Afrikan Egyptian people."[51]

Afrocentric scholars prioritize three objectives: establishing the antiquity of history and civilization in Africa; affirming the influence of Egyptian civilization on ancient Greece, and by extension, Africa's superiority over European civilization; and finally proclaiming the universality of the African worldview. Consequently, they substitute Afrocentric diffusionist theory for the Eurocentric, proclaiming Africa the epicenter of world civilization.

Most telling, Afrocentric scholars represent ancient Egypt as the birthplace of science, philosophy, and mathematics, the place to which Greek scholars went to study, before returning to shape Western civilization.[52] The Greeks, acclaimed progenitors of Western civilization, were tutored by, and borrowed copiously from, ancient Egyptians (Africans).[53] This is the basis for what Shavit describes as Afrocentric "Greek dependency theory." The logic of this theory is simple and simplistic: if ancient Greece is the fountain of Western culture, and if it could be proven that Greek culture was heavily influenced by Egypt, it seemed reasonable then to depict Western civilization as a product of nonwhites (Africans).[54] The recognition of Greek science and philosophy absent acknowledgment of Egyptian influence compelled Afrocentric scholars to invoke the "stolen legacy" theory. They characterize Western civilization as the product of "stolen" ancient Egyptian and African legacies, identifying the Alexandrian conquest of Egypt as epochal in the theft. Greek scholars allegedly accompanied Alexander on his rampage through Egypt and pilfered the ancient libraries and temples.[55] This theory is discussed in detail in George G. M. James's *Stolen Legacy* (1954), a book that has become a standard text of the Afrocentric genre. The underlying purpose of the *Stolen Legacy*, as the author contended, is "an attempt to show that the true authors of Greek philosophy were not the Greeks; but the people of North Africa, commonly called the Egyptians."[56]

Developing and establishing affinity with a heritage of grandeur and opulence became an obsessive preoccupation of Afrocentric "historians." This called for embellishing and at times willfully misrepresenting African historical and cultural realities. This was also accompanied by a reluctance or refusal to acknowledge and engage historical *change*. In *The Souls of Black Folk* (1903), Du Bois described black Americans as peoples of dual identities who are constantly battling with, and in fact tormented by, the conflicting demands of the duality (African/American). This conflict and torment notwithstanding, Du Bois warned against privileging either of the identities.[57] Some critics characterize the duality paradigm as an accurate and perceptive representation of the complexity of the black American experience.[58] Afrocentric scholars, however, disagree. Anxious to deny any lasting European influence on blacks, they contest the duality, proclaiming instead the permanence and immutability of the African identity. Asante, for example, insists he was never afflicted by double consciousness. Deemphasizing the duality, Asante affirms, "I was never affected by the Du Boisean double-consciousness. I never felt 'two warring souls in one dark body' nor did I experience a conflict over my identity."[59] The true Afrocentrist, therefore, according to Asante, retains his/her *Africanness* intact. According to W. D. Wright, Asante accepts "only an African parentage for blacks in America," while completely blacking out the Euro-American parentage.[60] As Yaacov Shavit underscores, a major problem of Afrocentric historiography is the attempt to split the duality of the black American, to magnify one dimension of identity (African) and deny the other (American).[61] Such dehistoricizing enables Afrocentric scholars to construct a monolithic identity for diaspora blacks, regardless of location, ignoring the multiple, complex, and complicated historical and cultural experiences.

Afrocentric exaltation of ancient Egypt is a continuation of a tradition characteristic of nineteenth-century black nationalism. The novelty of Afrocentrism, however, lies in its ethnocentric overtone, a trait that has provoked the most criticisms. To enhance black self-esteem, Afrocentric scholars advance a monolithic construction of black diaspora identity and a romanticized view of the African past.[62] They portray precolonial Africa as a period of harmony and advanced cultural and civilizational achievements. They depict Africa as a continent inhabited by people who are morally and ethically superior to Europeans. In his scathing criticism of Afrocentrism, Shavit rightly notes that Afrocentrists use "strategies of cultural self-affirmation to offset a sense of collective inferiority by boosting national self-esteem or express a sense of collective superiority."[63] But the Afrocentric ideology was not meant purely for enhancing black self-esteem. It also targeted white cultural arrogance. Paradoxically, despite its anti-Eurocentric and antihegemonic character, Afrocentrism soon developed its own hegemonic, and some would argue, racist tendencies: the claim of Africa's preeminence and superiority in history and civilization. One such grandiose "theory" was Leonard Jeffries's curious dichotomy between the so-called superior "Sun people" (Africans), and inferior "Ice people" (Europeans)![64] Thankfully, this embarrassing "theory" has crawled deservedly into obscurity.

As Shavit contends, the quest for validation in antiquity is a driving force of Afrocentric historiography. Afrocentric scholars desperately seek to establish originality and distinctiveness in antiquity, a preoccupation undoubtedly driven by Eurocentric denial of African antiquity. Shavit describes this search for authenticity in antiquity as "an important tool in a vanquished nation's struggle for pride, dignity and status."[65] Ancient Egypt enables Afrocentric scholars to establish both the genesis and evolution of civilization and culture in Africa and authenticity in antiquity. But Egypt also serves another function, that of constructing what Shavit terms a grand scale universal history. Afrocentric scholars use Egypt to affirm the authenticity of African culture both "among black and non-black people around the globe."⁶⁶ They researched ancient Egypt, "in the hope of finding within it the origins of a black centered philosophy, a foundation for group unity and identity, a source of resistance to alien domination, and a basis for independence and creativity."⁶⁷

Clarence Walker attributes Afrocentric proclamation of ancient Egypt as the primal cite of world civilization to a problematic conflation of two concepts—*life* and *civilization*. The claim that *life* began in Africa is often mistaken for another—that *civilization* began in Africa. The truth of the former, Walker suggests, did not necessarily establish the latter. He offers the possibility that civilization could have had multiple origins.⁶⁸ Walker seriously questions the Negroid construction of ancient Egyptian civilization, accusing Afrocentric scholars of reading too much of racial essentialism into ancient Egypt. He proposes a much more complex origin of ancient Egyptian civilization, one that includes Mediterranean and Asia Minor influences.⁶⁹ He accuses Afrocentrists of "a selective reading [of] Egyptian cultural production as biological" and applying modern racial categories to a context (ancient Egypt) that did not recognize those categories.⁷⁰

AFROCENTRISM, PAN-AFRICANISM, AND IDENTITY

Afrocentric scholars also forcefully defend the Pan-African and identity paradigms. According to Asante, Africans and diaspora blacks have a "collective consciousness" not impacted by centuries of separation.⁷¹ Underlining this global unifying identity, he declares, "We have one African Cultural System manifested in diversities . . . We respond to the same rhythms of the universe, the same cosmological sensibilities, the same general historical reality as the African descended people . . . All African people participate in the African Cultural System."⁷² Invoking Maulana Karenga, Asante asserts, "Our Africanity is our ultimate reality."⁷³ Furthermore, he envisions a "Pan-African" world based on African cultural retentions (Africanisms) among black Americans and rejects any notion of *difference* between continental Africans and blacks in America. As he reasons, "There are some people around who argue that Africans and African-Americans have nothing in common but the color of their skin. This is not merely an error, it is nonsense."⁷⁴ Asante proclaims a single "African Cultural System" to which all blacks, regardless of location, respond. In his words, "There exists an emotional, cultural, psychological connection . . . that spans the ocean."⁷⁵

In the opinion of W. D. Wright, the Afrocentric "Pan-African" construction of identity establishes no boundaries separating continental Africa and the black diaspora. It is one global world.[76] Afrocentric scholars justify this Pan-African conflation of continental Africa and the black diaspora on the basis of shared history and culture. As a result, both supposedly confront similar problems and challenges: economic marginalization, political domination, and cultural alienation in the United States; political instability, poverty, and neocolonialism in Africa; challenges directly or indirectly linked to Eurocentrism. Afrocentric scholars presume the antiquity of Pan-Africanism, which they depict as a movement defined by unifying ethos: that black Americans and Africans have always been drawn together by common interests and have historically cooperated in furtherance of those interests. Asante's numerous publications, especially those written since the 1980s, testify to the depth and strength of his faith in Pan-African identity and unity.[77] The identity paradigm unequivocally declares black Americans "Africans" premised on residues of African traditions and values (or what some scholars call "Africanisms") found among blacks in diaspora. These cultural retentions or survivals confirm the African essence of diaspora blacks, ethnically and culturally, despite centuries of exposure to, and acculturation in, Western/European values and civilization.[78]

Marimba Ani is a leading advocate of the African identity paradigm. She represents black Americans and blacks in the Caribbean and South America as Africans based on vestiges of indigenous African traditions in their music, religion, and lifestyles. According to her, Africans and blacks in diaspora share the three essential elements of identity—spirituality, ethos, and worldview.[79] In her judgment, these unifying and immutable African elements underscore shared identity. As she explains;

> Africa survives in our spiritual make-up; that it is the strength and depth of African spirituality and humanism that has allowed for the survival of African-Americans as a distinctive cultural entity in New Europe; that it is our spirituality and vitality that defines our response to European culture; and that that response is universally African.[80]

The African identity paradigm contradicts the Du Boisean duality. While acknowledging the American experience, Afrocentric scholars seek to delegitimize its identitarian significance. In their judgment, American blacks are Africans. Black Americans supposedly came out of slavery and the American experience with their African identity intact. This is not true. The identity and

Pan-African paradigms are historically flawed. The portrayal of black Americans and Africans as one people united by cultural attributes and historical experience is both theoretically and practically problematic. Regardless of the degree and depth of African cultural retentions, black Americans are undeniably products of the American historical experience, an experience that profoundly and indelibly altered their identity.

Furthermore, the black experience in the diaspora is culturally transforming and revolutionary. It is difficult to superimpose a "Pan-African" identity on this complex historical reality. It should be noted that not all black Americans embrace the Afrocentric bandwagon. Some critics object to the location of identity exterior to America. For example, slavocentrists define black American identity exclusively within the American context. Deemphasizing, and at times rejecting, Africa, they identify *slavery* as the substantive identitarian element. In their judgment slavery was far more profound and consequential than the fact of African ancestry. A modern amplification is found in Keith Richburg's provocative book *Out of America: A Black Man Confronts Africa* (1996). Former *Washington Post* Africa Bureau chief Richburg rejected "Mother Africa," and thanked God profusely that his ancestors "got out." On identity, he wrote, "Thank God that I am an American."[81] Furthermore, reflecting on his stay in Africa, he said, "I know now that I am a stranger here. I am an American, a black American, and I feel no connection to this strange and violent place."[82] Richburg loathed the concept "African American," preferring "Black American," which he insisted more accurately reflected the reality. He doubted if there was "anything really 'African' left in the descendants of those slaves who made that torturous journey across the Atlantic."[83] "African-American" in his words, "never existed in the first place."[84] Underlining his slavocentric identity, Richburg declared, "Condemning slavery should not inhibit us from recognizing mankind's ability to make something good arise often in the aftermath of the most horrible evil."[85]

Richburg is not alone in contesting the continuing relevance of the African heritage. Despite the problematic character of race, some blacks continue to prefer a racial construction of identity. For example, in a recent study advocating a new philosophy of black identity Michael Eric Owens also rejects "African American," and projects race as the central element of his "new philosophy." As he argues,

> Regardless of how poetic African-American sounds to our ears, it tells us nothing about "who we are and how we fit in American society"

> ... *Black America* is our title. It alone speaks of our contributions and commitment to the American experience, not the African experience ... The name "African-American," tells us absolutely nothing about who we are or what we shall become (emphasis added).[86]

The racial underpinning of Afrocentrism is perhaps its most provocative character. Economist Glenn Loury, for instance, is opposed to what he terms, "invented ethnicity." In his view, "a personal identity wholly dependent on racial contingency falls tragically short of its potential because it embraces too parochial a conception of what is possible, and what is desirable."[87] Insisting that blacks are only "partially" descended from Africa, cultural critic Stanley Crouch urges blacks to construct their identity within a much broader framework. He believes that "Euro-American ancestry, far more than anything from Africa itself, also fuels the combination of ethnic nationalism and evangelical liberation politics domestic Negroes bring to high-pitched rhetoric over the issue of Nelson Mandela and his struggle."[88] This suggests a strong opposition to essentializing the African connection among black Americans. It also underscores a potent crisis of identity among black Americans and negates Afrocentric homogenizing of black identity. Richburg and Owens represent one extreme. Most critiques of the Afrocentric and Pan-African paradigms do not jettison the African background. While they acknowledge the historicity of Africa, they are opposed to romanticizing it. It is noteworthy that even among Afrocentric or "Africancentric" scholars, there is now a growing objection to a monolithic African identity. Denouncing what he terms Asante's "100 percent African parentage," W. D. Wright, a self-proclaimed "Africancentric" scholar, criticizes Asante for "ignoring, or down-playing ... and even suppressing ... historical, cultural and social reality."[89]

AFROCENTRISM AND GLOBALIZATION

Globalization and the attendant shrinkage of spatial distance have given rise to optimism about the prospects for greater human interdependence and interactions. Enthusiasts predict the imminence of global "cultural citizenship" as globalization erodes national, ethnic, racial, or other primordial constructions of identity.[90] The notion of global "cultural citizenship" suggests the possibility of transcending the limitations of national, racial, or ethnic constructions of identity. It also implies the capacity to engage multiple cultural experiences without being boxed in, or restrained, by one's *original* identity. As Robin Cohen further argues, "the scope for multiple affiliations and associations that has been opened up outside and beyond the nation-state has also allowed a diasporic allegiance to become both more open and more acceptable."[91] There is a widespread belief that the world is becoming one "global village" and that technology is breaking down cultural barriers. Consequently, increased interactions inexorably lead to the realization that *engagements, contacts, interactions, mutuality,* and *shared experiences* rather than *differences,* define the human experience. Afrocentric scholars, however, deem this broadening of the human experience pregnant with hegemonic implication that could perpetuate a global system of unequal relationships. They discern the threat of a "colonial situation" within this global framework, which would facilitate European and super-power dominance over, and threat to the survival of, weaker nations and peoples. Afrocentric scholars magnify this image of a supra-European hegemonic and destructive cultural force. To highlight the magnitude of this threat and mobilize blacks, Afrocentric scholars advance a monolithic and hegemonic portrait of European culture. According to this perspective, Europeans are uniformly and insatiably driven by an unrepentant and arrogant culture of imperial greed. Europeans have used, and would continue to use, culture as a weapon of domination. They have objectified and denigrated Africans and successfully constructed a hegemonic world order in the past, and nothing in the new global horizon suggests a different outcome. To Afrocentrists, therefore, Europe's cultural threat to blacks is perpetual and absolute.

Afrocentric scholars are deeply suspicious of any global cosmopolitan construction of identity (cultural citizenship). They deem the global context an extension of the hegemonic domestic American reality and a greater threat. Thus, the cultural implications of globalization have given an added urgency and poignancy to the Afrocentric notion of cultural threat, since culture is perceived as a critical front in the war against Eurocentric hegemony. Asante's cultural paranoia is worth recalling; "We are seriously in battle for the future of our culture. Afrocentric vigilance is demanded to preserve our culture."[92] The cultural agenda of Afrocentrism, therefore, is to socialize blacks to recognize the dangers of white American and European cultural values and regard any notion of intercultural dialogue with deep suspicion, while privileging African culture as the essential basis of identity. Afrocentric scholars counterpoise a racialized ideology for black survival against what they characterize as a new global order in which Europeans are united and uniformly driven by hegemonic ambitions. In their judgment, therefore, globalization has rendered blacks more susceptible to Western and European hegemonic interests. Strengthening and expanding, rather than shrinking, the global color line becomes an existential imperative. Race becomes, for them, a potent weapon of constructing a global unifying identity for Africans and diaspora blacks. They portray globalization as fundamentally a disguised European hegemonic force, a postmodern metamorphosis of nineteenth-century imperialism. In their perception, this new global imperialism has shed the blatantly racist arrogance and ideological and militaristic characters of the past and is now cleverly disguised as an internationalist, worldwide phenomenon that supposedly would benefit all of humankind.

Leading Afrocentric scholars, including the late Chancellor Williams and John Henrik Clarke, laid the groundwork for the cultural projection of a racialized Manichean global order. In his critically acclaimed study of how the West "destroyed Black Civilization," Williams advocated the creation of a "race organization," which he described as "a nation-wide organization of Blacks only."[93] He called on blacks to begin "building step by step, a race organization so great that it will not only be the voice of a united people but will carry on effectively an economic program to assist them [to] advance on all fronts."[94] Arguably the leading modern philosophical advocate of this genre, Asante's Afrocentric paradigm embodies the separatist vision in Williams's "organization." As he pontificates,

> Eurocentrism in its most extreme form has generated an entire cacophony of voices that have been arrayed against the best interests of international cooperation and mutuality. It has generated a view toward the world of domination, hegemony, and control. Every aspect of the gross Eurocentrism seems articulated toward this end, ultimately the subverting of international relationships. Thus, slavery, apartheid, Nazism, segregation, imperialism, intellectual arrogance, racial murders, and military and technological domination have been expressions of Eurocentrism.[95]

As already established, Asante firmly situates the black experience upon an African cosmological foundation. This mandates cultural vigilance and unity against an ever-threatening Eurocentric force. Based essentially on race and ethnicity, such unity, Asante contends, was critical to black survival and triumph in a world order still dominated by Europeans.[96]

In his own study, Haki Madhubuti underlines the ever-present threat of "white world supremacy" and the need for blacks to strive toward "total separation." He defines this "white world Supremacy" as "the supremacy of whites worldwide *finally* and *undiluted.*"[97] Madhubuti enjoins blacks to limit contacts with whites in a social and cultural context and presented a litany of reasons. Primarily, whites have proven themselves to "be traditionally and historically enemies of black people."[98] Looking toward the future, he advocates organizing and preparing "for a future not dependent on the concepts and visions of others who do not have our best interests in mind."[99]

Perhaps no other Afrocentric scholar has defended the paradigm and condemned the global hegemonic character of Eurocentrism as fervently and scathingly as Marimba Ani, whose seminal publication *Yurugu* (1996) is a devastating critique of the hegemonic character of Eurocentric history and culture.[100] She is also one of the most forceful defenders of the absolutist construction of African identity for diaspora blacks. Her study of identity deemphasizes the impact of New World transplantation and acculturation on black culture and identity. In her analysis, blacks retain their African essence and identity, centuries of transplantation in the new world notwithstanding.[101] In *Yurugu* she reaffirms a cardinal Afrocentric conviction: the inherent and absolute hegemonic character of Eurocentric culture. She calls for the "de-Europeanizing" of culture. This would render culture much more relevant to the political needs of blacks. Her book underlines the urgency of racial and cultural vigilance in a global context in which, she contends, blacks remain threatened by Eurocentric values and cultural contacts.[102]

More than any other Afrocentric scholar, Ani highlights the global, or what she calls the international character of the Eurocentric threat. In a rather tragic misrepresentation of European culture as monolithic, Ani discerns a unified and homogeneous European world order. According to her, Europeans are driven by the urge to dominate, and in furtherance of which they fraudulently invoke "universalism" and "internationalism" as weapons for expansion into, and domination of, other societies. She warns blacks against embracing "internationalism" of any kind, particularly one spearheaded by and involving Europeans. Since European culture is, in her view, monolithic, inherently expansionistic, and hegemonic, she counterpoises black cultural unity and vigilance.[103] In her analysis, two culturally monolithic worlds confront, and have always confronted, each other: African and Eurocentric, both inherently and diametrically opposed. "Europe," she writes, "is a culturally homogeneous" entity and thus threatening to blacks.[104] She wants to dispel any illusions of cultural harmony. Culture, she insists, is ideological, political, and hegemonic. Furthermore, she argues, European culture is also "extremely cohesive and well-integrated" with a deceptive veneer of heterogeneity.[105] Ani depicts the world order as an arena of perpetual cultural antagonism and conflict. Black survival is conceivable only in the context of perpetual opposition to, and vigilance against, and not in association with Eurocentric values and influences. Asante echoes similar conviction. He draws a simplistic portrait of Europeans and describes Eurocentrism as a force for global "domination, hegemony, and control. Every aspect of the gross Eurocentrism seems articulated toward this end, ultimately the subverting of international relations."[106] Although he acknowledges that "all people of Europe are not racists and imperialists," Asante insists that "it is very difficult for Europeans to escape the conditions of their historical realities."[107] Given this construction of Europe, Asante concludes, "Europe is dangerous; it is five hundred years of danger for Africans."[108]

Afrocentric scholars, therefore, remain indomitably opposed to a "global context," in which, as H. V. Perlmutter suggests, "Multiple cultures are being syncretized in a complex way. The elements of particular cultures can be drawn from a global array, but they will mix and match differently in each setting."[109] Afrocentrists are concerned that the "mixing" and "matching," could potentially destroy black cultural originality. The call for cultural vigilance and unity and the projection of a monolithic African cultural world and identity, therefore, represent a response to the cultural implications of globalization. Culture has become an arena of irreconcilable conflict and antagonism between blacks and whites. Consequently, Afrocentric scholars urge blacks to maintain a respectable distance from, and vigilance against, white cultural contacts. They understand "Cultural citizenship," to mean distinct antagonistic cultural zones with no grounds for discourses and exchanges. Instead of cultural understanding, Afrocentrism defends a world of cultural isolation, suspicion, and antagonism, one in which citizenship is defined not by cultural connectedness, or attempts to discover such connections, but by cultural disharmony and disengagement, foreclosing dialogue and communication across cultural spaces.[110]

In opposition to the intercultural implications of globalization, therefore, Afrocentric scholars advocate racial distinctiveness preserved through a strict observance of the color line on a global scale, in which blacks, regardless of sociopolitical experiences and geographical locations, are compelled to forge a united racial front.[111] Of course, besides race, the emblematic factor is culture: the depiction of black diaspora culture as quintessentially African. Due to its problematic character, some Afrocentric scholars deemphasize *race* as an identitarian construct and highlight *culture* instead, arguing essentially that centuries of transplantation had not fundamentally altered the original

African culture. This cultural *continuum* therefore constitutes the bedrock of unity between Africans and peoples of African descent in the diaspora.

Challenging this homogenizing *weltanschauung,* some scholars advocate acknowledging the dynamic, complex and complicated nature and character of the African and black diaspora worlds. As Jack Greene describes it, "the flow and mixture of peoples and cultures and implied a process of social and cultural formation that, far from being imposed from the top-down, derived from a continuing process of negotiation or exchange among the various peoples and cultures involved."[112] The emphasis here is on the growing complexity of the diaspora and the need to interrogate the complexity in different locations. As some critics contend, "At the general and specific levels of African Diaspora formation, there is variation by geographical location, by generations, by material and institutional conditions, and by socio-economic and demographic patterns."[113] In fact, more recent studies of the global black experience underscore the imperative of transcending both the diaspora and black Atlantic frames and the tradition of homogeneity-heterogeneity discourse.[114] The shift is toward acknowledging expansive and complex terrains of the human experience, as well as undertaking microanalytical studies of new forms of diasporas within and without Africa, diasporas that grew out of what Manger and Assal describe as "the decay in the contemporary African postcolonial state."[115] These microanalyses focus on new diasporas such as Eritrean refugees in Germany, southern Sudanese in the United States, and Somali and Sudanese refugees in Norway, among many others.[116] This illuminates the complex and multilayered nature of the global black diasporic world, the consequence of what Ruth Hamilton and others call "proliferations of departures across time and space, conditioned by, and within, a changing global culture and political economy."[117] There are undoubtedly shared experiences relating to "persistence of oppression, racialization, prejudice and discrimination, political disenfranchisement, and hostile social environment."[118] However, as Ruth Hamilton and others suggest, "Such *continuity* should not be interpreted to mean *fixed*. Collective identities are contested, negotiated, conflictual and dynamic. They are paradoxical and contradictory, generating internal 'differences.'"[119]

The black diaspora is neither monolithic nor culturally isolated and distinct. Afrocentric construction of an isolationist black world is, therefore, ahistorical. The construction of a distinct community "We" is a relational category. "We" cannot exist without "They." In Ruth Hamilton's words, "Even the extent to which the mobilized actions of a people can be conceptualized as 'acts for itself' implies a contradiction: people stand (act) in opposition to the forces that have conditioned their existential reality and material circumstances."[120]

In their attempts to construct a uniform and monolithic black world, Afrocentric scholars deemphasize complexities and paradoxes of the African and black diaspora worlds. A major challenge "in any project to construct a global identity and hence a global culture," Anthony Smith opines, "is that collective identity, like imagery and culture, is always historically specific because it is based on shared memories and a sense of continuity between generations."[121] This generational continuity should not be construed in isolation from the broader human experiences. It does not, and should not be presumed to, privilege isolation, racial and cultural essentialism.

CONCLUSION

Afrocentric scholars assumed leadership of the ideological and intellectual struggle to authenticate African/diaspora black history and culture with crusading zealotry. Blinded by ideology, they saw racial conspiracy in almost every historical lens and responded with an equally conspiratorial worldview. To combat Eurocentric historiography, Afrocentric intellectuals position blacks on an essentialist ahistorical pedestal. To effectively contest and unravel Eurocentric historiography, it was necessary to revisit and refight old battles, the most critical and urgent of which is the epic battle over history and civilization. This is because much of the rationale for European hegemony and claims of European superiority from slavery in the Americas, through colonialism in Africa to the present, derived from a negative construction of African history and culture. Africans and diaspora blacks were depicted as peoples without a viable and credible past. Europe was the cradle of civilization, and Europeans were the bearers of civilization to "Dark Africa." Paradoxically, the "White Man's Burden" equally saddled black intellectuals with a historical burden (the Black Man's Burden?) the burden of reconstructing a counterhegemonic history, a regenerative and empowering history with which to obliterate the negative, oppressive, and debilitating consequences of Eurocentrism. Emboldened, Afrocentric intellectuals assumed this burden of history and strove to establish a credible and legitimate foothold for Africa and diaspora blacks in the sands of history. For this, they turned to antiquity.

The quest for legitimacy in antiquity became the driving force of much of Afrocentric historicism. Civilizations in the Nile Valley and other parts of

West and Central Africa became building blocks for establishing legitimacy in antiquity and constructing what Shavit aptly describes as "Afrocentric Universal History," characterized by claims of originality, preeminence, and superiority buttressed by a "stolen legacy" theory. For Afrocentric scholars, the claim to antiquity became a means of affirming "distinctiveness, uniqueness and self-proclaimed central role in the world's history."[122] However, in their quest for authenticity in antiquity, Afrocentric scholars made bogus and dubious claims of historical preeminence and universality. In the process, they were the Afrocentric replica of the racist Eurocentrism they opposed. They developed a conspiratorial and Manichean historicism derived from slavery, racism, colonialism, and their legacies. Though slavery and colonialism ended, Afrocentric scholars insist that blacks in the United States and peoples of African descent globally continue to suffer from their destructive legacies. More than ever before, they contend, Africans and diaspora blacks remain threatened by the same global enemy. While Africans languish in the cesspool of neocolonialism, blacks in postslavery and post-civil rights America, and globally, continue to endure the debilitating legacies of slavery and racism. Against these forces, Afrocentric scholars advocate Africa–black diaspora black unity. They justify this "Pan-African" unity also on the basis of shared identity, which they advance as perhaps the key historical force for developing a unified framework of global struggle. This monolithic global Afrocentric identity is premised on the conviction that the essential *Africanness* of blacks survived the vicissitudes of history and centuries of transplantation in different regional locations. Invoking and building on this supposedly immutable and unifying *Africanness*, Afrocentric scholars suggest, would enable blacks to not only rehabilitate their much maligned heritage, but also unleash an effective counterhegemonic resistance.

Solidifying a global Pan-African monolithic and supposedly homogeneous entity equally required homogenizing the Other. That is, Europeans (the ideological enemy) had to be presumed homogeneous in order to fully expose the magnitude and potency of their threat. To appeal for global black unity, therefore, and rationalize conflating and homogenizing the African and black diaspora worlds and experiences, Afrocentric scholars portrayed the Other, that is the ideological enemy and nemesis (Europeans) as equally homogeneous and monolithic. The attempts to conflate the experiences of blacks in the United States, Africa, and globally entailed dehistorization, that is, deemphasizing or refusing to acknowledge historical changes and transformations both within the United States and globally. Likewise, the homogenizing of Europe, even in the face of obvious and glaring complexities, is a curious and inexplicable ahistoristic exercise. Assuming the burden of history led Afrocentric scholars to everything but respect for, and acknowledgment of, the complexities of the histories of Africans, diaspora blacks, and Europeans. They chose to manipulate history. In consequence, they compromised the one force that could in fact have validated and authenticated their work, one which, as John Hope Franklin recognized, would have provided a clearer glimpse into the realities of the complex experiences and issues they engage.

It is the primal responsibility of historians to offer interpretative insights into historical events from a critical study of historical data and facts. This does not suggest the total nullification of personal biases. As humans, historians bring to their vocation shades of personal biases and experiences. Yet, the measure of "objective" history is not the absolute elimination of biases but the degree to which the historian succeeds in making those biases secondary to the fundamental task of historical interpretation. This is what John Hope Franklin underscored and reflected in his scholarship. Afrocentric scholars, however, define the duty of the black historian as essentially ideological—to use historical data and facts to affirm, legitimize and advance socioeconomic, cultural, and political agendas. In other words, they advocate subordinating historical interpretation to the ideological agenda of the black struggle. This explains Asante's almost pathological disdain for objectivity, prioritizing consciousness (subjectivity) instead. In his view, black historians could not afford the luxury of objectivity. As he explains it,

> The . . . relationship between our consciousness and our history is the true character of Afrocentricity. If we are Afrocentric, then we know that objectivity and subjectivity while not arbitrary designations are not ironclad. We determine what constitutes objectivity and subjectivity by deciding what is necessary in order for the relationship between history and consciousness to work.[123]

Concurring, Terry Kershaw, another Afrocentric scholar writes, "Praxis must be observed first and then explained as theory if the discipline of Black Studies wishes to maintain its ties to the struggles of Black people."[124] This disregard for objectivity is reflected in Afrocentric romanticized, mythologized, simplified and simplistic interpretations of African and diaspora black historical and cultural experiences. The resultant "feel-good" history serves fundamentally an ideological function and is thus of little intellectual relevance. Though "Applied Negro History," as the late Earl Thorpe described it, has some purpose, its ultimate value as history, however, is very much dependent on acknowledgment of, and respect for, established and recognized canons of historical inquiry. Though Afrocentric delegitimating of objectivity and prioritization of praxis resulted in "good popular history," they have yet to produce "good history."

The imperative of constructing history as a "philosophy of change" has become even more evident with globalization. As the world shrinks into this "global village," historians and other scholars in the humanities and social sciences perforce have to acknowledge and contextualize *change* in their research. Acknowledging the expanded parameters of human encounters compels recognition of the transient, fluid, flexible, and ever-changing character of culture and identity. Recognizing *change* as a critical defining aspect of history mandates understanding of how *change* occurred through historical *time* and *space*. Renowned historian E. H Carr defined history as "an unending dialogue between the present and the past."[125] This definition reflects a longstanding African conception of history as a continuous dialogue between the past, present, and future. The essential elements of the dialogue are the actual historical facts and data, not a selective production of the historian's ideological convictions. This conception of history mandates scholarship grounded in a methodology that acknowledges as well the complex and often multilayered and complicated character of the human experience. Those who manipulate history are vulnerable to distorted historical lenses and interpretations which produce and nurture equally distorted epistemological, existential, and cosmological consciousness. Paradoxically, Afrocentric mythologizing and romanticizing of Africa violate a cardinal principle of African philosophy of history: the dialogue between the past, present, and future accents *change*. Afrocentric scholars choose to devalue this dialogical relationship while constructing history instead as *changeless*.

Afrocentric scholars, mostly trained in disciplines other than history, not surprisingly, completely jettison a critical canon of historical research (objectivity), which as historian John Hope Franklin recognized, is crucial to the validation of their writings. Questioning objectivity as itself a Western/Eurocentric tool, they boldly call for prioritizing ideology and advocacy. They advance racial and cultural essentialist interpretations of the African and black diaspora experiences. A major problematic of Afrocentric historiography, therefore, is the refusal to acknowledge *change* as a critical element of history, the construction instead of an ideological edifice for an historical experience with disregard for the dynamic character. This has compromised scholarly credibility. Afrocentric academics have seen their work dismissed as propagandist and unscholarly. Fundamentally, works within this genre have not attracted intellectual respectability. Assuming the burden of history, as Afrocentric scholars do, mandates recognition and acknowledgment of *change*. This means historicizing, rather than dehistoricizing the African and black diaspora experiences. Afrocentric scholars have yet to take this injunction seriously.

NOTES

1. J. M. Blaut, *The Colonizer's Model of the World: Geographical Diffusionism and Eurocentric History* (New York: Guilford, 1993); Audrey Smedley, *Race in North America: The Origins and Evolution of a Worldview* (Boulder, CO: Westview, 1993); Paul G. Lauren, *Power and Prejudice: The Politics and Diplomacy of Racial Discrimination* (Boulder, CO: Westview, 1988); A. E. Afigbo, *The Poverty of African Historiography* (Idanre: Afrografrika, 1977); Okon E. Uya, "Trends and Perspectives in African History," in *Perspectives and Methods of Studying African History*, ed. Erim O. Erim and Okon Uya (Enugu, Nigeria: Fourth Dimension Press, 1984), 1–9.

2. Earl Thorpe, *Black Historians: A Critique* (New York: William Morrow, 1971); W. D. Wright, *Black History and Black Identity: A Call for a New Historiography* (Westport, CT: Praeger, 2002), chs. 1, 2; John Ernest, *Liberation Historiography: African American Writers and the Challenge of History, 1794–1861* (Chapel Hill: University of North Carolina Press, 2004); August Meier and Elliott Rudwick, *Black History and the Historical Profession, 1915–1980* (Urbana: University of Illinois Press, 1986); Stephen Hall, *A Faithful Account of the Race: African American Historical Writing in Nineteenth-Century America* (Chapel Hill: University of North Carolina Press, 2009).

3. Earl Thorpe, *Black Historians*, 33–61.

4. G. N. Grisham, "The Functions of the Negro Scholar" in *The Voice of Black America: Major Speeches by Blacks in the United States, 1797–1973*, ed. Philip S. Foner, ed. (New York: Capricorn Books, 1975), 1:629–30.

5. Ibid., 632–33.

6. Andrew G. Paschal, ed., *A W. E. B. Du Bois Reader* (New York: Collier-Macmillan, 1971), 31–51.

7. Hall, *A Faithful Account*; Ernest, *Liberation Historiography*.

8. Ernest, *Liberation Historiography*.

9. Hall, *A Faithful Account*, chap. 6; Meier and Rudwick, *Black History and the Historical Profession*, chap. 1.

10. Meier and Rudwick, *Black History and the Historical Profession*, chap. 1.

11. John Hope Franklin, "The Dilemma of the American Negro Scholar," in *Soon, One Morning: New Writings by American Negroes, 1940–1962*, ed. Robert Hill (New York: Alfred A. Knopf, 1963), 64.

12. Ibid., 65.

13. Ibid., 68.

14. Ibid., 69.
15. Ibid.
16. Ibid., 73.
17. Ibid.
18. Ibid.
19. Ibid., 74.
20. Ibid.
21. Ibid., 74–76.
22. A. E. Afigbo, *The Poverty of African Historiography*. See also Smedley, *Race in North America*; Lauren, *Power and Prejudice*.
23. Ernest, *Liberation Historiography*; Benjamin Quarles, *Black Mosaic: Essays in Afro-American Historiography* (Amherst, MA: University of Massachusetts Press, 1988); Robert L. Harris, "Coming of Age: The Transformation of Afro-American Historiography," *Journal of Negro History* 67, no. 2 (Summer 1982): 107–21.
24. Martin R. Delany, "The International Policy of the World towards the African Race," in *Life and Public Services of Martin R. Delany*, ed. F. Rollin (Boston: Lee and Shepard, 1868), 323.
25. Ibid.
26. Ibid., 324.
27. Andrew G. Paschal, *A W. E. B. Du Bois Reader*, 31.
28. G. N. Grisham, "The Functions of the Negro Scholar," in *The Voice of Black America*, ed. Philip S. Foner, 632.
29. Ibid.
30. Ibid.
31. Meier and Rudwick, *Black History and the Historical Profession*, chaps. 1–2; Hall, *A Faithful Account*, chap. 5.
32. John H. Franklin, *From Slavery to Freedom: A History of African Americans*, 9th ed. (New York: McGraw Hill, 2010).
33. Vincent Harding, "Beyond Chaos: Black History and the Search for the New Land," in *Amistad 1: Writings on Black History and Culture*, ed. John A. Williams and Charles F. Harris (New York: Vintage Books), 1970, 269–92.
34. Sterling Stuckey, "Twilight of Our Past: Reflections on the Origins of Black History," in *Amistad 2: Writings on Black History and Culture*, ed. John A. Williams and Charles F. Harris (New York: Vintage Books, 1971), 261–95.
35. See also Molefi Asante, *Kemet, Afrocentricity and Knowledge* (Trenton, NJ: Africa World, 1990).
36. Molefi Asante, "The Afrocentric Idea in Education," *Journal of Negro Education* 60, no. 2 (1991): 171.
37. Ibid. See also Asante, "On Historical Interpretations" and "On Afrocentric Metatheory" in Asante, *Malcolm X as Cultural Hero and Other Afrocentric Essays* (Trenton, NJ: Africa World, 1993).
38. Molefi Asante, *The Afrocentric Idea* (Philadelphia: Temple University Press, 1987); *Afrocentricity*; C. Tschloane Keto, *Vision, Identity and Time: The Afrocentric Paradigm and the Study of the Past* (Dubuque, IA: Kendall/Hunt, 1995).

39. Asante, *Afrocentricity*, 49.
40. Asante, *Malcolm X as Cultural Hero*, 18.
41. Ibid., 48.
42. Na'im Akbar, "Africentric Social Sciences for Human Liberation," *Journal of Black Studies* 14, no. 4 (June 1984).
43. Asante, *Afrocentricity*. See also Asante, *The Afrocentric Idea*; *Kemet, Afrocentricity and Knowledge*.
44. Mary Lefkowitz, *Not out of Africa: How Afrocentrism Became an Excuse to Teach Myth as History* (New York: Basic Books, 1996); Stephen Howe, *Afrocentrism: Mythic Pasts, Imagined Homes* (London: Verso, 1998); Clarence E. Walker, *We Can't Go Home Again: An Argument about Afrocentrism* (New York: Oxford University Press, 2001). Yaacov Shavit, *History in Black: African-Americans in Search of an Ancient Past* (London: Frank Cass, 2001).
45. Shavit, *History in Black*, chap. 1.
46. Walker, *We Can't Go Home Again*; Howe, *Afrocentrism*; Shavit, *History in Black*.
47. Asante, *The Afrocentric Idea*; Asante, *Afrocentricity*; *Kemet, Afrocentricity and Knowledge*.
48. Amos Wilson, *The Falsification of Afrikan Consciousness: Eurocentric History, Psychiatry and the Politics of White Supremacy* (New York: Afrikan World Infosystems, 1993), 40–41.
49. Cheikh Anta Diop, *The African Origin of Civilization: Myth or Reality* (Chicago: Lawrence Hill, 1974). See also Diop, *Civilization or Barbarism: An Authentic Anthropology* (New York, 1001), 3; Ivan Van Sertima, ed., "Africa: Cradle of Humanity," *Nile Valley Civilization (Journal of African Civilization)* 6, no. 2 (1984); "Origins of the Ancient Egyptians," in *UNESCO General History of Africa*, vol. 2: *Ancient Civilizations of Africa*, ed. G. Mokhtar (Berkley, CA: University of California Press, 1981), 27–57.
50. Asante, *The Afrocentric Idea*, 9.
51. Wilson, *The Falsification of Afrikan Consciousness*, 25.
52. Ibid., 38. See also chaps. 4, 5. Although not counted among the Afrocentrists, leading Afrocentric scholars see Martin Bernal's work as incontrovertible intellectual corroboration of the Greek dependency theory. Bernal's work on Egyptian influence on Greece has become a standard reference on the Afrocentric genre. See his *Black Athena: The Afroasiatic Roots of Classical Civilization, vol.1 (The Fabrication of Ancient Greece 1785–1985)* (New Brunswick, NJ: Rutgers University Press, 1987); *Black Athena: The Afroasiatic Roots of Classical Civilization, vol. 2 (The Archaeological and Documentary Evidence)* (New Brunswick, NJ: Rutgers University Press, 1991); *Black Athena Writes Back: Martin Bernal Responds to His Critics* (Durham, NC: Duke University Press, 2001).
53. Howe, *Afrocentrism*; Shavit, *History in Black*; Walker, *We Can't Go Home Again*.
54. Shavit, *History in Black*, chap. 3.
55. Ibid., chaps. 6–7. See also Mary Lefkowitz, "The Origins of the 'Stolen Legacy,'" in John Miller, ed., *Alternatives to Afrocentrism* (Washington, DC: Manhattan Institute, 1994), 27–31.
56. Quoted in Walker, *We Can't Go Home Again*, xix-xx. See also George G. M. James, *Stolen Legacy* (New York: Classic House Books, 2009, originally published in 1954).

57. William E. B. Du Bois, *The Souls of Black Folk: Essays and Sketches* (Chicago: A. C. McClurg, 1903), 3–4.

58. Tunde Adeleke, "Contemporary Relevance of the Du Boisean Duality Paradigm," *Journal of American Studies* (Turkey) 16 (Fall 2002).

59. Molefi Asante, "Racism, Consciousness and Afrocentricity," in *Lure and Loathing: Essays on Race, Identity and the Ambivalence of Assimilation*, ed. Gerald Early (New York: Penguin Books, 1993), 127–43.

60. W. D. Wright, *Black Intellectuals, Black Cognition, and a Black Aesthetic* (Westport, CT: Praeger, 1997), 39.

61. Shavit, *History in Black*, chaps. 1–2.

62. Prince Justice, *The Black World: Evolution to Revolution* (London: AU, 2005); Chancellor Williams, *The Destruction of African Civilizations* (Chicago: Third World, 1976). See also Williams, *The Rebirth of African Civilizations* (Hampton, VA: U.B. and U.S. Communications Systems, 1993); Molefi Asante, *The History of Africa: The Quest for Eternal Harmony* (London: Routledge, 2007).

63. Shavit, *History in Black*, 3.

64. Joseph Berger, "Professor's Theories on Race Stir Turmoil at City College," *The New York Times*, April 20, 1990. Also quoted in Arthur M. Schlesinger Jr., *The Disuniting of America: Reflections on a Multicultural Society*. Rev. and enl. ed. (London: W. W. Norton, 1998), 73.

65. Shavit, *History in Black*, 23.

66. Ibid., 29.

67. Ibid., 38; see also chaps. 4–5.

68. Walker, *We Can't Go Home Again*, 40–41.

69. Ibid., 44.

70. Ibid., 46–50.

71. Asante, *Afrocentricity*, chap. 2.

72. Ibid., 2.

73. Ibid., 43.

74. Ibid., 67.

75. Ibid.

76. W. D. Wright, *Crisis of the Black Intellectual* (Chicago: Third World, 2007), 106.

77. Asante, *Afrocentricity*. See also Asante, *The Afrocentric Idea*; Asante, *Kemet, Afrocentricity and Knowledge*; Asante, *The Painful Demise of Eurocentrism*.

78. Joseph Holloway, ed., *Africanisms in American Culture*. 2nd ed. (Bloomington: Indiana University Press, 2005). See also Dona Marimba Richards, *Let the Circle Be Unbroken: The Implications of African Spirituality in the Diaspora* (Trenton, NJ: Red Sea, 1980); Asante, *Afrocentricity*.

79. Richards, *Let the Circle Be Unbroken*.

80. Ibid., 1.

81. Keith Richburg, *Out of America: A Black Man Confronts Africa* (New York: Basic Books, 1996).

82. Ibid., 227.

83. Ibid., 227–28.

84. Ibid., 237.

85. Ibid., xiii.

86. Michael E. Owens, *Yes, I Am Who I Am: A New Philosophy of Black Identity* (Tulsa: Yorkshire, 2009), 128.

87. Glenn Loury, "Free at Last? A Personal Perspective on Race and Identity in America," in *Lure and Loathing*, ed. Gerald Early, 1–12.

88. Stanley Crouch, "Who Are We? Where Did We Come From? Where Are We Going?" in *Lure and Loathing*, ed. Gerald Early, 80–94. See also Crouch, *The All-American Skin Game, or The Decoy of Race: The Long and The Short of It, 1990–1994* (New York: Pantheon Books, 1995), 45–57.

89. Wright, *Black Intellectuals, Black Cognition*, 38–39.

90. Robin Cohen, *Global Diasporas: An Introduction* (Seattle: University of Washington Press, 1997). See also Wenche Ommundsen, Michael Leach, and Andrew Vandenberg, eds., *Cultural Citizenship and the Challenges of Globalization* (Cresskill, NJ: Putnam, 2010).

91. Cohen, *Global Diasporas*, 157, 159.

92. Asante, *Afrocentricity*, 49.

93. Chancellor Williams, *The Destruction of Black Civilization* (Chicago: Third World, 1976), 362.

94. Ibid., 381.

95. Asante, *The Painful Demise of Eurocentrism*, vii.

96. Ibid. See also Asante, *The Afrocentric Idea*; *Afrocentricity*; *Kemet, Afrocentricity, and Knowledge*.

97. Haki Madhubuti, *Enemies: The Clash of Races* (Chicago: Third World, 1978), 187.

98. Ibid., 186.

99. Ibid., 190.

100. Marimba Ani, *Yurugu: An African-Centered Critique of European Cultural Thought and Behavior* (Trenton, NJ: Africa World, 1994).

101. Richards, *Let the Circle Be Unbroken*.

102. Ani, *Yurugu*.

103. Ibid., 528–70.

104. Ibid., 4.

105. Ibid.

106. Asante, *The Painful Demise of Eurocentrism*, vii.

107. Ibid.

108. Ibid., 7.

109. Cohen, *Global Diasporas*, 174.

110. Tunde Adeleke, "Against Euro-Cultural Hegemony: Black Americans, Afrocentricity, and Globalization."

111. Adeleke, "Against Euro-Cultural Hegemony," 12.

112. Jack P. Greene, "Beyond Power: Paradigm Subversion and Reformulation and the Re-creation of the Early Modern Atlantic World," in *Crossing Boundaries: Comparative History of Black People in Diaspora*, ed. Darlene Clark Hine and Jacqueline McLeod (Bloomington: Indiana University Press, 1999), 332.

113. Ruth Hamilton, Kimberly Simmons, Raymond Familusi, and Michael Hanson, "Rethinking the African Diaspora: Global Dynamics," in *Routes of Passage: Rethinking the African Diaspora* (East Lansing: Michigan State University Press, 2007), vol. 1, part 1, 8.

114. Gregory Smithers, "Challenging a Pan-African Identity: The Autobiographical Writings of Maya Angelou, Barack Obama, and Caryl Phillips," *Journal of American Studies*, February 4, 2011.

115. Leif Manger and Munzoul A. M. Assal, eds., *Diasporas within and without Africa: Dynamism, Heterogeneity, Variation* (Uppsala: The Nordic Africa Institute, 2006), 10.

116. Bettina Conrad, "'We Are the Warsay of Eritrea in Diaspora,': Contested Identities and Social Divisions in Cyberspace and in Real Life," in *Diasporas within and without Africa*, ed. Manger and Assal, 104–39; Roqaia Abusharaf, "Southern Sudanese—A Community in Exile," in *Diasporas within and without Africa*, ed. Manger and Assal, 140–64; Munzoul A. M. Assal, "Somalis and Sudanese in Norway—Religion, Ethnicity/Clan and Politics in the Diaspora," in *Diasporas within and without Africa*, ed. Manger and Assal, 165–96.

117. Ruth Hamilton, Kimberly Eison Simmons, Raymond Familusi, and Michael Hanson, "Rethinking the Diaspora: Global Dynamics," in *Routes of Passage*, ed. Ruth Hamilton, 12.

118. Ibid., 7.

119. Ibid., 8.

120. Ibid., 1–40.

121. Anthony D. Smith, "Towards a Global Culture?" in *Global Culture: Nationalism, Globalization and Modernity*, ed. Mike Featherstone (London: Sage, 1990), 180.

122. Shavit, *History in Black*, 23.

123. Asante, *Afrocentricity*, 51.

124. Terry Kershaw, "The Emerging Paradigm in Black Studies," in *Black Studies: Theory, Methods, and Cultural Perspectives*, ed. Talmadge Anderson (Pullman: Washington State University Press, 1990), 19.

125. E. H. Carr, *What Is History?* (London: Penguin Books, 1961), 30.

CONTRIBUTORS

TUNDE ADELEKE is a native of Nigeria who is presently professor of history and director of the African and African American Studies Program at Iowa State University. He researches and teaches African and African American history/studies. His most recent book was *The Case against Afrocentrism* (University Press of Mississippi, 2009).

BRIAN D. BEHNKEN is associate professor of history and Latino/a studies at Iowa State University. His research and teaching interests include comparative race relations, civil rights, and ethnic history, among other subjects. He is the author of *Fighting Their Own Battles: Mexican Americans, African Americans, and the Struggle for Civil Rights in Texas* (University of North Carolina Press, 2011) and co-author, with Greg Smithers, of *Racism in American Popular Media: From Aunt Jemima to the Frito Bandito* (Praeger, 2015). He has also edited three collections of essays: *The Struggle in Black and Brown: African American and Mexican American Relations during the Civil Rights Era* (University of Nebraska Press, 2012); *Crossing Boundaries: Ethnicity, Race, and National Belonging in a Transnational World* (Lexington Books, 2013) with Simon Wendt; and *Civil Rights and Beyond: African American and Latino/a Activism in the Twentieth Century United States* was published by the University of Georgia Press in 2016.

MINKAH MAKALANI is associate professor of African and African diaspora studies at the University of Texas at Austin. An interdisciplinary scholar working at the intersections of intellectual history, political theory, and literary studies, his interests lie in black political thought, racial formation, and the imaginary in the Caribbean, the United States, and Europe. He is the author of *In the Cause of Freedom: Radical Black Internationalism from Harlem to London, 1917–1939* and co-editor (with Davarian Baldwin) of *Escape from*

New York: The New Negro Renaissance beyond Harlem. His work has appeared in the journals *Souls, Social Text, Journal of African American History,* and *Women, Gender, and Families of Color,* as well as the collections *White Out: The Continuing Significance of Racism, Outside In: The Transnational Circuitry of U.S. History,* and *C. L. R. James' Beyond a Boundary Fifty Years On.* He is currently working on a study of C. L. R. James's return to Trinidad (1958–1962), giving particular attention to James's thinking about democracy, the arts, and Africa in conceptualizing a Caribbean political future beyond the liberal democratic structures inherited by the postcolonial state. This is tentatively titled *Calypso Conquered the World: C. L. R. James and the Politically Unimaginable in Trinidad.*

BENITA ROTH is an associate professor of sociology, history, and women's studies at Binghamton University. Her work focuses on the intersections of gender, social protest, race/ethnicity, and sexuality. Her first book *Separate Roads to Feminism: Black, Chicana, and White Feminist Movements in America's Second Wave* won the Distinguished Book Award from the Sex and Gender Section of the American Sociological Association and is in its fourth printing. She was an associate editor for *The Journal of Women's History,* editing its website (http://bingdev.binghamton.edu/jwh/?page_id=347) from 2010 to 2015. In 2012, she co-edited (with Jean Quataert) a special issue of the journal, *Human Rights, Global Conferences, and the Making of Postwar Transnational Feminisms,* on the impact of UN-sponsored global meetings of women for transnational feminism and human rights organizing. Her second book, entitled *The Life and Death of ACT UP/LA: Anti-AIDS Organizing in Los Angeles in the 1980s and 1990s,* is forthcoming from Cambridge University Press.

GREGORY D. SMITHERS teaches history at Virginia Commonwealth University. His research focuses on Native American and African American histories. He is the author of numerous books, the most recent being *The Cherokee Diaspora: An Indigenous History of Migration, Resettlement, and Identity* (Yale University Press, 2015) and a revised and expanded edition of *Science, Sexuality, and Race in the United States and Australia, 1780s-1940s* (University of Nebraska Press, 2017).

SIMON WENDT is assistant professor of American studies at the University of Frankfurt in Frankfurt, Germany. His research interests revolve around African American history, American gender history, memory, nationalism, and the history of heroism. He is the author of *The Spirit and the Shotgun: Armed Resistance and the Struggle for Civil Rights* (2007) and coeditor of a number of books, including *Globalizing Lynching History: Vigilantism and Extralegal Punishment from an International Perspective* (2011), *Crossing Boundaries: Ethnicity, Race, and National Belonging in a Transnational World* with Brian Behnken (2013), and *Masculinities and the Nation in the Modern World: Between Hegemony and Marginalization* (2015). He is currently completing a book manuscript on the history of the Daughters of the American Revolution.

DANIELLE L. WIGGINS is a doctoral candidate in history at Emory University. She received her bachelor's in history from Yale in 2012. Her research interests include African American conservatism and liberalism, black capitalism, and black urban politics in the post-civil rights era. Her doctoral research concerns crime, capitalism, and the politics of black neoliberalism in post-civil rights Atlanta.

INDEX

Adeleke, Tunde, 9, 15, 186, 206
African Baptist Missionary Society
 (ABMS), 16
African Blood Brotherhood, 44, 64
African Liberation Support Committee
 (ALSC), 66–68
African Methodist Episcopal Church
 (AME Church), 16, 18, 176
African Nationalist Pioneer Movement
 (ANPM), 182, 192
Akbar, Na'im, 209, 213
Alkalimat, Abdul, 67
Allen, James S., 41
Allen, Richard, 16
Allen, Robert, 56–57
Ani, Marimba, 223–24
Asante, Molefi, 209, 212–16, 222, 228
Association for the Study of Negro Life
 and History (ASNLH), 89

Baker, Ella, 145
Bambara, Toni Cade, 144, 148, 149–51
Baraka, Amiri (Leroi Jones), 65–66, 130,
 180, 182, 183, 184, 194
Beal, Frances, 139, 148–49
Bibb, Henry 17–18,
Black Arts Movement, 184
Black Belt Nation Thesis, 36
Black intellectualism: and Abolitionism,
 15–19; and Afrocentrism, 108, 185–86,
 195–96, 206–30; and black nationalism,
 9, 19, 65–66, 171–98; and Black Power,
 50, 56–57, 62, 64–68, 113–14, 147, 180–81,
 185, 192–93, 197–98; and black women,
 23, 26–27, 53–54, 69, 138–63, 192; and
 colonialism/postcolonialism, 54–64,
 170–72, 186–89; and conservatism, 5, 8,
 13, 18, 100–101, 107–31; and education,
 21–22; and feminism, 8–9, 138–63, 195;
 and gender, 191–96; historiographical
 misconceptions about, 5–7, 9, 35–38;
 history of prior to World War II, 11–27;
 and issue of legitimacy, 4; and liberalism 7, 8, 13, 80–102; and Marxism/
 Communism, 7–8, 26, 35–69, 139,
 141–43, 183, 188; and miscegenation,
 24; and Negro Convention Movement,
 16–17, 18; and Pan-Africanism, 43, 50,
 176, 178, 184–86, 217–20; and race/racial
 theories, 24, 181–84; and religion, 12–13,
 93–94, 110–11, 123–24, 142; and slavery,
 13–18
Black Lives Matter (BLM), 123, 140, 160–61
Black Panther Party, 65, 183, 188–89, 193–95
Black Radical Congress, 68
Black Women's United Front, 68
Blow, Charles, 160
Blyden, Edward Wilmot, 176
Boggs, James, 65
Bogues, Anthony, 38, 45, 50, 60
Briggs, Cyril, 26, 44–45, 50
Brooke, Edward, 109, 113
Brown, William Wells, 17, 206
Bruce, Blanche K., 20

INDEX

Cabral, Amílcar, 61–64, 66
Campbell, Grace, 40, 141
Carmichael, Stokely (Kwame Touré), 56, 57, 171, 180–81, 182, 183, 184, 186–87
Carson, Ben, 5, 131
Césaire, Aimé, 54–55, 60
Chisholm, Shirley, 140, 144, 146
Civil War, 20
Clark, Peter H., 40
Clarke, John Henrik, 209, 222
Cleaver, Eldridge, 194
Clinton, Hillary, 160, 161
Cobb, W. Montague, 24
Collins, Patricia Hill, 140, 142, 153, 156, 157
Combahee River Collective (CRC), 150–51
Communist Party of the United States (CPUSA), 36–37, 48, 50, 51, 141
Congress of African Peoples (CAP), 66, 180
Congress of Racial Equality, 114, 179, 188
Connell, R.W., 189
Connerly, Ward, 125
Cooper, Anna Julia, 23, 156
Cornish, Samuel, 15, 16
Cosby, Bill, 119
Crenshaw, Kimberlé, 152–53, 162
Crouch, Stanley, 220
Crummel, Alexander, 176
Cruse, Harold, 5, 27, 44, 56
Cuffee, Paul, 175
Cullors, Patrisse, 160–61

Davis, Angela, 64, 150, 155
Debs, Eugene V., 40
Delany, Martin, 19, 111, 176, 209, 210
Diop, Cheikh Anta, 214
Domingo, W. A., 40
Douglass, Frederick, 17, 18–20, 21, 209
Du Bois, W. E. B., 6, 22–23, 43, 47, 84–86, 112, 156, 207, 209, 210, 211, 215
Dyson, Michael Eric, 119, 157

Edelin, Kenneth, 151
Edwards, Thyra, 141
Ellison, Ralph, 108
Eugenics, 24

Fanon, Frantz, 35, 38–40, 43, 47, 55–56, 57, 58, 64, 172, 186, 187, 193
Fard, W. D., 177, 179
Farrakhan, Louis, 184, 196
Forten, James, 111, 175
Foucault, Michel, 38
Franklin, John Hope, 89–90, 91, 207–9, 211, 228, 229
Frazier, E. Franklin, 24, 90–91

Garnet, Henry Highland, 176, 209
Garrison, William Lloyd, 16
Garvey, Amy Jacques, 139, 140
Garvey, Marcus, 26, 44, 108, 112, 139, 176–77, 178, 182
Garza, Alicia, 160–61
Gates, Henry Louis, Jr., 97–98, 156
Gilroy, Paul, 15
Goldberg, David Theo, 5
Gordon, Lewis R., 3, 5
Grimke, Francis, 24
Grisham, G. N., 210–11
Guy-Sheftal, Beverly, 155–56

Hall, Prince, 175
Hall, Stuart, 15
Hamer, Fannie Lou, 145
Hamilton, Charles, 187
Hammon, Jupiter, 109, 110
Harding, Vincent, 211
Harrison, Hubert, 40
Haywood, Harry, 41, 65
Henry, Milton (Gaidia Obadele), 181, 188
Herbert, Robert, 99–100
Hernández, Aileen C., 145–46
Ho Chi Minh, 64
Holloway, Jonathan Scott, 5
hooks, bell, 150
Hooks, Benjamin, 130
Horne, Gerald, 36
Houston, Charles Hamilton, 91
Hull, Gloria, 150
Hurston, Zora Neale, 109

Innis, Roy, 179, 187–88
Ivory, Richard, 131

Jacobs, Harriet, 17–18
James, C. L. R., 43, 47, 48–50, 51, 58–60, 64, 65, 68
James, George G. M., 215
Johnson, Edward Austin, 11, 12
Johnson, Lyndon B., 116, 124
Johnson, Manning, 109
Jones, Claudia, 51–53, 64, 69, 140, 141–43
Jordan, Barbara, 95–96

Karenga, Ron (Maulana), 113, 184, 186, 195–96, 209
Kelley, Robin D. G., 37, 51, 64
Kennedy, Florynce, 140, 144, 146–47
Kennedy, John F., 124, 179
Kershaw, Terry, 228
King, Martin Luther, Jr., 80, 93–95, 108, 125, 159, 179, 193
Kirsanow, Peter, 122–23

League of Revolutionary Workers, 65
Lee, Grace, 65
Locke, Alaine LeRoy, 86–87
Long, Eddi, 123
Lorde, Audre, 150
Loury, Glenn, 107, 118, 120, 121, 122, 124–25, 126, 220
Louverture, Toussaint, 48–49
Love, Mia, 131
Lynch, John, 20
Lynching, 21–23, 26, 83–84, 102, 192

Madhubuti, Haki R. (Don L. Lee), 67, 222–23
Malcolm X, 56, 65, 108, 113, 130, 170, 171, 179–80, 181, 182–83, 184, 185, 192–93
Mandela, Nelson, 220
Mao Tse-Tung, 64
Marable, Manning, 5, 68–69, 119, 157
Marshall, Thurgood, 91–92
McKay, Claude, 26
McKissick, Floyd, 114, 187–88
McWorther, John, 101, 121–22, 126–27, 131
Moore, Audley ("Queen Mother"), 65
Moore, Richard B., 40

Morgan, Philip, 15
Morgan, Robin, 148
Morrison, Toni, 150, 156
Muhammad, Elijah, 179, 182, 192, 194
Murray, Pauli, 149

National Association for the Advancement of Colored People (NAACP), 84, 113, 119, 130, 177, 194
National Association of Colored Women, 27
National Black Feminist Organization (NBFO), 147
National League of Colored Women, 26
National Organization for Women (NOW), 145
National Urban League, 119
Nation of Islam (NOI), 170, 177, 179, 182, 184, 194, 196
Negro Convention Movement, 16–18
Nell, William Cooper, 206
New African Independence Movement (NAIM), 181, 189
Newton, Huey, 56, 171, 188–89, 193, 195
Nixon, Richard, 124
Nkrumah, Kwame, 56, 65
Nyere, Julius, 65

Obama, Barack, 4–5, 102, 131, 155
O'Dell, Jack, 56, 57
Owens, William, 123

Paraintellectuals, 171
Parker, Star, 118, 122, 123, 125
Patton, Gwen, 144
Pendleton, Clarence, 107
Pennington, James W. C., 81–82, 206
Peterson, Jesse, 129
Powell, Colin, 119, 130
Purvis, Robert, 16

Quarles, Benjamin, 211

Randolph, A. Philip, 26, 40
Reagon, Bernice Johnson, 150

Republic of New Africa (RNA), 181, 188
Revolutionary Action Movement (RAM), 65, 186, 188
Revels, Hiram, 20
Rice, Condoleezza, 130
Richards, Dona Marimba (Marimba Ani), 209
Robinson, Cedric, 37
Robinson, Pat, 149
Rodney, Walter, 58, 59–60, 64, 65, 68
Roosevelt, Franklin D., 116
Russwurm, John, 15, 16

Sadaukai, Owusu (Howard Fuller), 66
Schuyler, George, 109, 112–13
Scott, Patricia Bell, 150
Scott, Tim, 131
Seale, Bobby, 193
Sidbury, James, 15
Smith, Barbara, 150
Smith, James McCune, 16
Smith, Mark, 67
Socialist Party of America, 40
Sowell, Thomas, 100–101, 107, 115, 117, 120, 122, 124, 125, 128
Spivak, Gayatri, 171–72
Stanford, Maxwell (Muhammad Ahmad), 65, 188
Steele, Michael, 130
Steele, Shelby, 120, 126, 128
Steinem, Gloria, 144, 147
Stewart, Maria, 138, 140, 148
Student Nonviolent Coordinating Committee (SNCC), 148, 180

Terrell, Mary Church, 26–27
Third World Women's Alliance (TWWA), 139, 148
Thomas, Clarence, 107, 110, 130
Thompson, Louise, 141
Thorpe, Earl, 211
Tillich, Paul, 93
Todd, John, 86
Tometi, Opal, 160–61

Touré, Askia Muhammad (Rolland Sellings), 184
Trotter, William Monroe, 6–7
Truth, Sojourner, 18
Tubman, Harriet, 17
Turner, Henry McNeal, 176, 209
Tuskegee Institute, 6, 21, 112

Walker, Alice, 150
Walker, Clarence, 217
Walker, David, 15
Washington, Booker T., 6–7, 19, 21, 108, 109, 111–12, 113, 119, 121, 131, 177
Weathers, MaryAnne, 149
Wells, Ida B., 23, 26, 83–84, 156
West, Cornel, 5, 119, 156
Wheatley, Phillis, 15
White, Walter, 23
Wilkins, Roy, 194
Williams, Chancelor, 209, 222
Williams, Eric, 58
Williams, George Washington, 25
Williams, Walter, 107, 117, 124, 128
Wilson, Amos, 214
Wilson, William Julius, 98–99
Winfrey, Oprah, 140, 157–59
Woodson, Carter G., 87–89, 91, 94, 207, 209, 211
Woodson, Robert, 117, 120–21, 125, 126
Wortham, Anne, 125
Wright, Crystal, 131
Wright, Margaret, 149
Wright, Marion Thompson, 89, 91
Wright, Richard, 47
Wright, W. D., 220
Wynter, Sylvia, 43, 57, 64

www.ingramcontent.com/pod-product-compliance
Lightning Source LLC
Chambersburg PA
CBHW030619230426
43661CB00053B/2056